EAT & RUN

EAT & RUN

MY UNLIKELY JOURNEY TO ULTRAMARATHON GREATNESS

SCOTT JUREK

WITH **Steve Friedman**

HOUGHTON MIFFLIN HARCOURT
BOSTON   NEW YORK

A note to the reader:

My book presents my own research and ideas. And while I hope you'll be inspired by them to get the most out of yourself, and out of life, keep in mind that I'm not a doctor. So by all means use this book, but this book is not intended to substitute for consultation with a doctor or healthcare provider. Neither I nor the publisher can claim any responsibility for any adverse effects resulting directly or indirectly from information contained in this book.

Let me put it another way: If you decide to run 135 miles in Death Valley, no matter what advice of mine you do or do not follow, you do so at your own risk. But I'll be with you in spirit, every kickass step.

Library of Congress Cataloging-in-Publication Data
Jurek, Scott, date.
Eat and run: my unlikely journey to ultramarathon greatness / Scott Jurek, with Steve Friedman.
p. cm.
Includes index.
ISBN 978-0-547-56965-9
1. Marathon running — Training. 2. Marathon running — Physiological aspects.
3. Athletes — Nutrition. 4. Vegan cooking. I. Friedman, Steve, date. II. Title.
GV1065.17.T73J87 2012
796.42'52 — DC23   2012010581

Book design by Melissa Lotfy

Printed in the United States of America
DOC 10 9 8 7 6 5 4

To my parents, who first taught me to dig deep,
and to all those who taught me to dig deeper

Beyond the very extreme of fatigue and distress, we may find amounts of ease and power we never dreamed ourselves to own; sources of strength never taxed at all because we never push through the obstruction.

— WILLIAM JAMES

Contents

Prologue

I was a shy kid with high blood pressure. I grew into a skinny adoles-
cent whom other kids teased and called "Pee-Wee." I wasn't the fastest
kid in my school, or the strongest, or even the smartest. I was common as grass, longing for something I couldn't even name. I was like
everyone else, the same. Then I found something.

I'm not going to offer gauzy parables about inspiration and belief. I'm not going to promise you that if you want to achieve your
dream, all you need is faith. No, I am going to show you — in concrete
terms — how I transformed myself from the inside out and how you
can do it too. Whether you're a marathoner or weekend jogger, swimmer or cyclist, young or old, fit or fat, you can do this. I know because
I did it.

The story of my life is going to sound very familiar. Not in the details (unless you've found yourself face down in Death Valley, that is),
but in the desire. It's the tale of everyone who has ever felt stuck, of
anyone who has dreamed of doing more, of being more.

I was stuck like that a few years ago in one of the lowest, hottest
spots on the planet. That's where I'll start my story. That's where I'll
start *your* story.

1

Somebody

The best way out is always through.

— ROBERT FROST

M Y BRAIN WAS on fire. My body was burning up. Death Valley had laid me out flat, and now it was cooking me. My crew was telling me to get up, that they knew I could go on, but I could barely hear them. I was too busy puking, then watching the stream of liquid evaporate in the circle of light from my headlamp almost as fast as it splashed down on the steaming pavement. It was an hour before midnight, 105 incinerating, soul-sucking degrees. This was supposed to be *my* time. This was the point in a race where I had made a career of locating hidden reservoirs of sheer will that others didn't possess, discovering powers that propelled me to distances and speeds that others couldn't match. But tonight, roasting on the pavement, all I could summon was the memory of a television commercial I had seen as a child. First there's an egg in someone's fingers and a voice says, "This is your brain." Then the owner of the hand cracks the egg, and as it sizzles and crackles onto a hot skillet, the voice says, "And this is your brain on drugs." I saw that image in the scorching nighttime sky. I heard the disembodied voice. But what I thought was: "This is my brain on Badwater."

I had just run 70 miles through a place where others had died walking, and I had 65 more to go. I reminded myself that this was the point in the race where I was supposed to dust anyone foolish enough to have kept up with me in the first half. In fact, I had started this race intending to shatter its record, never mind worry about winning it. And now I didn't think I could finish.

There was only one answer: Get up and run. Whatever the problem in my life, the solution had always been the same: *Keep going!* My lungs might be screaming for oxygen, my muscles might be crying in agony, but I had always known the answer lay in my mind. Tired tendons had begged for rest in other places, my flesh had demanded relief, but I had been able to keep running because of my mind. But not now. What had gone wrong?

Running is what I do. Running is what I love. Running is — to a large extent — who I am. In the sport I have chosen as avocation, career, obsession, and unerring but merciless teacher, running is how I answer any challenge.

Technically speaking, I am an ultramarathoner. So I compete in any footrace longer than the marathon distance of 26.2 miles. In point of fact, though, I have fashioned a career from running *and winning* races of at least 50 miles, most often 100, and every so often 135 and 150 miles. Some I have led from start to finish; in others I have stayed comfortably back until the point when I needed to find another gear. So why was I on the side of the road vomiting, unable to go on?

Never mind my success. People had warned me that this race — this 135-mile jaunt through Death Valley — was too long and that I hadn't given my body enough time to recover from my last race — a race I had won just two weeks earlier, the rugged and prestigious Western States 100 Mile. People had said that my diet — I had been eating only plant-based foods for seven years — would never sustain me. No one had voiced what I now suspected might be my real problem — that I had underestimated the race itself.

Some ultras curve through level virgin forest, next to melodious streams, past fields of wildflowers. Some ultras occur in the cool melancholy of autumn, others in the invigorating chill of early spring.

Then there were the ultras like the one that had felled me. Its proper name was the Badwater UltraMarathon. Competitors called it the Badwater 135, and a lot of people knew it as "the world's toughest foot race."

But I hadn't taken such talk too seriously. I thought I had run more difficult courses. I thought I had faced much faster, tougher competition. I had raced in snow and rain, won events in far corners of the earth. I had scrambled up loose rock, over peaks of 14,000 feet. I had hopscotched down boulder fields, forded across icy streams. I was used to trails that caused deer to stumble and falter.

Sure, the Badwater flat-lined through Death Valley at the hottest time of the year. And yes, according to Badwater legend, one year when a shoe company handed out its product to all entrants, many of the soles supposedly melted on the scorching pavement.

But that was just a story, right? And though the Badwater did sizzle and though it was longer than I usually race, its brutality was unidimensional. I was used to forbidding terrain, climate, *and* competition. Other ultras inspire not just reverence but fear. The Badwater? The truth is, a lot of the most accomplished and well-known ultrarunners had never run it. Yeah, Death Valley made it sound ominous, if not fatal, but among elite ultrarunners, tales of danger and death aren't uncommon. Ultrarunners liked the stories but didn't dwell on them. We couldn't.

It wasn't that I hadn't prepared; in my line of work, lack of preparation was tantamount to self-abuse. I had purchased an industrial-sized sprayer so that I could be hosed down at regular intervals. I had worn specially designed heat-reflecting pants and shirt by Brooks Sports. I had guzzled 60 ounces of water (the equivalent of three bicycle bottles) every hour for the first 6 hours of the race. But those precautions were designed to shield my body. No industrial sprayer was going to protect my mind. And an ultrarunner's mind is what matters more than anything.

Racing ultras requires absolute confidence tempered with intense humility. To be a champion, you have to believe that you can destroy your competition. But you also have to realize that winning requires total commitment, and a wavering of focus, a lack of drive, a single misstep, might lead to defeat or worse. Had I been too confident, not humble enough?

Early in the race, after 17 miles, a marine who had dropped out saluted me as I ran past him because he knew my reputation. Another runner, a desert race veteran, dropped out about 30 miles later, right about the time he realized his urine was flowing dark as coffee. He knew my reputation, too. But my reputation wasn't helping me now. Neither was my earlier confidence.

The leader was a fifty-year-old ship pilot and cliff diver named Mike Sweeney, whose high dive training had included smacking himself on the head. Trailing him was a forty-eight-year-old Canadian baggage handler named Ferg Hawke, who was fond of quoting Friedrich Nietzsche.

Journalists in the running press called me "the Real Deal." But was I? Or was I a fraud?

Moments of questioning come to us all. It is human nature to ask why we put ourselves in certain situations and why life places hurdles in our path. Only the most saintly and delusional among us welcomes *all* pain as challenge, perceives all loss as harsh blessing. I know that. I know that I've chosen a sport stuffed with long stretches of agony, that I belong to a small, eclectic community of men and women where status is calibrated precisely as a function of one's ability to endure. Hallucinations and vomiting, to me and my fellow ultrarunners, are like grass stains to Little Leaguers. Chafing, black toenails, and dehydration are just the rites of passage for those of us who race 50 and 100 miles and more. A marathon is a peaceful prologue, a time to think and work out kinks. Ultrarunners often blister so badly they have to tear off toenails to relieve pressure. One ultrarunner had his surgically removed before a race, just in case, so he wouldn't need to bother later on. Cramps don't merit attention. Unless nearby lightning makes the hair on your arms and head stand up and dance, it's nothing but scenery. Altitude headaches are as common as sweat and inspire approximately the same degree of concern (the death by brain aneurysm of one runner in a Colorado race notwithstanding). Aches are either ignored, embraced, or, for some, treated with ibuprofen, which can be risky. Combined with heavy sweating, too much ibuprofen can cause kidney failure, which usually results in ghostly pallor and, if you're lucky, an airlift by helicopter to the nearest hospital. As an ultrarunner buddy and physician once said, "Not all pain is significant."

Ultrarunners take off at sunrise and continue through sunset, moonrise, and another sunrise, sunset, and moonrise. Sometimes we stumble from exhaustion and double over with pain, while other times we effortlessly float over rocky trails and hammer up a 3,000-foot climb after accessing an unknown source of strength. We run with bruised bones and scraped skin. It's a hard, simple calculus: Run until you can't run anymore. Then run some more. Find a new source of energy and will. Then run even faster.

Other sports take safety precautions, but in ultramarathons, we have death-avoiding precautions baked into the enterprise. Most ultras are dotted with aid stations, where runners are tracked, sometimes weighed, and provided with snacks, shade, and medical checkups. The majority of races also include pacers, who are allowed to accompany runners in latter sections of the course (but only for advice and to keep them from getting lost, not for carrying food or water). Ultrarunners can — much of the time — bring support crews, men and women who provide food, water, updates on competitors, and reassurance that you can, in fact, continue when you are sure you will collapse.

Nearly all ultras are run continuously, meaning that there is no point at which the clock stops and everyone gets to retire for a large plate of pasta and a well-deserved night's sleep, like competitors in the Tour de France do. That's part of the challenge and appeal of the event. You keep going in situations where most people stop. You keep running while other people rest.

But that was my problem — it was other people who stopped to rest. Not me. But now it *was* me. I simply couldn't go on.

My buddy and support crew member Rick was telling me he knew I could do it. He was mistaken. What had I done wrong? Was it my training and lack of recovery? Was it my race schedule? Had my men-

tal approach been wrong? Was it what I had been eating? Was I thinking too much?

Ultramarathons give you plenty of time to think — that is, when
you're not watching out for mountain lions, avoiding sheer drops, or
responding to grinning rocks and gibbering trees (which your mind
can't believe are mere phantasms). Stopping in an ultra, quitting, gives
you even more time to ponder. But perhaps I wanted time to stop.
Maybe I was meant to lie here on my back in the desert to question
why I was running through an oven. Why was I subjecting myself to
this torture?

I started running for reasons I had only just begun to understand.
As a child, I ran in the woods and around my house for fun. As a teen,
I ran to get my body in better shape. Later, I ran to find peace. I ran,
and kept running, because I had learned that once you started something you didn't quit, because in life, much like in an ultramarathon,
you have to keep pressing forward. Eventually I ran because I turned
into a runner, and my sport brought me physical pleasure and spirited
me away from debt and disease, from the niggling worries of everyday
existence. I ran because I grew to love other runners. I ran because I
loved challenges and because there is no better feeling than arriving
at the finish line or completing a difficult training run. And because,
as an accomplished runner, I could tell others how rewarding it was
to live healthily, to move my body every day, to get through difficulties, to eat with consciousness, that what mattered wasn't how much
money you made or where you lived, it was *how* you lived. I ran because overcoming the difficulties of an ultramarathon reminded me
that I could overcome the difficulties of life, that overcoming difficulties *was* life.

Could I quit and not *be* a quitter?

"You've done it before," Rick said. "You can do it again."

I appreciated the optimism. I also appreciated its idiocy.

At another time, on another summer night, in another race, I might
have gazed in wonder at the stars glittering against the velvety black
night. I might have swiveled my head to peer at the snowy Sierra Ne-

vada peaks looming like grouchy sentries on the edge of the endless desert and seen, not scowling defeat, but majesty. I would have moved toward the mountains' dark, disapproving bulk until it had transformed to welcome.

"My stomach," I moaned. "My stomach." A couple of my crew members suggested I should crawl into the coffin-sized, ice-filled cooler they had lugged up the road to get my core temperature down, but I had tried that already. Rick told me to put my feet in the air — that might help me feel better. He told me I should do it on the side away from the road so the other crews wouldn't be able to see me, because their reports would only embolden their runners. Didn't he realize that the other runners didn't need emboldening? The guy with the reputation wasn't going anywhere.

Not moving was actually pleasant. It wasn't nearly as shameful as I had imagined. It allowed me to ponder my hubris.

If it had been a movie, this was the place where I would close my eyes and hear the faint, strangled voice of my bedridden mother, telling me she loved me and that she knew I could do whatever I wanted, and I would have flushed with shame, and then I would have heard the authoritative voice of my father, telling me, "Sometimes you just do things!" I would have risen to my elbows, shut my eyes, and pictured all the middle school kids who had called me Pee-Wee, and they would have melted into all the naysayers who had questioned me at the beginning of my career, who said that I was nothing to worry about, I was nothing but a flatlander. In that movie I would have risen to my knees and suddenly remembered who I was — I was a runner! — and I would have pulled myself up, stood tall, and started walking, then loping, into the thick desert night, chasing down the two seasoned veterans in front of me as a wolf chases doomed field mice.

I tried to puke some more, but it was all dry heaving, the type that is excruciating with every empty pump of the stomach.

My crew and close friends told me to close my eyes and relax. Instead, I stared at the stars. Everyone and the desert disappeared. Loss of peripheral vision was one manifestation of dehydration and passing out. Was that what was happening? It was as if I was looking through a tunnel at a small circle in an infinite, glittery sky.

My crew told me to take some little sips of water, but I couldn't. I was thinking, "I don't think this is gonna happen," and then I heard a noise, and it was my voice saying what I was thinking: "I don't think this is gonna happen."

The stars didn't care. That's another pleasure of running an ultra: the absolute and soothing indifference of the land and the sky. So I made a mistake? It wasn't the worst thing in the world; the constellations weren't gossiping about me. Maybe this would help me with humility. Maybe dropping out and being defeated would renew my spirit. Maybe cutting one race short was a good thing.

If only I could have made myself believe that.

Should I have listened to the trainers and doctors who said that athletes needed to fill their bodies with animal protein? Should I have trained less? I had thought I was invincible. I closed my eyes.

I had been schooled by nuns, raised by a mother who had been sprinkled with holy water from Lourdes, hoping it would help her rise from her wheelchair. Now it was me who couldn't rise.

I hadn't always been the fastest runner, but I had always considered myself one of the toughest. Maybe acceptance of my limits was the toughest thing of all. Maybe staying where I was wasn't weak but strong. Maybe accepting my limits meant it was time to stop being a runner, to start being something else. But what? If I wasn't a runner, who was I?

I looked again at the stars. They had no opinion on the matter.

Then, from the desert, a voice, an old familiar voice.

"You're not gonna win this fucking race lying down in the dirt. C'mon, Jurker, get the fuck up."

It was my old friend Dusty. That made me smile. He almost always made me smile, even when everyone around him was cringing.

"Get the fuck up!" Dusty yelled, but I couldn't. I wouldn't.

"Sweeney is out there dying, and you're gonna take that dude. We're gonna take that dude!"

I looked at my friend. Couldn't he see that I wasn't going to take anyone?

He squatted, folded himself until our faces were inches apart. He looked into my eyes.

"Do you wanna be somebody, Jurker? Do you wanna *be* somebody?"

Rice Balls (Onigiri)

I first saw these seaweed-wrapped rice packets when I asked a Japanese runner to show me what was in his race pack. I'm grateful I did, because white rice is a great food for cooling your body, especially in hot climates like Death Valley. It's packed with carbohydrates, it's not too sweet, and it's soft and easy to digest. A great source for electrolytes and salt (via the seaweed), rice balls have always been a portable pick-me-up in Japan. These days, you can even find them at convenience stores in Asia. For a soy-free variation, substitute pickled ginger or umeboshi paste for the miso.

- 2 cups sushi rice
- 4 cups water
- 2 teapoons miso
- 3–4 sheets nori seaweed

Cook the rice in the water on the stovetop or using a rice cooker. Set aside to cool. Fill a small bowl with water and wet both hands so the rice does not stick. Using your hands, form ¼ cup rice into a triangle. Spread ¼ teaspoon miso evenly on one side of the triangle. Cover with another ¼ cup rice. Shape into one triangle, making sure the miso is covered with rice. Fold the nori sheets in half and then tear them apart. Using half of one sheet, wrap the rice triangle in nori, making sure to completely cover the rice. Repeat using the remaining rice, miso, and nori.   MAKES 8 ONIGIRI

2

"Sometimes You Just Do Things"

The only line that is true is the line you're from.

— ISRAEL NEBEKER OF BLIND PILOT

SAT ON A stool in our kitchen. My mother thrust a rough wooden spoon at me and told me to stir, but the batter was too thick. She told me to use both hands, but still I couldn't move the spoon. Suddenly it moved and kept moving. She had put her hands around mine. We made spirals of pale yellow out of sugar and butter, and I pretended I was doing it all by myself. It's one of my earliest memories.

I thought my mom was famous. She worked for the Litton Microwave company, showing women how to cook bacon and make chocolate cake with the new invention. The Minnesota Egg Council hired her to go on the radio to talk about eggs and that led to television commercials and that led to her own cable cooking show. Her motto (which I still believe): "You don't have to be a chef to cook great food." For her family she roasted pork, baked chicken, broiled steak, and whipped up mashed potatoes from scratch. In the childhood of my memory, there was always a pie cooling on the kitchen windowsill, the scent of pastry and fruit stealing into our kitchen, enveloping my mother and me in its thick embrace.

I don't remember anyone talking about a primal connection to food, or how by eating the vegetables we grew we were connecting ourselves to the place where we lived and each other. I don't remember anyone remarking that the act of catching and cleaning and frying and eating walleye together was akin to a family sacrament. At my mother's insistence, we did sit down together for a full hour at dinner. If someone had praised her for baking cookies from scratch rather than using a mix, she would have thought they were nuts. I didn't know it, but I was learning a lot about food and its connection to love. When we cooked together, she told me stories about when she was in college, and said she knew I would go to college, too. When my dad wasn't around, she would ask me to grab my baseball bat, and she'd take me into the backyard, next to the garden, and she'd pitch underhand to me. She told me she was proud of what a hard worker I was and not to let Dad's grouchiness bother me. He just worried a lot.

My father wasn't the only disciplinarian in the family. When I misbehaved, my mom would spank me — with the same wooden spoon with which we stirred batter. She was the one who limited my television watching to 5 hours a week. If I wanted to watch a football game, she made me choose between the first or second half. I always chose the second half.

I can't remember the first time I saw her drop a jar. I must have been about nine. After a while, it was hard to remember when she didn't drop things. Knives trembled in her once-sure fingers. Sometimes, just standing by the counter, she would wince. If she saw me watching, she'd wink and smile.

Here's another memory: When I was six, stacking firewood outside, a car pulled up to our house. I knew it wasn't a neighbor; we lived on a dead-end road at the edge of a woods, 5 miles from Proctor, Minnesota, which was another 150 miles from Minneapolis. I knew all the cars on our road, who was driving, and which brothers and sisters were probably sitting in the back seat punching one another. This car belonged to a friend from Proctor. His mom had driven him out to play with me. I yelped and ran toward the car, but a stern voice stopped me.

"You can play when we're finished stacking wood. From the looks of it, we've got two more hours to go."

It was Dad, and I knew better than to argue. So I whispered the news to my friend and he told his mom. She gave me a look, then gave my dad a look, and then they drove off. I went back to stacking wood.

When I was done with chores, on rare occasions my dad would take me for a walk in the woods. Once, when I was seven and my mom was taking a nap — she had been getting tired a lot — he picked up a handful of dirt and let it trickle through his thick fingers. He told me about the day that two of the smartest scientists in the world were walking in the woods — maybe woods just like these, right here in Minnesota — and God strolled up, right out of the trees. And God said, "If you guys are so smart, can you make dirt out of thin air, like I can?" I remember my dad smiling when he told me that story, but it was a sad smile. I think he was trying to tell me that no matter how hard a man thought or worked, some things in life would remain unknowable, and we had to accept that.

By the time I was eight, there were fewer walks in the woods with my dad. I was helping around the house a lot. I was pulling weeds from the big garden we had out back, or picking out rocks, or stacking wood, or helping in the kitchen, or making sure my sister, Angela, who was five, had a snack, or that my brother, Greg, who was three, wasn't getting into mischief. By the time I was ten, I could cook a pot roast in the oven by myself. Whenever I complained that I didn't want to pick rocks or stack wood, I just wanted to go play, my dad would growl, "Sometimes you just do things!" After a while, I stopped complaining.

He tempered his discipline with compassion and a sense of fun. He would challenge me to see how much wood I could haul into our "wood room" in 10 minutes or how many rocks I could pick out of the garden in the same time. I don't think I realized it at the time, but he was teaching me that competition could turn the most mundane task into a thrill, and that successfully completing a job — no matter how onerous — made me feel unaccountably happy.

When I was ten my dad bought me a .22-caliber rifle with a polished walnut handle and a barrel made from burnished steel. He told me to kill any animal I wounded, to skin and gut it, to always eat whatever I brought home. I already knew how to catch a walleye and gut it and clean it.

I was a great blueberry picker, too. It was a rite of passage in my family that when you turned six, you got to go blueberry and cherry picking with Grandma Jurek. My older cousins had told me stories about the great adventure and I couldn't wait. My cousins had forgotten to mention the clouds of mosquitoes, or stinky bogs, or the beating sun, or the ladder, which I fell off. I cried and said I wanted to go home, but that didn't happen. Grandma Jurek had raised my dad. When you went cherry picking with her, you were picking for hours. And when you went fishing with Grandpa Jurek, if you got bored, too bad, you were gonna stay and fish. I learned patience while doing the tedious tasks, but more important, I learned to find joy in repetitive and physically demanding work.

I didn't always feel happy or patient, of course. I was a kid. But those were the times I kept going. Why?

Sometimes you just do things!

My dad was working two jobs then — during the day as a pipefitter and during the night in maintenance at the local hospital. I knew that the coupons Mom was using when I went with her to the grocery store were really food stamps, that we were getting government cheese, and that Dad was having trouble making ends meet. When our television broke, we didn't replace it for a year. We had two cars, but one was usually not working at all, and sometimes both. I knew that Mom was tired more and more and our garden next to the house was getting smaller while the list of chores my dad put on the fridge for us — a piece of paper with grids and the names and duties for me, my brother, and my sister — was getting bigger and bigger. I knew that none of my friends had to weed the garden and cut grass when it was 90 degrees and humid or haul and stack wood for 2 hours before they could play. My mom stopped pitching to me behind the house. I learned not to ask her.

The worse my mom got, the more I had to help. The more I helped, the more I wondered why things were the way they were. Why was my mom sick? When would she get better? Why couldn't my dad be less grumpy? Why did the school nurse always single me out for a second look at our regular head lice inspections? Was it because we lived in the country? Or because she thought we were poor?

Things got much worse the summer after third grade. It was a hot, clear Minnesota day. My dad had gotten off his shift, and he and my mom were coming to see me play baseball. I was in left field, and I had just caught a fly ball. I flung the ball toward the infield, and that's when I saw the Oldsmobile station wagon pull up and my father get out. The passenger door opened and my mother got out too, but something was wrong. The door was opening in slow motion. Then I saw her stumble and my father rush around the car to help her. He had to help her walk the 30 yards to the bleachers, and I watched each slow step. I missed two batters, and when the inning was over, I was still in left field, watching.

The chore list got bigger. We knew Mom was sick, and she took more and more naps. One day when I was in sixth grade my dad told us Mom was seeing some specialists. Maybe he said "multiple sclerosis," but if he did, they were just words. It didn't change who my mom was or what was happening to her. If I thought about it at all, it was along the lines of "Multiple what?" She would stay in Minneapolis for treatment from time to time. Dad said there was always hope.

One day, a physical therapist came to help Mom. It was an acknowledgment that her condition wasn't going to go away or be cured. She didn't see specialists after that.

I was cooking meatloaf and potatoes by then and chopping wood before I stacked it. I made lunches for my brother and sister and helped Mom get around the house. Sometimes I helped her with the exercises the physical therapist showed me.

I wish I could say something different, that I was grateful to be of service, that I appreciated the opportunity to help the woman who loved me, but the truth is, I hated the chores. I hated what was happening to my mom. None of us could say anything, though, because of my father, who had served in the Navy and believed in military discipline, and I know now that he was more stressed out than ever. *Don't ask why. Sometimes you just do things.* So my brother and sister, and especially I, basically lived in fear. Once, after I spent an hour stacking the wood, he said it was sloppy and knocked it down. Then I had to start over.

I began spending more and more time in the woods. I built trails and passageways to hidden tree forts with scrap wood left over from my father's projects. I took my rifle out every chance I could get, my fishing pole every other chance. Much of the time I went empty-handed, just me, and I walked under the cool green canopy until I knew every foot of those woods by heart.

I don't think they knew it at the time — and I certainly didn't — but my parents were training me to be an endurance athlete. By the time I started running, I knew how to suffer.

IN THE BEGINNING

Running efficiently demands good technique, and running efficiently for 100 miles demands great technique. But the wonderful paradox of running is that getting started requires no technique. None at all. If you want to become a runner, get onto a trail, into the woods, or on a sidewalk or street and run. Go 50 yards if that's all you can handle. Tomorrow, you can go farther. The activity itself will reconnect you with the joy and instinctual pleasure of moving. It will feel like child's play, which it should be.

Don't worry about speed at first or even distance. In fact, go slow. That means 50 to 70 percent of your maximum effort. The best way to find that zone is to run with a friend and talk while you're doing so. If you can't talk, you're run-

ning too fast and too hard. Do a combo of running and walking if needed. Don't be afraid to walk the uphills. Over time,
add distance. Your long, slow runs will strengthen your heart
and lungs, improve your circulation, and increase the meta-
bolic efficiency of your muscles.

Minnesota Mashed Potatoes

*As a child, I had a glass of milk with every meal and could pile mashed
potatoes higher than anyone in my family. I still love the dish, but now
I use homemade rice milk, which is just as creamy and rich as the stuff
from cows, much less expensive, and doesn't produce any plastic container waste. There's no better comfort food.*

5–6	medium red or yellow potatoes
1	cup rice milk (see recipe, below)
2	tablespoons olive oil
½	teaspoon sea salt
½	teaspoon crushed black pepper
	Paprika (optional)

Wash the potatoes; peel or leave the skins on as you prefer. Place in a
pot and add enough water to completely cover, 1 inch above the potatoes. Bring to a boil, covered, over high heat. Lower the heat and simmer for 20 to 25 minutes. Check the potatoes with a fork. If the fork
goes into the potatoes easily, they are ready.

Remove from the heat and drain. Mash the potatoes with a potato
masher or hand mixer. Add the remaining ingredients and continue
to mash until a smooth, fluffy consistency is reached. Season with a
dash or two more salt and pepper and paprika if desired.

MAKES 4–6 SERVINGS

Rice Milk

1 cup cooked brown or white rice
4 cups water
⅛ teaspoon sea salt
1 tablespoon sunflower oil (optional)

Combine the rice, water, and salt in a blender. If you want a creamier milk, add the oil. Blend on high for 1 to 2 minutes, until smooth. Pour into a container, cover, and refrigerate. Rice milk will keep for 4 to 5 days.   MAKES 5 CUPS

3

For My Own Good

> You never know how strong you are until being
> strong is the only choice you have.
>
> — ANONYMOUS

WAS JUST A fourth-grader, and I was trapped.

There were fourteen runners ahead of me and only twenty-five in the field. I was panting, cramped. Runners on either side of me swung their elbows, boxing me in. Others were on my heels, shoving. It was autumn, chilly. Leaves, deep red and orange, were carpeting the banks of Caribou Lake. Yellow flags marked the ¾-mile course, two laps around the baseball and soccer fields of Caribou Lake elementary school. I could see the puffs of warm air from the other runners clouding in the chilly north woods evening. I was wearing my maroon and gold St. Rose T-shirt and my long blue cotton pants, with shiny gold stripes down the side and elastic hems that my mother had sewed.

I couldn't play Little League anymore because that would have required a ride into town, and my dad was working too many hours to drive me. I couldn't play football because we couldn't afford the equipment. So I ran. I was tall and lean, and I didn't complain, so my school said I would be their representative in the school district meet. But I had never run as far as a mile before, and I wasn't fast. That's why, by the halfway mark of the race, I had fallen back to twentieth, out of twenty-five.

I kept running, though. I didn't ask why. I knew it was a useless question. *Sometimes you just do things!* And a couple of the elbow swingers next to me slid out of my peripheral vision. I kept running, and I didn't feel anyone shoving me from behind. My cramps got worse and my panting turned to gasps, but I kept running and then smacked into a clot of kids in front of me, and a couple of them yelled, "Hey!" and then I broke from the pack. Then there were only five kids ahead of me. A quarter of a mile to go, and now there were four kids, then one.

I didn't win. The guy in front was way too fast. I couldn't envision ever being that fast. It would be a long time before I even thought about winning a race. But on that chilly afternoon I realized something. I realized that while most kids my age slowed down during a race and fell back, I made up ground. I seemed to gain strength

By the time I entered middle school, sixth grade, I knew how to hold an egg between my forefinger and thumb so I could crack it with one hand. I could separate a load of white clothes from colored clothes, wash them, dry them, and fold them without a wrinkle in 60 minutes. I could do a hundred sit-ups in a row and run up and down the road three times without stopping (my brother and sister helped by sitting on my feet for the former and counting for the latter). I could cook spaghetti and pork chops and tuna noodle casserole and make wreaths from ground pine. (My brother and sister and I sold them for holiday money. We'd get five bucks for each one.) I could burp a baby and change a diaper, and I knew the principles of a basketball zone defense and the different motions needed to throw a perfect curveball. The first two I'd practiced on my brother and sister. The second two I knew from reading books in the library. I couldn't really play a lot on those teams — no transportation — but just in case, I wanted to know *how* to play.

. . .

At the beginning of seventh grade I wanted to be perfect. Part of that was because I saw my mom getting weaker and weaker and working harder and harder — on her exercises, on making sure all of us got nutritious meals, on creating little fun things for us to do around holidays: We had Mexican wedding cakes and Christmas spritz cookies that came out of a cookie shooter that we would form in different shapes, dye with food coloring, and decorate with sprinkles. When it was my turn to dry the dishes, I wanted to be the fastest dryer in the family. When I rolled fresh walleye in breadcrumbs and fried it in butter, I wanted it to be the most delicious walleye anyone had ever tasted. I got good grades and worked hard for them, but that wasn't enough. I wanted the *best* grades, and even that wasn't enough. We had multiple-choice reading proficiency tests every month, and I wanted to be the first one finished. So did one of my best friends, Dan Hamski. He beat me every single time and it drove me crazy. It took me a while, but finally I figured out what was going on. He'd rip through the tests, and when he got to a question he couldn't answer, he just skipped it and moved on. If the same thing happened to me, I'd bear down and work on that question until I had figured it out, even if it took the rest of the allotted time. I never got anything wrong . . . but I never beat Dan. I had to get everything right, no matter what it cost.

The only place I didn't have to try so hard was the woods. There I could run, walk, or do whatever I wanted. The trees didn't care how hard I worked, whether I stacked wood the right way, or how fast I was. The sky wasn't depending on me to make sure my mom didn't get worse. The ground wasn't testing me. It was just me and the sighing wind and the silence. In the woods I was alone with my questions of why and the utter lack of answers. The lack didn't seem so frightening in the woods. I wanted to be a game warden. Years later, my parents showed me something I wrote that said I wanted to be a doctor, but I don't remember that. More likely, I just wanted my mom to get better.

We all did. But what could we do? It would have been nice to take my mom out for dinner, but meals out were only for birthdays or when dad got a raise. It would have been great for Mom to have a computer, and every year my dad would talk about buying one, but we never did. It wasn't until I was in eighth grade that he sprung for an Apple IIe.

I tried to help. I entered poster and coloring contests where the prize was twelve gallons of ice cream from Bridgeman's. I won that ice cream, and later I won poster contests sponsored by the state department of fish and game. That made my dad and mom happy. She was happy, but she was still tired all the time. "Mom has the flu," Dad would say, or "She really needs to rest today."

I had learned in school that if you put a frog in a pot of water, then gradually heat the water until it's hot enough to kill the frog, the animal won't move because he doesn't pay attention to gradual changes. That's how it was with me. It's not like one day my mom was great and then, after she got diagnosed with multiple sclerosis, everything sucked. Maybe even with a healthy mother and gentler father, I would have worried a lot. I'll never know.

At my annual checkup when I was twelve, the doctor took a deep breath when he read my blood pressure. He took it again and breathed even deeper. Then he told me to go sit in the waiting room and he whispered to my dad. After that, my dad took me to a specialist who took my blood pressure at least three times, sitting down, lying down, and standing up. He asked me how I was sleeping and if I ever felt faint, and I told him the truth, that I felt okay. But by the time I left I was scared — mostly because my dad looked scared, too.

When I got home, my dad told me to go outside and play — and that was particularly frightening because he *never* told me to play — while he and my mom talked. Then he called me in, and they told me that I was going to have to start taking some pills every morning.

"Why?" I hadn't said the word out loud in years.

"Your blood pressure is high," my mom said. "This might help."

I knew what taking pills meant because my mom took them every day. I said I wasn't going to take them, that I could lower my blood pressure myself. I would read some books on it. My mom smiled at that. I don't think I ever saw my dad look so helpless.

It wasn't just pills, they said. From now on, no more salt. That news was as bad as the pills. I loved Campbell's Chicken Noodle Soup, and that was out. I loved mounds of butter and piles of salt on mashed potatoes. Nix on that, too. (I hated vegetables, with a few exceptions, notably canned corn, raw carrots, and potatoes.)

I insisted. Really, I would study up, I could beat this thing. I pleaded for them to give me a chance. Of course they said no.

The next night after dinner, I saw the big white bag from the pharmacy with my name on it. It was sitting in the bathroom cabinet with all my mom's pills, and when my dad reached up for the bag and handed it to my mom, I started crying.

"Scottie," my mom said, "you have to take these. It's for your own good."

Sometimes you just do things! But *why?* I kept bawling and then I started screaming. She took the pills out of the bag and looked at me, then sighed and put them back.

"We'll try to figure something out, Scottie, but you have to cooperate a little bit."

The next week, my dad took me to another specialist. This doctor turned off the lights in his office and told me I should imagine somewhere where I was happy. I thought of the woods in the summer, the great green hush. He told me to close my eyes and to stay where I was — in the woods — and then after a while he turned on the lights and called my dad in.

"Your son can get his blood pressure down by himself," the specialist said. "If he can do it again, at his pediatrician's office, we can wait on the medication."

That night my dad told me I didn't need to be so "wound up." He told me I should relax more, that I was just a kid, that I couldn't save the world. My dad, Mr. *Sometimes you just do things!*, was a complicated guy. He also told me that he had confidence in me, that I'd always been a good worker, and that he knew I could get my blood pressure down when we visited the pediatrician's office. I wasn't so sure. He promised that afterward he would buy me my own skis.

The next afternoon, at my pediatrician's office, I walked back into the woods, toward the green trees and the dirt and the quiet. Afterward, the doctor told my dad that he should hold on to the medicine but that I didn't need to start taking it. Not yet. He didn't say anything about stress or meditation or controlling your body with your mind, but I figured it out. Every week my parents would take out the inflatable blood pressure monitor they had bought and wrap it around my arm, and every week I would close my eyes and imagine trees and quiet. I learned that I could control my blood pressure with my brain. I remember thinking that talent might come in handy some day for something other than avoiding pills and getting to eat what I wanted.

I knew downhill skis were for rich kids, the kids who went to Duluth East, the ones whose parents were doctors and lawyers and who boarded planes to go on ski vacations. In my school, we called the people from that side of town "cake eaters." But my dad bought me those skis — used red, white, and blue K2s, used boots, and new poles — and even then I knew what a sacrifice it was.

That summer, my dad announced one night at dinner that the next week we were all going up to northern Minnesota to stay in a lodge. A lodge! He might as well have said we'd be going to Chicago to have a steak dinner. And not only that, but we would be at a lake and we could swim — in the lake next to the lodge or in the swimming pool — and fish and ride our bikes. There would be pontoon boat rides, too, and we could go by ourselves and paddle boat wherever we wanted on the lake. Angela and Greg and I felt as though we had won the lottery.

What my dad didn't tell us is that there would be other families there, and other kids, and professionals who would talk to all the kids while the adults met somewhere else.

The grownups brought the kids all together and asked us a series of questions. Questions like "How do you feel about your mom having MS?" And "What's it like at home? How do you feel about your friends and schoolmates visiting?" And "Do you feel different?" I was already reading a lot then — about blood pressure and soccer and even cooking. But I hadn't read anything about multiple sclerosis. I knew all I needed to know about it. Angela and Greg didn't say anything to the social worker — they were shy, anyway, and I think they were scared. I didn't say much either. No one in my family talked much about things like that. What good would it have done? What would it have helped? I had learned by then that all the whys in the world wouldn't change what was happening to my mother. I didn't start crying or anything, like some of the other kids there. My sister just stared at the social worker. My little brother, who was already becoming a handful, kept tugging at me, asking when we were going to go back to the paddle boats. He was a badass even then.

The truth is, I don't remember feeling much at that moment. It was like, "Mom has MS, tough luck, that's the way it is. You just keep going."

Lentil-Mushroom Burgers

For any reluctant vegan who worries that nothing will ever replace the taste or texture of a juicy beef patty, consider the lentil burger. It might not matter so much that lentils are an excellent source of protein, that they are one of the fastest-cooking legumes, or that they are consumed in large quantities all over Europe, Asia, and Africa (even Idaho!). What will impress you is how tender, juicy, and "meaty" they taste. I grew up grilling over campfires, and I know burgers. These are as delicious as they come. Sometimes I'll even take a few patties with me on long training runs and races.

    1 cup dried green lentils (2¼ cups cooked)

2¼ cups water

    1 teaspoon dried parsley

  ¼ teaspoon black pepper

3   garlic cloves, minced

1¼   cups finely chopped onion

¾   cup finely chopped walnuts

2   cups fine bread crumbs (see Note)

⅓   cup ground flax seed (flax seed meal)

3   cups finely chopped mushrooms

1½   cups destemmed, finely chopped kale,
      spinach, or winter greens

2   tablespoons coconut oil or olive oil

3   tablespoons balsamic vinegar

2   tablespoons Dijon mustard

2   tablespoons nutritional yeast

1   teaspoon sea salt

½   teaspoon black pepper

½   teaspoon paprika

In a small pot, bring the lentils, water, parsley, 1 garlic clove, and ¼ cup of the onion to a boil. Reduce heat and simmer, partially covered, for 35 to 40 minutes, until the water is absorbed and the lentils are soft.

While the lentils are cooking, combine the walnuts, bread crumbs, and flax seed in a bowl. Add the nutritional yeast, salt, pepper, and paprika and mix well.

Sauté the remaining onion, remaining garlic, the mushrooms, and greens in the oil for 8 to 10 minutes, then set aside. Remove the lentils from the heat, add the vinegar and mustard, and mash with a potato masher or wooden spoon to a thick paste.

In a large mixing bowl, combine the lentils, sautéed veggies, and bread crumb mixtures, and mix well. Cool in the refrigerator for 15 to 30 minutes or more.

Using your hands, form burger patties to your desired size and place on waxed paper. Lightly fry in a seasoned skillet, broil, or grill until lightly browned and crisp, 3 to 5 minutes on each side. Extra uncooked patties can be frozen on wax paper in plastic bags or wrapped individually in aluminum foil, making for a quick dinner or whole-some burger for the next barbecue.

MAKES A DOZEN 4-INCH DIAMETER BURGERS

Note: To make the bread crumbs, you'll need about half of a loaf of day-old bread (I use Ezekiel 4:9). Slice the bread, then tear or cut into 2- to 3-inch pieces and chop in a food processor for 1 to 2 minutes, until a fine crumb results. The walnuts can also be chopped in the food processor with the bread.

4

"Pain Only Hurts"

TO ADOLPH STORE AND BACK, 1990

> A journey of a thousand miles begins
> with a single step.
>
> — LAO-TZU

T TURNED OUT those secondhand skis would take me places.
I liked sports but had avoided the school teams in middle
school. Only twelve of us had graduated from the sixth-grade
class at St. Rose, and even though I would have liked to play football
or basketball on the middle school team, the thought of getting on the
late bus with a whole lot of older, athletic kids scared me. I was shy
and I was skinny, and other kids called me "Pee-Wee." Kids pushed
and shoved me and challenged me to fights on the school bus. I think
it was because my mom always made me wear a button-down shirt to
school. Probably because word got around that I did well in class, too.
Studying hard at a northern Minnesota redneck school was not cool.
If they had known how much I hunted and fished, it might have been
different. But they didn't, and it wasn't.

Once a guy on the bus spit in my face. But I didn't fight. I knew
no matter what happened — whether I won or, much more likely, got
beat up — I would get it worse from my dad when I got home.

I played basketball in our church league when I was in seventh
and eighth grades because the travel and uniforms were taken care of

(and church league teammates aren't exactly known for stealing any-one's lunch money), and even though I knew all about trapping zone defenses and backdoor picks, I wasn't anything special. What I re-member most about those basketball games is how my mom needed help getting to the bleachers. I hated seeing that. It sounds awful to say, but I hated how slow she moved. I felt as if we were a really odd family and I was a really odd kid because of that. At church, we all sat up front. My dad would drop us off and say, "You kids go up and get seats and I'll bring Mom in." So everyone in the church got to watch our mom shuffle to the front of the church.

By the time I was a sophomore, I had good grades, a part-time job at the Dry Dock Bar & Grill (where I had been promoted from dishwasher to short-order cook), and not a lot of friends. I could cook shrimp and French silk pie, chili, burgers, clam chowder, and a kick-ass Philly cheesesteak. Something was burning in me, but I don't think I'd call it ambition. It was too vague, too shapeless. I still wanted to know why things were happening the way they were. I wanted to know what I would become. Concentration had helped me in every activity of my life, but it didn't help me find those answers. I wasn't sure what would.

It was the skis. My high school formed a boys cross-country ski team when I was a sophomore, and because I liked being outside and figured I wasn't going to be a star point guard or tailback, I joined. The coach, a tough Norwegian named Glen Sorenson, showed us some fundamentals, took us to meets where we piled up losses, and ordered us to spend the summer before our junior year building our endur-ance. He said that he didn't care how we did it as long as we did it. I didn't own a road bike or inline skates, so I ran.

If my shift at the Dry Dock started early, I'd run in the afternoon. If I had to help my mom in the afternoon, I'd run at night. I'd go a lit-tle farther each day. One day I made it 4 miles out and 4 back, and my dad said, "You ran out to Adolph Store!" He and my mom were both blown away.

I didn't run because it always felt good. My muscles ached, I had blisters, and I was having to go to the bathroom on the run — that was

the summer I learned about the runner's trots (cramps, gastrointesti-
nal distress, and the urgent need to move your bowels). That was the
summer I got honked at and run off the roads of northern Minnesota. I enjoyed the sense of movement and progress, discovering that
I could reach places on my own without anyone driving me. But that's
not why I kept running. I ran because I wanted to ski.

Coach Sorenson told us stories about how he and his brother would
go up to the Arctic Circle and fish from canoes for weeks. He also told
stories of chasing deer on foot until they (the deer) collapsed from
exhaustion. Coach Sorenson was one of the only people I had ever
met who asked why as relentlessly as I had and then explained the answers. Why alternate sprints with distance training? Why move your
arms one way and not another? Why lag back rather than take the
lead early? Coach was usually asking the questions and providing the
answers, but if one of us asked something he didn't know, he seemed
even happier. Knowing pleased him not nearly as much as wondering.
Finally, a place where — and a man who — I could ask why.

To call our team motley would have been a lavish compliment.
Duluth had three school districts. There were the cake eaters on the
East Side, and in the middle were the greasers, the city kids, the ones
who hung out on street corners and who we were sure carried switch-
blades and pulled stickups. Then there was us, the poor kids, so far
out of town that we weren't even technically part of the Duluth school
district. The tough redneck kids.

There was Jon Obrecht, whose parents thought sports built charac-
ter, and the Szybnski brothers, Mark and Matt, who were both around
6-foot, 225. They wore tights and long baggy shorts over them. They
looked like a cross between linebackers and ballerinas. And there was
lanky me. Before Coach Sorenson, not one of us had ever been on
cross-country skis before.

We might not have been as experienced as the other teams, and we
definitely weren't as well equipped, but we were focused. Coach had
only three commandments: Be in shape. Work hard. Have fun. They

were the perfect fundamentals for a bunch of poor redneck Minnesotans. His motto was, "Pain only hurts."

Other teams had bigger squads and nicer uniforms, but we'd show up in our blue jeans and flannel shirts, and by the time I was a junior we'd kick their asses. Or at least some of their asses. The cake eaters at Duluth East were in a different class than everyone else. They wore red Lycra uniforms, and each one of them carried two or three pairs of skis. They were our version of the Evil Empire, or the New York Yankees, or whatever group was rich and powerful and had everything they ever wanted but wanted more. They showed up at meets in privately hired buses. Of course we hated them.

I was probably the best skier on our team then, and a lot of it was because of all the endurance and fitness base I had built up running. We did interval training on the skis — racing up hills — and Coach Sorenson told me it was the first time anyone younger than him had ever beaten him. He seemed happy about it.

It wasn't just our team that was winning. I started collecting individual prizes that season. My parents would come to the meets, and because they took place in the woods, my dad built a sled. He'd put my mom in it and wrap her up in a sleeping bag and put big mittens on her hands, and he'd pull her so she could watch me. That felt good.

I was ranked fifteenth best cross-country skier in the state, and my dad had found steady work as a boiler operator at the University of Minnesota–Duluth. Even though my mom needed a wheelchair now, and even though I still had to stack wood and do the laundry and cook and clean, I had learned that if *sometimes you just do things,* well, sometimes things worked out.

The trouble was, sometimes they didn't. One day in March, I drove my brother and sister over to our great-grandmother's to take her out for lunch and shopping. When we got home, my mom was lying on the floor. She had fallen when she was trying to get up from the toilet, and she had broken her hip. We called my dad, and we called for an ambulance. My mom never walked after that. My dad changed, too. First he gave us — especially me — hell. He said he counted on me to take care of things at home when he was working and I had let him down. I tried to explain that Mom had insisted we go to Grandma's. She said she'd be fine. But he was not having any part of it. He was pissed.

Soon, a new physical therapist came to help my mom; the help she needed now was much more intensive. His name was Steve Carlin, and twice a week he worked with my mom on some pretty involved exercises. He saw me watching them, and one day he said, "Hey, you're an athlete, you can help out here, you'd be good at this." That's when I first thought of being a physical therapist instead of a game warden. So I started being Mom's physical therapist, too. I'd always felt close to her, ever since the days she had pulled my hands around the cookie bowl, and I think my helping meant a lot to her. My brother hated how things were at home, and he spent all his time skiing and causing trouble with his little buddies. Those were his ways of escaping. My sister kept her head down. My dad withdrew.

That summer I was nominated to go to the Team Birkie ski camp for the best high school cross-country skiers in the state. It was held in Cable, Wisconsin, at Telemark Lodge, and all the skiers stayed in a youth hostel in the woods. There were kids from all over the Midwest and coaches from all over, too. The three-time Olympic medalist Nikolai Anikin and his wife, Antonina, were our guest coaches. Antonina spoke almost no English and communicated in yips and yells. She said things with this great accent, like "ski valking" instead of "ski walking," like Drago from *Rocky IV*. We imitated that stuff, and I tried to soak up every Russian-sounding word.

I learned about VO_2 max, the maximum amount of oxygen we can use for aerobic respiration. I learned about different kinds of waxing and finishing kicks and plyometric strength training and lactate threshold, the point at which our muscles accumulate lactic acid faster than they can clear it. I learned about pacing and how to wear a heart rate monitor to measure how hard I was working. We watched videos of the Norwegians, Swedes, and Finns who were the best skiers in the world, and I was amazed. It was like finding the best book in the world on cross-country skiing.

As much as I focused and listened to the instructors, I think I might have learned even more at mealtime. The camp served vegetable lasagna, all kinds of salads, and freshly baked whole wheat bread. At the time, anything more than iceberg lettuce with some cucumbers and creamy ranch dressing seemed bold to me, if not amazingly sophisticated. Whole wheat anything and cooked spinach? That was flat-out exotic.

I didn't have any choice, so I ate it all. And I couldn't believe how good it tasted! What was even more amazing was how great I felt. I trained more, and more often, at that camp than I ever had before. And I had never felt better, stronger. I suspected that what I was eating had something to do with how I was feeling, but it wasn't until years later, when I began to study the connection between diet and exercise, nutrition and health, that I learned the importance of diet for everyone — not just athletes.

I would learn that a plant-based diet meant more fiber, which sped food through the digestive tract, minimizing the impact of toxins. The same diet also meant more vitamins and minerals; more substances like lycopene, lutein, and beta carotene, which helps protect against chronic disease. And it would mean less refined carbohydrates and trans fats, both implicated in heart disease and other ailments.

When I got home, I couldn't stop talking about the camp. My dad built me a slide board out of Formica and plywood and two-by-fours. I spent hours in the basement on that thing, going back and forth, back and forth, trying to replicate the skating movements of the Norwegians and Finns. Dad welded me a bicycle, too. He got an old girls' bike and welded a bar across the top. When I wasn't in the basement on the slide board or riding my bike or logging mile after mile running, I was studying the Finnish videotapes and the Swedish books on exercise physiology that I'd managed to get through interlibrary loan (that took some doing).

I continued my dietary education, too. The winter of my senior year, I joined my ski team buddy, Ben Deneen, and his stepdad, Ben Croft, on a ski trip to Minoqua, Wisconsin. They brought coolers and canvas bags full of whole wheat pasta and spinach salads and black bean chili. We stopped at the house of a friend from Team Birkie ski camp named Kurt Wulff, and his mom served us homemade granola. I asked her for the recipe, and when I got home I told my dad I wanted to make granola for everyone, and I showed him the ingredients. He told me to call a cooperative run out of an old house, with the name Whole Foods Co-Op (no affiliation with the national chain), to see if they had soy flour and wheat germ and barley flakes. I wasn't eating granola and salads because I wanted to make a better world (that would come later) or be nice to cows. I was just noticing that the more I ate what I thought of then as hippie food, the better I felt — and the better I raced. Before high school races, on the morning bus ride I began to eat a big bowl of brown rice I had made the night before. I hid the rice as I ate it because I knew the grief I'd get if anyone noticed. (I tried to educate my family, but slowly. I suspected spinach lasagna might be too much, so I stuck with granola and occasional brown rice for many months at home.)

By the time I was a senior, I was ranked ninth in the state. There was only one local kid who was faster. He was not only the best skier around, he was also the best swimmer and bicycle racer. He had already won the regional championship in cross-country running and was a top competitor at the state meet. That would have been enough, but the word was, he had been expelled from school at least a few times, as well as been thrown off the team for skipping class and mouthing off to coaches.

I had first seen him two years earlier, when our school bus was going through Duluth. Outside on a street corner stood a guy in a bright pink and yellow ski outfit — *no* school wore those colors — with a yellow ribbon hanging out the back. He carried three pairs of skis and had a punk hairdo, with half of his head shaved, the other half in a ponytail. As if he needed to call any more attention to himself, he was yelling and waving for us to stop. It turned out his coach had left him behind to teach him a lesson because he was such a rebel (he refused to wear his school's colors; his uniform was a personal creation). So he had called up Proctor, told them where he would be, and asked if they would pick him up. Coach Sorenson agreed; he always had a weak spot for outsiders.

Everyone had a story about this guy — how he never trained, how he would race hungover, all kinds of things. But man, could he ski! I had never seen someone with so much talent. The word around town was, he never made it past regionals because he was such a screw-up and was always on the verge of flunking out (report cards came out after regionals but before state). I remember thinking that if I had his talent, there is no way I'd let my grades slip.

When he climbed the stairs of our dinged-up yellow bus, he didn't know any of our names. But we knew his. He was the bad boy legend, the greatest athlete in the state, the juvenile delinquent parents warned their kids to avoid. He was the rogue prince of the cake eaters.

His name was Dusty Olson, and he was going to change my life.

STRETCHING

Some people needn't bother with stretching. If you have good biomechanics, don't spend a lot of time in front of a computer, and have the kind of lifestyle where you can nap or take a dip in the ocean whenever you want, you might be one of them. Otherwise, stretch.

Focus on the "runner's five": hamstrings, hip flexors, quadriceps, calves, and the iliotibial (IT) band, or connective tissue that runs from your hip down the outside of the leg. These are the muscle groups that tighten even when people aren't running, from bad posture, sitting, repetitive activities, and just living.

Though there are myriad exercises to choose from for each area (I suggest *The Whartons' Stretch Book* for clear instructions and diagrams), what's important is to do them correctly and regularly.

For example, to stretch the hamstring, lie flat on your back and loop a belt or piece of rope around the ball of one foot, holding the ends of the rope in each hand. Keeping your legs straight, lift the roped leg (without pulling on the rope) as high as you can. Keep lifting until you feel a slight stretch in the back of the thigh, then use the rope to pull until the stretch is slightly — but just slightly — deeper. The stretch should be neither difficult nor painful. Hold for 2 seconds. Then relax and lower your leg to the floor. Repeat five to ten times.

This exercise uses the Active Isolated Stretching (AIS) technique, which I prefer and which is quick (you can do your daily routine in 5 to 10 minutes), easy, and effective. Whether you stretch before exercise or after (as I do), using the active isolated technique, there's no excuse not to stretch.

Apple-Cinnamon Granola

The secrets to this recipe are the soaked oat groats and the hemp milk. Soaking the oat groats (the whole-grain form of oats) promotes the release of enzymes that aid digestion. Hemp seeds are high in omega-3 fatty acids, and hemp milk creates a creamy, light accompaniment to the crunchy granola. It's perfect for before or after a morning workout or race.

1–2 teaspoons coconut oil

4 cups raw oat groats, soaked in water for 6 to 8 hours or overnight, then drained

1 apple, cored and sliced

½ cup dried coconut flakes

2 teaspoons ground cinnamon

2 tablespoons maple syrup or 1 tablespoon agave nectar

1 teaspoon vanilla extract

½ teaspoon sea salt

½ cup raw almonds, chopped

½ cup pumpkin seeds, chopped

⅔ cup raisins

Preheat the oven to 250°F. Grease two baking sheets with the oil.

Process the oats, apple, coconut, cinnamon, sweetener, vanilla, and salt in a food processor for 30 seconds. Scrape sides, process for another 30 seconds, and repeat one more time. Transfer the mixture to a large mixing bowl and combine with the almonds, pumpkin seeds, and raisins. Mix thoroughly with a spoon.

Spread the mixture in a thin layer on the prepared baking sheets. Bake for 2 to 4 hours, turning the granola over a few times with a spatula, until dried and crisp. You can set the oven temperature higher and reduce the baking time, but be sure to check frequently to avoid burning.

Cool and stir in the raisins. Serve with non-dairy milk and sliced banana or fresh berries. Keeps for 3 to 4 weeks in an airtight container.   MAKES 8-10 SERVINGS

Hemp Milk

¼ cup raw shelled hemp seeds

4 cups water

¼ teaspoon sea salt

1-2 teaspoons agave nectar or maple syrup (optional)

Place the hemp seeds, water, and salt in a blender and blend on high for 1 to 2 minutes, until smooth and milky. For sweeter milk, add agave nectar or maple syrup to taste. Hemp milk keeps for 4 to 5 days in the refrigerator.   MAKES 5 CUPS

5

The Pride of the Cake Eaters

> Wanting to be someone else is a waste of the
> person you are.
>
> — KURT COBAIN

DUSTY'S DAD SPENT his days at the bars, and his mom — who worked at the Lutheran church — would give Dusty a quarter and tell him to go play. That was when he was *five years old*. He rode his BMX bike to the Y and spent the day there, swimming, running around, getting into trouble. When Dusty was twelve, his dad drove the family car to a bar and never came back. Soon after that he divorced Dusty's mom, and Dusty didn't see his father for years. His mom started dating a guy who hated Dusty and kicked him around. Dusty didn't spend much time at home.

I, on the other hand, was either studying, helping my mom around the house, skiing, lifting weights (something I learned about at ski camp), or hanging out with my girlfriend. (It seemed that girls liked athletes.)

Dusty drank. All the kids knew that. We also knew (or thought we knew) that he mouthed off to cops and seduced not just high school girls but barmaids and coeds. He didn't just beat people in races but called them names, laughed at them, and insulted their families when he did it. He had no discipline and was wasting his prodigious talent. We all knew that: cake eaters, greasers, and rural rednecks alike.

But in the spring of 1992, when Dusty and I were seniors, I learned how much I didn't know.

Dusty and I stayed together at the USSA Junior Nationals in Rumford, Maine. There were cross-country skiers from every state where it was a sport. The conditions couldn't have been worse. It was 55 degrees, and the snow was like frozen yogurt. The next day it rained 2 inches, and a cold snap the following night froze the trails into skating rinks. But every day the coaches would put us through training exercises. And every day Dusty would talk back. He wanted to know why we were doing this drill or that drill. He wanted to know why we weren't doing more kilometers. He told all of us that the coaches were a joke. He told the *coaches* they were a joke. I couldn't believe they didn't kick him out the first day. I had never talked back to an adult. I had never questioned a coach. He read my face and told me to relax, they were just a bunch of pussies anyway. He called me "Jurker" and a "dumb Polack," but the way he said it, I didn't feel insulted.

The first day of competition, in a 10K race, Dusty took a really bad fall on an icy hairpin turn with only 2K to go. He took some time getting up, and I knew something was wrong because he was in third place and closing. He calmly announced that he had broken his ankle. The coaches told him to suck it up, no one had broken an ankle. They knew all that they needed to know about Dusty. He was just trying to get attention. They told him to get a good night's sleep and to be ready to race the next day.

In his room that night, when he took off his boot, his foot was so purple it was almost black. It looked like a black volleyball, but Dusty didn't say anything. There were no wisecracks. I was actually a little disappointed. Maybe the guy wasn't such a badass after all. When he showed up for his start the next day, his ankle was so swollen, he couldn't even pull his boot on. But he tried. He didn't say a word, just tried to yank that boot up so he could race. Finally one of the coaches from another team, who happened to be a doctor, saw what was going on and yelled at him to stop, that they were driving to the hospital. Dusty got X-rayed and sure enough, it was broken.

That's when I realized I had been wrong about Dusty. He was one tough bastard.

The rest of the week was vintage Dusty. First he snuck into the Alaskan team's room and stole their Nintendo game. When they found out, he told them they were pussies and launched a water fight with them that lasted all week. Every night Dusty would hold forth at the hotel bar over Cokes and ginger ales. He told stories about getting chased through the woods by cops and their K-9 units. He talked about all the women he'd slept with. He told us about how he had befriended a guy who knew which janitors' closets were open at the University of Minnesota at Duluth and how he'd steal ninety rolls of toilet paper at a time, then TP the houses of people he wanted to piss off. He said he never ran out of houses. He said he once ran 18 miles from his house to the start of the Grandma's Marathon in Duluth, then ran the marathon, then ran the 5 miles home.

I said "yes sir" to adults and Dusty asked coaches, "Why the hell are you making us do this?" I wore button-down shirts and Dusty shaved half his skull. Our differences were obvious to anyone who was looking. What wasn't so apparent was the hunger we shared, the way we defined ourselves by our effort. When Dusty regaled everyone with outlandish tales of superhuman endurance, they all hooted and hollered. Except me. Dusty was hilarious, but everyone thought he was totally full of shit. I wasn't so sure. He had something that allowed him to keep going when everyone else stopped. I wasn't sure what it was, but I wanted it.

When graduation rolled around, with some money I'd saved from the Dry Dock Bar I bought my grandpa Ed's beige Toyota Corolla so I could drive the 2 miles to work rather than run or ski. I was president of the National Honor Society, and I had read Solzhenitsyn and Thoreau. I was thinking about life beyond Proctor and Duluth and Minnesota — life way beyond our house on the dead-end road — but I couldn't quite see it. I definitely didn't know how I'd get there. I wanted to ski cross-country in college and to study physical therapy.

I had become pretty good at helping my mom and had become friends with her physical therapist. Steve Carlin was a real down-to-earth guy, not like the doctor who wanted to put me on blood pressure medicine. Steve would help get my mom up, and when she didn't want to, he would help me motivate her. She had a big wound on her hip from the surgery after her fall, but that didn't scare me. Steve said that was another reason I'd be good at physical therapy — I wasn't squeamish.

In my valedictory speech I said, "I would like to leave you with four messages to help you and others benefit from life." (I still have the speech.)

"First of all, I ask you to be different.

"Second, find a way to help others rather than thinking solely of yourself.

"Third, everyone is capable of achieving. Never let anyone discourage you when trying to pursue a goal or a dream.

"And finally, do things while you're young. Be sure to pursue your dreams and goals even if they seem impossible."

It all sounded good, but the truth was, I wasn't sure what my own goals and dreams were beyond skiing and a job as a physical therapist. I knew I wanted to go to college, but my dad had made it clear I would have to pay my own way. I dreamed of going to Dartmouth, but the Ivy League was financially out of the question. I ended up choosing the College of St. Scholastica, my mom's alma mater. It was a small private liberal arts school and had a highly regarded physical therapy program. Best (and worst) of all, it would allow me to stay at home, to continue helping around the house. Mom's spasticity was getting worse, and Steve had stopped coming as much. There just wasn't a lot he could do anymore. When I started taking classes, it was a relief to be out of the house. (That might sound like an awful thing to say, but it was the truth.)

Only one in five kids from Proctor attended college, so most of my friends stayed around and took jobs. I took a job, too, at the NordicTrack shop at the Miller Hill Mall in Duluth. I would put on a polo shirt and demonstrate and sell NordicTrack machines. I was polite, and I knew about the movements of cross-country ski machines. Nick the Greek, who worked a few evening shifts, wanted to fix me up with his daughter. I took medieval history and chemistry and freshman composition. I ate at McDonald's at the mall at least four times a week. I'd get two McChicken sandwiches, extra-large fries, and a Coke. As a kid, I had rarely had fast food. Between my mom's dedication to cooking and my dad's dedication to saving, it was a luxury we couldn't afford. So being able to buy a burger or chicken sandwich whenever I wanted felt like freedom. And it tasted good. While salads and veggie stir-fries might have been okay for some people, I was an athlete, and everyone said serious jocks needed serious protein. That meant meat.

I ran cross-country in the fall but only lasted about half the season, three meets. It was a total junk show. The baseball coach was coaching the team. We wore uniforms that the girls' team had thrown out a decade or two earlier. To stay in shape for the coming ski season, I ran on my own or, more and more often, with Dusty.

We would drive to ski races in my car, and while I would be getting gas, he would be shuffling out of the convenience store attached to the station with a package of baloney or potato chips in his pants. I'm surprised we never got arrested. While I drove down the freeway in my old wagon, Dusty would hang out of the passenger window and high-five fellow skiers on their way to races. He loved the all-you-can-eat buffets. He taught me how to stuff my jacket full of slices from Godfather's Pizza after our stomachs could hold no more.

When Dusty wasn't stealing stuff, getting into trouble, or running, he was working at the Ski Hut, which sold ski gear. He would ride his bike to work (his skis strapped to his bike) in –15-degree weather. That guy could endure.

And of course Dusty always beat me on our runs. He was faster and stronger, and I — I remembered that broken ankle — would never be that tough. We both knew it. But we both knew that I was changing. Dusty skied a 90K training day every year during winter break, the week after Christmas. It was called "the 90K Day." The guy who organized it was Rick Calais, the coach at St. Paul Central High School, whom everybody called "the Ricker." Only the hardest of the hardcore skiers did it. The last year of high school, Dusty asked if I wanted to join him. Of course he beat me, but afterward he told me that he and the Ricker had been looking back every minute or so of the last 10 miles, amazed at how close I was. He knew I had never had blazing speed, and he couldn't believe I was keeping up. To this day the Ricker says, "The 90K Day is what made the Jurker!"

Dusty still gave me shit — about college, about what a nerd I looked like in my polo shirt at NordicTrack, about how straight I was. I envied him. I wondered what it would be like to have no responsibility, no worries. I wondered what it would be like to have his life.

One night in March of freshman year, I came home a little later than I had said I would. My dad had told me that when I said I would be home at a certain time, I had better be home then. I told him he had to realize I had a life outside the house. I was working full time and going to school and I had a lot going on, but he didn't want to hear it. He said, "If you don't like it here, you can go live someplace else. This is the way we do things around here."

I was sure he wasn't serious about my living someplace else. But he was. He really meant it. He said, "I don't want you around here anymore." We were both yelling at each other and Mom was crying. Even when she was well, I don't know if she could have intervened. I had a chemistry test the next day, so I grabbed my books — I didn't even take any clothes — and threw them in my bag and walked out. I drove to an overlook at a nearby rise called Thompson Hill, pulled into a rest area overlooking Duluth, and just sat there. It was freezing. I didn't think about where I was going to live or how my life was changing. I knew what I had to do. I pulled my car below one of the rest area lights. I pulled out my chemistry book and opened it. I started studying.

Long Run Pizza Bread

When I was an omnivorous teenager in northern Minnesota, the idea of pizza without cheese would have sounded like winter without snow: interesting, but impossible. As a plant-eating adult, finding a tasty vegan pizza is about as easy as clocking a three-hour marathon, off the couch (with no training): very rare. That's why I make my own pizza. This one is not only delicious and hearty, it's incredibly fast and easy. The secret ingredient is the nutritional yeast — aka hippie dust — yellow flakes that provide a buttery, cheesy flavor to anything they're sprinkled on. As a bonus, they pack lots of B vitamins, including the crucial B-12.

Tofu "Feta"

8 ounces firm tofu

2 tablespoons light miso (yellow or white)

3 tablespoons nutritional yeast

1 teaspoon lemon juice or apple cider vinegar

Drain and lightly squeeze the water from the tofu. In a small bowl, combine all the ingredients and mash with a potato masher or wooden spoon until they are thoroughly mixed and form a feta-like consistency. Set aside while you make the sauce.

Sauce

1 6-ounce can tomato paste

1 teaspoon onion powder

½ teaspoon garlic powder

1 teaspoon Italian seasoning

1 teaspoon sea salt

¼ cup water

½ teaspoon crushed red pepper (optional)

In a small bowl, combine the tomato paste, onion powder, garlic powder, Italian seasoning, salt, and water, and mix well. Add the crushed red pepper if you like a spicier sauce. Set aside.

Crust

Use any fresh or day-old bread of your choice (my favorite is olive bread).

1 loaf bread

Slice the bread into ½- to 1-inch slices.

Toppings

The vibrant color and pungent flavors make spinach, sundried tomatoes, and olives a favorite combination. Feel free to substitute any 3 to 5 of your favorite veggie toppings.

1½ cups chopped fresh spinach
¾ cup chopped sundried tomatoes
¾ cup chopped kalamata olives

Preheat the oven or toaster oven to 425°F. To assemble the pizza, spread a thin layer of sauce on each piece of sliced bread. Next, add a small amount of the spinach, followed by the tomatoes and olives. Last, crumble the tofu "feta" on top. Bake 10 to 12 minutes, until the bottom of the bread and the toppings are very lightly browned. Leftovers can be cooled to room temperature, placed in small plastic bags, and refrigerated overnight for the next long run or lunch. MAKES 4-6 SERVINGS

6

The Wisdom of Hippie Dan

MINNESOTA VOYAGEUR 50, 1994

> The more you know, the less you need.
> — YVON CHOUINARD

EOPLE ARE ALWAYS asking me the same question. Why, when I could stay in shape with a 25-minute jog, do I train for 5 hours at a time? Why, when I could run a perfectly civilized marathon, would I choose to run four of them back-to-back? Why, instead of gliding over shaded tracks, would I take on Death Valley in the height of summer? Am I masochistic? Addicted to endorphins? Is there something deep down inside that I am running from? Or am I seeking something I never had?

At the beginning of college I ran because of Dusty. It was the summer after my freshman year. Dusty was living with guys in a place they called the House of Gravity. One of his roommates was a champion downhill skier, another was a world-class mountain biker. Dusty was bunking in the attic, where the temperature could drop to −20 degrees, and slept in a down winter sleeping bag from the army surplus store. They called it the House of Gravity because they smoked from a gigantic bong so often that much of the time they couldn't get up. They decided the field of gravity was greater in that house than anywhere else. They even attached the bong to a rope so they could swing it from one person to another.

Meanwhile, I was staying with the Obrechts, the family that had re-formed the Proctor High School boys' ski team. To see my mom and little brother and sister, I had to sneak back to the house when I knew my dad was working. Dusty and his housemates lived day-to-day. I couldn't stop thinking about the future. I knew my skiing career was coming to an end; I didn't have Dusty's talent, and while I could hone my technique until a casual observer would think I was born in Norway, I also had figured out that guys like Dusty — and there were a lot of them at the upper levels of cross-country skiing — could almost always sprint faster than I could. No matter how hard I worked, I could never attain the pure speed that others could. I think whoever — or whatever — gave me determination and a good work ethic forgot to throw in fast twitch muscles. Then Dusty called and told me he had won a 50-mile race called the Minnesota Voyageur. He said he was going to run it next year, too, and asked whether I wanted to train with him. Of course I said yes. (I always said yes to Dusty.) I told myself it was to get in shape for the next ski season. But in reality Dusty was living the life I envied: free, fun, and fast. He was a dirtbag, and I wanted to be a dirtbag, too.

So we dirtbags trained. We would run for 2, 2½ hours, Dusty giving me shit the whole way. Jurker this and Jurker that, telling me I studied too hard, that I thought too much, I needed to loosen up, who cared if I was a fucking valedictorian. We picked up mud along the way and flung it at each other with various insults. Then one day, just when I was getting used to running distance, Dusty said we should mix up the training, and he threw bike riding into the equation. My experience riding was on the hunk of metal my dad had welded for me. Dusty promised it would be fun. He persuaded a friend of his to sell me his old bike — a Celeste green steel Bianchi. It was too small for me, so Dusty helped me put on an oversized mountain bike seat post. We'd go 70, 100 miles. Dusty knew how to ride, knew all the mechanics. He had raced against George Hincapie a few years earlier; Hincapie would eventually compete in the Tour de France. There I was, my giant seat post jabbing the seat into my nuts every time I hit a rock, ready to quit every 5 minutes. Except I didn't. Maybe because it was such a relief to be away from studying and the sadness of my family, from watching my mom deteriorate and sensing my dad get sadder and more angry. I didn't have the skills, and I didn't have the bike, but I discovered something important during those rides with Dusty. I learned that even though I was a hack, even though I didn't know anything about riding—I hadn't read a single book on it, hadn't studied a single essay on spinning or gear ratios—I could gut out those long rides. I wondered what else I could gut out.

I moved into the dorms my sophomore year. I signed up for a class with a Sister Mary Richard Boo, who was a notorious hardass, even among St. Scholastica's hardass nuns. The first day of class she told us to get *Crime and Punishment*. We had five days to read it. It was a struggle between my other classes, my 30-hour-a-week Nordic-Track job, sneaking home to help my mom, and training for what I was sure would be my last season of cross-country skiing.

I looked at my classmates (the student body was 70 percent female), laughing on their way to class. I didn't think many of them were on scholarship. They always seemed to have plenty of time. It seemed to me their life was school and intramural sports and parties. I felt out of place. It wasn't the first time.

It didn't help when Dusty would come over from the House of Gravity reeking of marijuana, hair down to his shoulders, making googly eyes at the coeds. He'd say, "Hey, maaaaaaaaaaaaaaan," and they'd blush. They all asked me, "Who's your stoner friend?" Dusty was always a hit with the ladies. One day he slapped a sticker on my door that read: THANK YOU FOR POT SMOKING. I left it up, and the visiting students would laugh as they passed by, but I'm sure their parents didn't.

If someone had asked me at the time what I liked about Dusty, I probably would have shrugged. He was my friend, and that was enough. Now, though, I suspect it was because he embodied the worldview that was pulling at me. I had started delving into existential literature in high school and was continuing in college. Writers like Sartre and Camus described the plight of the outsider who felt like a stranger in an incomprehensible world. Hermann Hesse wrote about the search for the sacred amid chaos and suffering. The existentialists did not believe in living life from the neck up. They challenged me to reject artifice and the expectations of others, to create a meaningful life.

Back then, while my life never strayed from the conventional lines of socially approved behavior, the people I chose to hang out with created their own conventions — people like my uncle, my mom's younger brother, nicknamed "the Communist," who wore a Malcolm X cap, demonstrated to protect the rights of the homeless, slept on the beaches of Hawaii, worked on the Alaska pipeline, and usually had a copy of Mao's Little Red Book in his pocket. And people like Dusty, of course, who now had a puke-green Chevy van emblazoned with a bumper sticker that read: HEY, MISTER, DON'T LAUGH, YOUR DAUGHTER MIGHT BE IN HERE.

The most unconventional of all might have been the Minnesotan known as Hippie Dan, a modern Henry David Thoreau.

Dan Proctor was forty-five years old when I met him in 1992 at the co-op where he worked and which he co-owned, the Positively Third Street Bakery. He was 5-foot-10, all legs and long, gangly arms. He wore a T-shirt that said BIKES NOT BOMBS, partly hidden by a beard that would have looked at home on a Hasid. He moved as if he was dancing at a Grateful Dead concert. His hair was plaited into two braids that hung over each shoulder. He talked fast — about the environment, and wheatgrass juice and whole grains, and living a mindful life. He spoke with a Scandinavian twang, and when he laughed, he sounded like a loon at dusk.

Hippie Dan made Thunder Cookies that were like chocolate chip cookies on steroids, with oatmeal and whole wheat flour and peanut butter and tons of butter. They were the best cookies I had ever tasted. (Rumor has it he once ran a secret bakery in the back of the shop, long since closed, and Dusty and his stoner pals used to sample those goods a lot.)

He was also a local running legend. People said that when he was younger, he would ride his bike to the local races. Then, wearing blue jeans, he would leave all the people wearing shorts gasping as he shot ahead of them. Even Dusty seemed in awe of Hippie Dan. Dan had been running for twenty years. He didn't have a car or a phone. Eventually he would get rid of his refrigerator. He talked about solar energy and living off the grid and minimizing impact—he produced one small garbage can of trash over an entire year. He also talked a lot about fossil fuels and the foolishness of humans. Essentially, he was trying to lessen his impact on the earth long before that became the trend. Some people called him the Unabaker.

Once Hippie Dan invited me to run with him. We followed his yellow labs, Zoot and Otis, and he told me to watch how effortlessly they ran. He encouraged me to notice how they seemed connected to their surroundings. Simplicity, he said, simplicity and a connection to the land made us happy and granted us freedom. As a bonus, it made us better runners. I didn't know it, but it was a lesson I would learn years later in a hidden canyon in Mexico.

I longed for happiness and freedom as much as the next guy, probably even more, considering my schoolwork and jobs and the situation at home. I could see the wisdom in a simpler-is-better philosophy. But simple for me had never been, well, simple. I had always tackled problems by study and focus. Consequently, when I began training with Dusty for his upcoming Voyageur, I suggested we read up on race strategy and training techniques. Maybe, I said, we should do some intervals or alternate sprints and jogs. Maybe we should count our strides. I think I mentioned heart rate monitors and lactate thresholds. Dusty told me I was full of shit. He said I thought too much. Do monster distances, he said, work your tail off, and that's what will save your ass. He mimicked the Ricker's voice as he beamed, "If you want to win, get out and train, and then train some more!"

So we spent that spring chugging monster distances that lasted 2, 3, 4 hours, runs all through and around Duluth. Dusty would come by and knock on my dorm door, and I'd take a break from *The Brothers Karamazov*, or *War and Peace*, or upper-level physics and anatomy and physiology, and we'd head out. We ran on paths that would narrow to trails and on trails that would narrow to almost nothing. We were running where deer bounded, where coyotes rambled. We ran through calf-deep snow and streams swollen with spring melt so cold that after a while I couldn't feel my feet. Somewhere between my agonized, gasping high school forays to Adolph Store and now, running had turned into something other than training. It had turned into a kind of meditation, a place where I could let my mind — usually occupied with school, thoughts of the future, or concerns about my mom — float free. My body was doing by itself what I had always struggled to make it do. I wasn't stuck on my dead-end street. No bully was spitting in my face. I felt as if I was flying. Dusty knew all the animal paths in the area, and after that spring, I knew them, too. We ran free all spring, sometimes talking, sometimes silent. We ran the way we always ran, Dusty in the lead, me behind. I knew my place, and it was fine. It was all quite fine.

I know a novelist who says he was never happier than when he was working on his first book, which turned out to be so bad that he never showed the manuscript to anyone. He said his joy came from the way time stopped and from all he learned about himself and his craft during those sessions. Running with Dusty that spring — not racing, *running* — I understood what the writer had been talking about.

I also thought I might do all right in a race. I entered Duluth's Grandma's Marathon in June, and all the training with Dusty paid off. I finished in 2:54. Not bad. I thought that, with focus and training, I could get faster.

Instead, with Dusty's recommendation, I decided to go farther. I would enter my first ultra.

The day of the 1994 Voyageur we were both ready, and when Dusty — the defending champion — shot off the starting line, I shot off, too. Dusty didn't call me Jurker or give me shit about my studies. We ran, and not just free. We ran hard. Minnesota in late July can be a muggy 90 degrees and muddy, and this day it was both of those, but we kept cranking. Then, at about mile 25, in a particularly gooey mud puddle, Dusty's left shoe came off. He stopped to fetch it, and for a second I hesitated. How was I supposed to run without Dusty in front of me? He was the legend. I was the sidekick. He was the runner. I was just a stubborn Polack. I wasn't sure what to do, so I did what I had been doing. I kept running. I ran for a few seconds, then a few minutes, and I looked back over my shoulder and didn't see Dusty. I kept running.

Maybe my ski career was over. Maybe my dad would never be happy. Maybe my mom wasn't going to get better, and maybe I'd always lead a dual life, split between diligence and the wild ways that Dusty represented. But at the moment I crossed the finish line, it didn't matter. I had completed one of the hardest things I had ever attempted, and I told myself "never again." I lay face down in the grass, panting, happy but feeling sick, totally drained. I didn't have anything left. Was this what being a runner meant? Putting everything into a single race until you had nothing left to give? I had sensed a long time earlier that I had a talent for gaining speed when others gave ground, and I had wondered how that talent might ever serve me. In the rocky hills outside Duluth, bouncing on my cruel, nut-crunching green Bianchi, I had realized that no matter how much something hurt, I could gut it out. I wondered what that skill would ever be good for. I finished second in my first Voyageur, beating Dusty (who finished third) for the first time.

Hippie Dan had told me that we all had our own path, that the trick was to find it.

I think I had found mine.

⟹ EASIER, NOT HARDER

Coming from the flatlands, I had to learn to run uphill. Sharpening that skill, I improved all my running. You can, too, with or without hills. Next time you're running, count the times your right foot strikes the ground in 20 seconds. Multiply by three and you'll have your stride rate per minute. (One stride equals two steps, so your steps per minute will be twice your stride rate.)

Now comes the good part: Speed up until you're running at 85 to 90 strides per minute. The most common mistake runners make is overstriding: taking slow, big steps, reaching far forward with the lead foot and landing on the heel. This means more time on the ground, which means the vulnerable heel hits the ground with more force on landing, creating more impact on the joints. Training at a stride rate of 85 to 90 is the quickest way to correct this problem. Short, light, quick steps will minimize impact force and keep you running longer, safer. It also will make you a more efficient runner. Studies have shown that nearly all elite runners competing at distances between 3,000 meters and marathon distances are running at 85 to 90-plus stride rates.)

I used to train runners with a metronome. Nowadays there are plenty of websites that list music by BPM (beats per minute)—try http://cycle.jog.fm/. Either 90 or 180 BPM songs will do the trick. ▬

Green Power Pre-Workout Drink

Hippie Dan first taught me the importance of greens like spirulina and wheatgrass. Spirulina is a green algae said to have been carried into battle by Aztec warriors. Used for centuries as a weight-loss aid and immune-booster, it has lately been studied and shown promising results as a performance enhancer for long-distance runners. Because spirulina is marketed as a dietary supplement rather than a food, the FDA does not regulate its production; buy it only from a health food store and a brand you trust.

Packed with protein (spirulina is a complete protein) and rich in vitamins and minerals, this smoothie is an excellent source of nutrition. For a little extra carbohydrate boost, replace 1 cup water with 1 cup apple or grape juice.

2 bananas

1 cup frozen or fresh mango or pineapple chunks

4 cups water

2 teaspoons spirulina powder

1 teaspoon miso

Place all the ingredients in a blender and blend for 1 to 2 minutes, until the mixture is completely smooth. Drink 20 to 30 ounces (2½ to 3¾ cups) 15 to 45 minutes before a run.

MAKES TWO 20-OUNCE SERVINGS

7

"Let the Pain Go Out Your Ears"

MINNESOTA VOYAGEUR 50, 1995 AND 1996

Always do what you are afraid to do.

— GEORGE BERNARD SHAW

MET THE WOMAN who helped turn me into a vegan in line at McDonald's. She was waiting for a refill of a Diet Coke. I was picking up my lunch. Leah was blonde and smiled a lot. Because she had what seemed like a million pairs of Birkenstocks, some of the guys at the mall called her Birkenstock Girl. She worked at a clothing store, was a student at the University of Minnesota Duluth, and rode her bike everywhere. And she was mostly vegetarian (which made her eating at McDonald's sort of odd, I suppose). She and I hit it off, and between Leah and Hippie Dan and some of the books he was giving me (like Wendell Berry's *The Unsettling of America,* about how the loss of agriculture is the loss of culture, how we've gone from knowing where our food comes from to not even thinking that the packages of chicken we buy in the grocery store come from anywhere), I was changing.

I began to put Havarti cheese and spinach on my sandwiches instead of summer sausage. I cut down on breakfast sausage egg biscuits, but not much. I would make granola once in a while. I cooked brown rice and broccoli in my grandmother's Litton microwave (my mom gave it to me when I moved into my own apartment). I made the rice just as she had taught me.

Still, I was an athlete and a young man who felt invincible. So when I was a junior, beginning to embrace the earth-conscious sensibilities of people like Hippie Dan, I was also shoving down two McChicken sandwiches and a large order of fries (as well as the occasional Big Mac) at least four times a week. I figured I needed the protein and that a little junk food never hurt anyone. I loved to grill and was always cooking up sausage, steaks, bratwurst, pork chops, and whatever other animal flesh I could find, all on a giant grill I had bought at a garage sale and lugged to the apartment I shared with my pal Damon Holmes. I was the grill master. Besides, I worried that a plant-based diet would ensure round-the-clock bland food.

It's not that I was totally ignorant. The brown rice had helped me carb up before a race. I had tasted the wonders of granola. The salads and other vegetables at the Team Birkie ski camp helped my endurance. And Hippie Dan had been trying to sell me on the nutritional and ecological benefits of drinking wheatgrass juice and eating more fruits and veggies. Serious student that I was (and frugal), I even planted a little wheatgrass.

I promised myself to keep reading up on the whole plant-based diet thing, but in the meantime, Damon and I spent many a night on our back porch, feet on the banister, barbecued steak (or burgers, or brats) in our mitts, downing a tin of Planters Cheese Balls and a box of Malted Milk Balls in a single sitting.

I was occasionally hunting and fishing and I was still committed to protein and what I thought was the fastest way to get it — through eating dead animals. I didn't want to risk running my second Voyageur without it.

I needn't have worried about getting enough protein. The average 19- to 30-year-old American consumes 91 grams a day, nearly twice the recommended daily amount (56 grams for an adult male, 46 for an adult female). I wasn't aware that too much protein stresses the kidneys (an organ long-distance runners worry about in the best of times, due to our careful attention to water consumption, retention, and elimination) and can leach calcium from the bones. I didn't quite believe that you could get an adequate supply of protein — even if you're an ultrarunner — from plants. I certainly didn't think it would be easy.

So I had the occasional sausage egg biscuit, the random burger. Like it or not, I was still a Minnesota redneck, a hunter and fisherman. I was still my father's son. When Leah would show up with organic apples or milk and I would see the price tag, I went berserk. I'd yell, "You paid how much for that? What's in it, gold dust?"

Leah and I saw a lot of each other that year. I had landed a second job at a running store called Austin Jarrow, named for Jarrow (who had legally gotten rid of his last name, like Madonna) and Bill Austin, both local standout runners. With my two jobs and Leah and studies and at least 2 hours of running every day, I didn't have time for much else.

I stopped visiting my mom and brother and sister very often. Even if I had wanted to, I wasn't willing to go there when my dad was home. I often talked to Mom on the phone. She told me that Dusty called there sometimes, too, and that she was always glad to hear from him, but that Dusty had a hard time understanding her. Her vocal cords were getting weak from the MS.

In the spring of 1995, my mom told me she was moving to a nursing home. She had decided it would be better that way.

As angry as I had been at my father, it was nothing compared to how I felt when she delivered that news. How could he let this happen? *A nursing home!* She was only forty-four. What if I had never left? Could I have prevented this? Again, I had questions for which there were no answers.

She told me it was for the best, that I shouldn't worry, that I should study hard, that everything would be okay.

So I studied hard and ran harder. Dusty noticed. I was tearing up ground. I was assaulting hills and attacking animal trails, the more weed-choked the better.

I ran the game trails Dusty had shown me and across rivers. I ran through rain and snow and blistering heat. Now I was the one in front, and Dusty was right behind me. He kept saying the same thing, over and over: "Let the pain go out your ears, Jurker, let the pain out your ears."

I didn't, though. I held on to the pain. In my second Minnesota Voyageur, I made the pain mine. I used it. All through the 50 miles of the race, I listened to it. *You could have done more. You can do more. Sometimes you just do things!* I ran away from the pain, but it seemed as if I were running toward it. I thought of my mom, crippled. I thought of my life, my ridiculous, petty worries. I thought of the distances I had gone, all the work I had done. I didn't even have to ask myself the question. It was a part of me now. *Why?*

I shot off the starting line — just me this time, no Dusty. And I swallowed that course. I had never run harder. I finished in second place again.

Somehow, I would have to run faster. But I couldn't run harder. What was the secret?

A sick old man told me part of it. He had just shuffled back from his physical therapy session and was slowly climbing back into his hospital bed. With each painful step he took, I could see his frustration, feel his anger. It was my senior year at St. Scholastica, which doubled as my first year in physical therapy school. As part of my training I was an intern at a hospital in Ashland, Wisconsin. I was supposed to be helping the old man, and we both knew I was failing.

He climbed into bed and looked at the lunch tray waiting for him: Salisbury steak drenched in something brown and congealed, instant potatoes, iridescent-looking canned peas. His expression said it might as well have been a tray of rocks. He didn't say anything, but it was as though he was shouting. That's when I heard part of the secret.

What we eat is a matter of life and death. Food is who we are.

I had listened to Hippie Dan. I had remembered my grandmother showing me how good carrots pulled fresh out of the garden tasted. I knew that cutting down on meat and sugar was better for me. But watching a frail, sick man look at his lunch with a cross between nausea and indifference made me think of something else.

The food they served at the nursing home where my mother was bedridden was processed, filled with starches and sugars. The meals my clients ate at hospitals were heavy on meat, low on vegetables. As an athlete, I was ostensibly dedicated to health. As a physical therapist, I was supposed to be helping people with their bodies, but I didn't spend a second focusing on their diet. The healthier I had eaten, the faster and stronger I had become. Was it a coincidence that sick people were being served starchy, crappy food? If a balanced diet could make someone faster, could a bad diet make someone sick?

The answer, I discovered, was yes. I learned that diabetes now affects nearly 10 percent of Americans, and that type 2 diabetes, once nearly unheard of in children, is on the rise, bringing with it a host of complications such as kidney failure, blindness, and amputations, not to mention increased chances of stroke and heart disease in adults. The three most common causes of death in our country — heart disease, cancer, and stroke — have all been linked to the standard Western diet, rich in animal products, refined carbohydrates, and processed food.

Another part of the secret was revealed to me when I did my second internship the next spring in Albuquerque, New Mexico. I was shopping at a grocery store — possibly even getting a steak — waiting in the checkout line when I picked up a magazine to pass the time. There was an article about a doctor named Andrew Weil and one of his books, *Spontaneous Healing*. He said the human body possessed an enormous capacity to take care of itself as long as we took care of it by feeding it well and not putting toxins in it. Shortly after, I sought out that book and devoured it, cover to cover.

Neither my reading nor the old man's lunch marked a come-to-Jesus moment for me. But they did open my eyes to the benefits — and importance — of a plant-based diet. I didn't realize it then, but that spring marked the beginning of my lifelong commitment to learning about food, to eating better, and to living more consciously.

Cutting out processed foods and refined carbohydrates was not difficult. I had grown up eating bread my grandmother baked and fish my dad had caught. Meat and dairy were other matters. I didn't want to consume either — because of stress to my kidneys, possible loss of calcium, increased chances of prostate cancer, stroke, and heart disease, not to mention the chemicals and hormones injected into the country's food supply and the environmental degradation caused by cattle farms — but I was racing now, not just running with Dusty for kicks, so I was even more conscious that I still needed fuel to burn.

I knew I had to figure out a way to get enough protein, to marry my healthy eating with my long-distance running.

Combining vegetarian protein sources like legumes and grains every meal — until recently an article of faith among vegetarians — seemed too labor intensive. And it might have been. But I learned that our bodies pool the amino acids from the foods we eat over the course of the day. I didn't have to sit down and do the math every time I ate. As long as I ate a varied whole-foods diet with adequate caloric intake, I would get enough complete protein. Even the conservative American Dietetic Association, the largest organization of dietary profes sionals in the world, has stated in no uncertain terms: "Appropriately planned vegetarian diets, including total vegetarian or vegan diets, are healthful, nutritionally adequate, and may provide health benefits in the prevention and treatment of certain diseases. Well-planned vegetarian diets are appropriate for individuals during all stages of the life cycle, including pregnancy, lactation, infancy, childhood, and adolescence, and for athletes."

Those last two words were music to an almost-vegetarian ultra-runner's ears.

The next summer, I won the Voyageur on my third try, eating more plants and less meat. I didn't run harder. I had been right: I couldn't run harder. But I had learned something important. I could run smarter. I could eat smarter. I could live smarter. I knew I could keep going when others stopped. I knew I had good legs and good lungs. I wasn't just a runner now, I was a racer. And I was a mindful eater. How many races could I win with my newfound secret? I aimed to find out.

≋ LANDING ZONE

In an ideal world, all runners would land on their forefoot or midfoot when they run. In an ideal world, though, all runners would be lean, healthy, and have spent most of their lives clocking 5-minute miles.

There's no question that forefoot striking is more efficient than heel striking. It uses the elasticity of the Achilles tendon and the arch of the foot to translate the body's downward force into forward motion. Less energy is lost to the ground. It's also a given that landing on the forefoot, as barefoot runners do, prevents the heel striking that cushioned shoes enable, which can lead to so many joint and tendon injuries.

But it's also true that it's not a perfect world. Beginners run. Out-of-shape people run. And for them forefoot striking might increase the risk of tendonitis or other soft tissue injury. That's especially true for anyone who hasn't grown up running barefoot through rural Kenya.

Most researchers would say that a midfoot landing is the most efficient and shock-absorbing technique. But there are people who fall on both ends of the spectrum—heel strikers and those who run on the balls of their feet—and they do fine.

What's important isn't what part of the foot you strike but where it strikes. It should land slightly in front of your center of mass or right underneath it. When you have a high stride rate and land with the body centered over the foot, you won't be slamming down hard, even if you connect with the heel. ≋

"Buttery" Omega Popcorn

Who says vegans can't have fun or that ultrarunners don't like to kick back? Certainly not me. I ate a lot of junk food in college, and an evening with a bowl of this popcorn takes me back to those enjoyable evenings — without the junk or guilt. All popcorn is fun and flavorful. With this version, you're getting essential fatty acids and B vitamins as well. The Udo's Oil makes it taste buttery.

> ½   cup unpopped popcorn
>
> 2–3   tablespoons Flora Oil 3-6-9 Blend
>
> 1   teaspoon sea salt
>
> 3–4   tablespoons nutritional yeast

Using an air popper, pop the popcorn into a large mixing bowl. Sprinkle the popcorn with the oil, salt, and nutritional yeast to taste, mixing thoroughly.   MAKES 4 SERVINGS

8

Attack of the Big Birds

ANGELES CREST 100, 1998

> Strength does not come from physical capacity.
> It comes from an indomitable will.
>
> — MAHATMA GANDHI

DUSTY WAS SCREAMING at me in Spanish. It felt as if I had stepped into a familiar nightmare. I was tired and sore, trying to will myself up a mountain trail at 7,000 feet. Dusty was already there, on the ridge, and he was hurling insults my way, just as he had hurled them at me for so many years in Minnesota. But it wasn't a nightmare. And why Spanish?

My dad and I had started talking again. No big hugging, I'm-so-sorry-now-I-see-what's-important moment. We weren't those kind of people. Leah and I had gotten married at her folks' house on August 17, 1996, just west of Duluth, and my dad brought my mom from the nursing home. Dusty was there, too, wearing a black suit and a tie printed with a reproduction of the Sistine Chapel ceiling. He called it his going-to-court outfit. Dusty and my dad were both pissed that I was getting married and there was no alcohol, so they went back to my dad's place and drank Milwaukee's Best.

Soon after that my folks divorced (I found out later it was my mom's idea to move to the home and her idea to divorce — she didn't want to be a burden). I was starting my second and final year of physical therapy training, still skiing, but just for fun and to keep in shape for running, and still eating meat four or five times a week. I was making clam chowder and grilling chicken and pork chops. I was dipping into a few of the less crazy–sounding recipes from *The Moosewood Cookbook*, but I was still an animal protein athlete.

And then another epiphany hit me. This time it came in a giant bowl of chili. It was December, a cold Wednesday night, and fifteen of us had just finished a 10-mile ski through Duluth's Lester Park. It was a regular gathering of some of the local ski crowd, usually followed by burgers and beers at a nearby pub. That night we went to a microbrewery, where the cook had a reputation for being adventurous — in Duluth it meant he might serve burgers on something other than white bread. One of the guys suggested I try the vegetarian chili, and even though I had never liked regular chili, I agreed.

I couldn't believe the taste. The chilies, the tomatoes, and the beans combined into a spicy winter ambrosia. I suppose it's possible that I was overtired or in such a good mood after a long ski that anything would have tasted good, but that vegetarian chili was about the best thing I had ever eaten. And because of the bulgur wheat, it had the texture of beef chili (see page 70 for the recipe).

Meanwhile, I ran farther. I ran faster. The periods of soreness and fatigue that resulted were shorter and less severe. I was convinced it was the result of the plants I was eating and the meat I was not eating. The chili showed me I could recover faster without abusing my taste buds.

In the spring of 1997, I left for my final physical therapy internship, at an orthopedic clinic in Seattle. Leah stayed in Minnesota, and to save money, I stayed at a hostel on Vashon Island. Every morning I would wake at six, drive to the ferry, then, after the 20-minute ride through Puget Sound to Seattle, ride my bike the 8 miles to the clinic.

Seattle is where I became almost completely converted into a vegetarian. Part of it was the city itself. It seemed like every grocery store I visited was filled with information about local produce or a new vegetarian restaurant around the corner. The grocery stores all sold grains and spices I had never heard of. In Duluth, ethnic cuisine meant Chinese or Mexican restaurants, usually run by Midwesterners. In Seattle, though, there was Japanese, Ethiopian, Indian, and just about everything else. Back in Minnesota I had hidden my brown rice before ski race meets to avoid ridicule, but in the Northwest, it was the carnivores who weren't cool.

I absorbed the culture there — the notion of leaving a small footprint, of living low on the land. My grandparents had actually lived that way, with their gardens and the way they killed the vast majority of the meat they ate. I wanted to live that way, too.

I hung out with South Africans and New Zealanders at the hostel, and they told me about couscous curry and peanut stew. On the ferry I met a guy doing his physician assistant internship, and he introduced me to polenta. I read more of Doctor Weil. On the ferry, I would plug in my earphones and listen to audiobooks that talked about the connection between heart disease and a diet high in animal fat and low in vitamins and minerals.

By the time I drove back to Duluth that fall, I was almost completely a vegetarian. But not quite. I stopped three times at McDonald's for chicken sandwiches and a few sausage-egg biscuits. What can I say? I was hungry.

I stopped long enough in Duluth to pack my bags and write my thesis, and then, in April 1998, Leah and I moved to Deadwood, South Dakota, where I took my first full-time job as a physical therapist. It turned out that Deadwood was where my meat eating reached its dead end.

That I could change in Deadwood isn't so strange, but that I could move from meat and toward plants is something that people still don't believe. To get even a simple cheese pizza in Deadwood, you had to drive 20 minutes. To shop for something organic or whole grains like barley? Not in Deadwood. So I shopped for the week in Rapid City and planted a garden. My neighbor was a former Navy SEAL who told me I wouldn't be able to grow even a weed in the rocky hills, but I proved him wrong. We had squash, beans, tomatoes, and peppers.

I ran nearly every day, anywhere from 10 to 35 miles, through the ponderosa pine forests of the Black Hills and across occasional open plains of grass. One day I found myself surrounded by wild echinacea and picked some. We had echinacea tea that night. My craving for meat had left me, but not my worries about the limits of a meatless diet. My body became a laboratory. I tried combining vegetables and grains, fruits and nuts. One of my more ill-advised experiments involved carrying a small flask of olive oil on a 35-mile run, reasoning that my body needed energy and that oil and fat are the most concentrated forms of calories. A few big swigs, a few episodes of diarrhea, a lot of gas and bloating, and general nausea forced me back to the drawing board.

At every opportunity, I ran out my back door into the surrounding hills or drove to the Bighorn Mountains, where I'd spend hours running through the wild mountains of Wyoming. I loved those runs, but I didn't love my life. Many of the people I was trying to help were smoking two packs of cigarettes a day, ignoring their exercises, and eating junk. It was frustrating, but it was hard to blame them. They didn't know any better. Deadwood was lonely for a pair of newlyweds, especially when one of them worked at a job that seemed like pushing a rock up a hill. I brought my worries home with me. I didn't know what to do with them, and neither did Leah. I began to spend more and more time running in the hills with my training partner, Tonto, an Alaskan husky who loved to run free as much as I did. I felt a calling from those hills, a primal urge to run, something that kept beckoning me.

I had been reading more about Buddhism and self-actualization. I wanted the peace that these mystics talked about. I wanted the serenity I found in movement, the calm that spread through me the longer I ran and the more fatigued I got. Winning had thrilled me, but what thrilled me more was forgetting my worries, losing myself.

Every day I ran 10 to 15 miles; every weekend, 20 to 30. After a long talk with Leah, I flew to races in Virginia and Oregon, going deep into credit card debt in order to pay my travel expenses. I wanted to push my boundaries, to explore my potential. I was passionate, but I was also practical. It was still debt. For a kid who grew up eating government cheese, it was terrifying. But I won the McKenzie River 50K and the Zane Grey 50-Miler. Then I set a new record in the Minnesota Voyageur 50-Miler. Was it compulsiveness or just the determination of a Minnesota redneck or, as Dusty described my heritage, "Norwegian stubborn, French arrogant, and Polish stupid"? Or was it something more pure inside me, something good? I wasn't sure. To find out, I needed a test. I needed to run a 100-mile race. I decided on the Angeles Crest 100, held on a Saturday in late September. It was one of the hardest 100-mile races in the country, climbing 22,000 feet and descending 27,000 feet through the San Gabriel Mountains of California. I logged more distances and refined my diet even more. And I made a call to the man I wanted to be my pacer.

Now, waiting to meet me at 50 miles in Chilao Campground, he was screaming at me again. But this time it wasn't "You're a pussy, Jurker," or "C'mon, you Polack," or any of Dust Ball's other charming greetings.

It was Spanish.

I looked over my shoulder, finally realizing who he was yelling at. There was a knot of sinewy, coffee-colored men with ink black hair wearing loose shirts, long things that looked like skirts, and huarache sandals made from discarded tires. They looked to be in their forties. I had first heard about them from a friend from New York, Jose Camacho, whom I had worked with at the VA Hospital in Albuquerque during one of my PT internships. He had a quote taped to his locker: "When you run on the earth and with the earth, you can run forever."

Anyone who had competed in more than one ultrarace in the United States had probably heard of these men. They were the Tarahumara Indians of Mexico's Copper Canyon, an ancient people who supposedly could run hundreds of miles without even breaking a sweat. As the story went (and as the bestseller *Born to Run* would later document), they didn't talk much, subsisted on a mostly plant-based diet, and grew up running the way American kids grew up watching television or playing video games. Dusty and I had seen them at the starting line, smoking cigarettes (or joints; we weren't sure). They stood apart from everyone else, neither smiling nor frowning. While other runners stretched and warmed up, they just stood there. Some of their skirts were obviously put together recently. One of them had fashioned his from a sheet printed with Big Bird.

A runner named Ben Hian, who had won the race three of the past four years and was one of the best 100-milers in the country, had sidled up to Dusty and me. Ben was a recovering drug addict who loved tattoos: men crawling out of coffins, skulls, that sort of thing. His entire upper body was covered in ink. He wore a Mohawk, loved Ozzy Osbourne, and ran a business where he took tarantulas, snakes, and lizards to libraries and Girl Scout troops, among other places. Oh, and he taught preschool.

"Those guys don't even get warmed up till 100 miles, and they stop at the top of each ridge and all smoke something. Peyote, marijuana, I'm not sure what," Ben said with a grin. Or was it a smirk? He stretched a little, flexed his tattoos.

Was he screwing with us or was he serious? I didn't know.

"Yeah, right," Dusty had replied. "That is total bullshit." Then he told Ben that I was going to beat his ass. Good old Dusty.

But now he was yelling Spanish at them. (Later I learned it was something along the lines of "Fuck you, you slow Big Bird–wearing idiots.") I glanced back again and did a double-take. They really did seem to be floating up the mountain with no effort. *Had* they been smoking something? If so, I wouldn't have minded some.

Before the race, I had confessed my concerns about running 100 miles, and Dusty had told me not to be a pussy, that "this is just a 50-mile race, then another 50-mile race after. And you get stronger the longer you run."

As I suspected, Ben Hian was my main competition. The other

guy I knew I had to beat in order to win was Tommy Nielson, aka Tough Tommy. Tommy was known for his grit and a particular trick. If he was pursuing someone at night, he would switch off his headlamp until he was next to his quarry, then flash it on and move into a near sprint. It had demoralized runners who thought they had the lead, only to be passed before they knew they were even being chased.

I chased Ben Hian the first 50 miles of the course, and the Tarahumara chased us. Every steep incline, I'd gain ground on Ben, but the Tarahumara would *gulp* ground on me. How were they doing that floating thing? Every downhill, Ben and I would crash over rocks and bushes, and the Tarahumara would gingerly pick their way. I suspected it was the huaraches. But I also knew if they ever figured out the trick to descending in a race, they'd be invincible.

As the miles added up — Dusty joined me at mile 50 to pace me the rest of the way — I kept waiting to seize with cramps or for my knees to blow up or to look down and see I had swollen hands. I had never run so far, and I wasn't at all sure I could take the distance.

The Tarahumara chased me all the way to mile 70, gliding up mountains, tiptoeing down. After that, they slowed.

At 90 miles, it was the middle of the night, and Dusty and I saw lights behind us and ahead. That's when we decided to pull a Tough Tommy, and we shut off our lamps. Evidently, though, Tommy pulled a Tommy, too, because suddenly the light chasing us had disappeared. Ben also pulled a Tommy. We ran that way until the end, chasing invisible Ben, running from invisible Tommy. It was an amazing feeling, and somehow I didn't feel my tired legs and sore feet. I ran as if I had run only 10 miles instead of 90. We finished with 10 minutes between each of us.

When we got to the finish line, I had a second-place finish. I had defeated the members of a legendary tribe and almost caught the Man of Tattoos. I had almost won my first 100-miler.

Now I knew I could run this distance. I knew I could win, too. But few others knew it.

It was my little secret.

≋ GETTING ENOUGH PROTEIN

One of the biggest questions I had as an ultrarunner contemplating a vegan diet was how to get enough protein. Here are a few of my tricks: In my breakfast smoothie, I add some nuts and a hit of plant-based protein powder (brown rice, hemp, pea, or fermented soy protein). I'll also have a grain source for breakfast, such as sprouted-whole-grain toast with nut butter or sprouted-grain cereal or porridge. Lunch is always a huge raw salad—I love my Lacinato kale—and I'll up the protein content with a soy product (tempeh, tofu, or edamame), a big scoop of hummus, or maybe some leftover cooked grain or quinoa. Dinner might be beans and whole grains, maybe some whole-grain pasta. If I didn't have soy at lunch, I might have it with dinner. Add in some Clif Bars and trail mix as snacks throughout the day and some soy- or nut-based vegan desserts and I get more than enough protein to maintain my muscle tone and help my body recover.

I seek out traditional whole foods rather than highly refined meat substitutes. I look for products that have been sprouted, soaked, or fermented to help break down the indigestible cellulose in plant cell walls. Among soy sources, I favor tempeh, miso, and sprouted tofu, which are all more digestible and have less phytoestrogen (a naturally occurring substance that some—in spite of medical evidence to the contrary—suspect might mimic estrogen's effects in humans) than isolated soy protein. I eat sprouted-grain breads and tortillas, and at home I often soak my whole grains and beans before cooking. ≋

Minnesota Winter Chili

The night I tasted this chili is the night I decided I could be a happy, athletic vegetarian. One mouthful made me realize that vegetarian food could taste just as good, and have just as hearty a texture, as meat-based foods. The bulgur wheat is a source of complex carbohydrates, and combined with the other ingredients, it makes a complete protein. There's nothing like it after exercise, especially on a cold winter night.

2	tablespoons coconut oil or olive oil
2	garlic cloves, minced
1	cup finely chopped onion
8–10	medium mushrooms, finely chopped
½	cup finely chopped green bell pepper
½	cup finely chopped red bell pepper
½	cup finely chopped carrots
1	jalapeño pepper or other hot pepper, seeded and minced (optional)
1	cup frozen corn kernels
1	teaspoon ground cumin
½	teaspoon ground coriander
2	tablespoons chili powder
2	teaspoons sea salt, plus more to taste
½	teaspoon black pepper
1	28-ounce can diced tomatoes
1	15-ounce can tomato puree
1	15-ounce can kidney beans, drained
1	15-ounce can black beans, drained
1	15-ounce can red beans, drained
2½	cups water
½	cup dry bulgur wheat
	Hot sauce or cayenne pepper (optional)
¼	cup minced fresh cilantro, for garnish

Add the oil to a large pot. Sauté the vegetables and spices in the oil over medium to medium-low heat for 10 minutes or until tender. Add a few tablespoons of water if the veggies begin sticking to the pot. Add the remaining ingredients except the cilantro and simmer over medium-low heat, covered, for 30 minutes. Stir and simmer for an additional 20 to 30 minutes until the veggies are cooked through. Season with salt and, if more spice is desired, hot sauce or cayenne pepper to taste. Serve, sprinked with the cilantro. Leftover chili freezes well.

MAKES 8-10 SERVINGS

9

Silent Snow, Secret Snow

WESTERN STATES 100 TRAINING, 1999

> The mountains are calling and I must go.
>
> — JOHN MUIR

TIPTOED UP THE stairs from the basement, careful not to wake the family still sleeping, pulled a curtain, and watched dry flakes glinting in the watery light of a crescent moon. It was mid-December, 1998, 5 A.M., no warmer than 10 below. I pulled on polypropylene long underwear, a windbreaker, and a fleece, then my warm-up pants and thick wool socks. The path I had chosen — the path I hoped would fulfill me — would eventually take me through canyons of 100 degrees, deserts so hot that scorpions scuttled for shade. But the path started here, now.

Another layer: Nordic ski hat, Finnish ski gloves. It was a path not many other people could discern. High school valedictorian, college graduate, licensed physical therapist, and husband, and I was back in Duluth, about $20,000 in debt, squatting in my in-laws' basement, riding my bike 10 miles a day, five days a week, to Ski Hut. I earned $5 an hour. It was still warm inside my bed. Outside: black night, white ground. I *thought* it was my path. I laced up my trail running shoes. Shortly after returning to Minnesota, to help with traction in the snow, I had added sheet metal screws to the soles.

We had returned to Minnesota earlier that month. I reunited with

Dusty and Hippie Dan and we ran and occasionally skied together. Often joining us were Jess and Katie Koski, two other local athletes and, just as important to my future, both vegans. The Koskis knew about my Voyageur victories, and Hippie Dan had told them how much I read, how interested I was in nutrition and health. They gave me the book *Mad Cowboy*, by Howard Lyman, in which he argues that factory-farmed meat, fish, and dairy pollutes the earth, poisons the body, and sickens the soul. I thought, if this conservative third-generation Montana cattle rancher thinks plants are the best way to get clean food, then maybe I should take my plant-based diet to the next level. I stopped complaining to Leah about her buying organic produce. I considered eating well to be good, cheap health insurance.

I still worried about getting enough protein, but all the health arguments against meat seemed compelling enough that I thought I would chance it. The only obstacle to going totally vegan was the taste factor. I couldn't imagine going too long without cheese, butter, and eggs. I had too much of a sweet tooth and loved my cheese pizza.

I dabbled with soy and rice milk and thought about the philosophical and nutritional reasons to stop eating animals altogether. Then one Sunday morning, after a 20-mile run with Dusty and the Koskis, I served them my first batch of banana-strawberry vegan pancakes (see page 79 for the recipe). They were golden brown and sweet, dense, and hearty. The fruit flavors met on my tongue, then tangled together in a way fruit flavors had never done before. That's when I decided I could live without butter and eggs.

Milk was a little tougher; I had grown up drinking it with nearly every meal. My Grandma Jurek would take her empty glass bottles to a nearby farm and get them refilled with fresh whole milk. But the milk I was drinking as an adult was not from a nearby farm. It was more likely from a gigantic operation where cows were routinely injected with bovine growth hormone (rBGH), housed in cramped, unsavory conditions, and regularly dosed with antibiotics. No thanks.

(I also cut out fish when I realized that unless I caught them myself in a body of water I knew was clean, I was likely going to be getting some hormones and other chemicals along with my salmon or cod.)

To my delight (and, I admit, surprise), subtracting some things from my diet actually allowed me to expand the number of foods I ate and to discover incredible and delicious new foods. My new diet included fresh fruits and vegetables, beans, nuts, seeds, whole grains, and soy products like miso, tofu, and tempeh. I sought out vegetarian cookbooks and ethnic supermarkets to expand my repertoire. Since I had grown up a reluctant vegetable eater in the homogeneous Midwest, I was blown away by the bounty of Japanese sea vegetables that I discovered when I later raced in that country, the simplicity of a homemade corn tortilla, and the complexity of Thai red curry.

I'm a serious vegan. (I usually avoid that word; to many people it connotes a certain crabby, self-righteous zealousness.) And I'm a serious athlete. But I won't starve for my principles. Although I always have protein powder with me, there were a few times in Europe that I ate cheese out of desperation, and there were occasions in remote villages in Mexico when I consumed beans that I knew had been cooked with lard. I once took a snorkeling trip in Costa Rica and was assured that there would be a vegetarian option, but that turned out to be vegetables that had been grilled *inside* a giant fish! I was hungry and I had a race coming up, so I ate them. On the extremely rare occasions I've diverged from plant-based foods, it's always been a matter of survival, never because I craved animal products or felt incomplete without them.

Those compromises would come later, though. I wouldn't be faced with the difficult choices of a renowned ultrachampion until I *became* a renowned ultrachampion. That's why I was lacing up my running shoes with the sheet metal screws on their soles.

I eased myself out the door into the frigid almost-dawn. I was aiming for the mountains, but now this gently rolling snowmobile path would have to do. It was late enough that the partiers wouldn't be racing their machines, early enough that even the recreational users would be too hung-over to rev up. I took my first steps onto the path and sunk to my ankles. Good. Difficulty would help. It had always helped. I was finally figuring that out. All the whys in the universe hadn't granted me peace or given me answers. But the asking — and the doing — had created something in me, something strong. I pulled my feet out, kept going, sucked in the last bits of night sky, and tilted toward the lunar blade low on the horizon as birch trees slid past.

After the Angeles Crest, I knew I had passed a test. And I knew what the next one would be.

I had heard about it the way minor-leaguers hear of Babe Ruth or teenage climbers learn of Everest, which is to say I don't remember the moment someone said "Western States 100."

People spoke of its difficulties, how it broke spirits as well as bodies. I wanted to train in the most challenging place I knew. That's why I didn't loathe returning to Minnesota for the winter. That's why I was out in the snow, thinking of Northern California.

By the time I had decided I would conquer it, the Western States 100 was probably the most well-known ultramarathon in the world. The course had been featured on ABC's *Wide World of Sports* twice in the 1980s. It had twenty-one aid stations and six medical checks (both high numbers among ultra events, indicating the course's difficulty). Runners finishing in under 24 hours received a sterling silver buckle proclaiming 100 MILES, ONE DAY; those finishing in under 30 hours got a bronze buckle. The male and female winners took home bronze cougars. Every year, the race attracted 1,500 volunteers and 369 long-distance runners who had completed at least one 50-miler in the previous year and who had made it through the Western States lottery system.

Since it began, the race had been a source of local pride. Only one non-Californian had ever won in the men's division, and he was a secret hero of mine. In the past decade, as Northern California had become known as the hub of long-distance running, the race seemed to exude a kind of tribal turf protectiveness. A local (and ultra) legend named Tim Twietmeyer had won five times. People said Twietmeyer didn't care what kind of lead someone might have on him — he knew the course and the course was his. But in 1997 someone took it from him. A navy diver from Maryland named Mike Morton had dropped out of the 1996 race, confirming to many the widely held belief that unless you trained at (and preferably lived near) the Western States course, you didn't stand a chance. When he showed up in 1997, people admired his spunk, but many doubtless pitied his obstinance. Then he beat Twietmeyer by 1 hour and 33 minutes, setting a new course record of 15 hours and 40 minutes.

I wanted to accomplish what the diver had done. I wanted to use the Western States to prove to the Northern Californians and other ultra-distance hotshots that I was worthy of their fraternity. To prove to *myself* that I was worthy. I knew it would be difficult. Twietmeyer had come back and reclaimed his crown in 1998. But now that I knew the rewards of pain, I wanted more pain. I wanted to use it as a tool to pry myself open. Pitting myself against 100 miles of terrain and the best trail distance runners in the world would provide that pain.

The race had started in 1955 when a local businessman named Wendell T. Robie rode a horse 100 miles in a single day. Later, he said he did it "because he could." Every year thereafter, horsemen and horsewomen from all over the area would gather for the Tevis Cup — named after another successful local capitalist, Lloyd Tevis. Anyone who finished the torturous path in 24 hours or less on a mount "fit to continue" would receive a silver buckle.

A remarkable man named Gordy Ainsleigh and his not-quite-so-remarkable horse inadvertently transformed the event into a footrace. Ainsleigh, a chiropractor, outdoorsman, logger, equestrian, wrestler, and scientist, was also a formidable runner. He had long hair, a shaggy beard, and a large, muscled frame that wouldn't have looked out of place on a rugby player or linebacker. He once held the "Clydesdale division" record for the best marathon time by a runner weighing more than 200 pounds (2:52).

But Ainsleigh's favorite race was the Tevis Cup. He had buckled in 1971 and 1972 but the same year gave his trusty steed to a woman he loved. She soon left him, taking the horse. He rode again in 1973, but his replacement steed pulled up lame about 30 miles into the race at a stretch of wood-enclosed meadow called Robinson Flat. The next year, because he didn't want to injure another horse, the mountain man decided to travel the course on foot.

It was a particularly hot day. One horse died. Ainsleigh finished in 23 hours and 42 minutes. He received a buckle and a medical check from a veterinarian.

Another man tried to run the course in 1975 but dropped out after 96.5 miles. In 1976 another longhair, Ken "Cowman" Shirk, set out on foot and finished in 24 hours and 29 minutes. Then, in 1977, the Western States Endurance Run (commonly known as the Western States 100) was born. Fourteen men ran alongside their equine counterparts (three of the guys finished). The next year, the race organizers decided to separate human and horse and move the Western States earlier, to a cooler month, and since then it's run the last weekend in June.

The course begins in Squaw Valley, and the first thing any racer does is climb to 8,750-foot Emigrant Pass, an ascent of 2,550 feet in 4½ miles. She will spend the rest of the 100 miles climbing another 15,540 feet and descending 22,970. Racers follow trails once used by the Paiute, Shoshone, and Washoe, who scraped their living from the harsh land by scavenging nuts, berries, insects, and lizards, digging for tubers, trapping small game like rabbits and squirrels, and very rarely killing a pronghorn antelope. The Native Americans left, victims of smallpox, bullets, and other byproducts of a young nation's Manifest Destiny. Next came the settlers and the gold miners. Not far from the course was Donner Pass, named for the unfortunate group of settlers who had also followed their dreams west, failed to finish their course, and in the winter of 1846–47 suffered fates much worse and more memorable than not getting a buckle.

The moon had set. A pale, watery gray sky promised a pale, watery winter day. I crunched on past more stands of birch and empty, barren fields. My feet sank. I pulled them out. I pumped my arms, sank again, and pulled them out again. Timeless silence, except for the crunching of my feet, the heavy, rhythmic breathing of the forest's only moving creature — me. I would run an hour and 15 minutes this morning — 10 miles at a 7:30 pace. I would run another 10 miles the next morning, and the next. Weekends, I would run 25-mile-long runs.

A few people who knew about my training and also knew what I was eating told me I was crazy. My dad — who had ballooned to over 280 pounds — suggested that if I was going to run long distances, I needed steak, and when I replied that his health might improve if he ate more vegetables, he told me to wait until I was forty and to see how I felt and looked. My grandpa Ed — my mom's dad — told me no one could survive on "fruits and nuts" and that, furthermore, I would need new knees by the time I was forty.

But I felt better than I had ever felt before. I had always had pretty good endurance, but now the soreness I had always experienced after long runs was gone. The resting times I had always needed between hard workouts were shorter than ever. I felt lighter. I felt stronger. I felt faster. And I felt as young as ever.

When I returned to my doorway, the pale gray dawn had turned paler, but the sun seemed a vague memory, not even a promise. Wet little clouds of exhaust coughed from the cars of early shift workers. I would go in, stretch, shower, and change. Then I would start my day.

THE CORE

Your legs propel you, but it's your back and abdominal muscles that enable a lot of the power. For the back, do pulldowns and rows at a gym, with your shoulder blades pinched together. If you practice yoga, concentrate on backbend moves like the locust, the bridge, and the boat.

For the abs, work exercises into your routine that involve keeping your pelvis still while moving your legs. Planks are some of the simpler and most effective of these exercises. For the front plank, lie flat on a mat, face down, then raise your hips and pelvis, keeping your forearms and toes on the floor with your body straight from head to toe. The side plank is the same, except the points of contact between the body and floor are the side of one forearm and the side of the same foot. These starter exercises can be made more challenging with arm and leg movements or by adding a stability ball or disc. Any yoga position will be of tremendous value to the runner if you make sure to focus on and engage your core. Any Pilates routine — which by its nature emphasizes engaging the core — will make you a stronger and more efficient runner. ▬▬

8-Grain Strawberry Pancakes

I first cooked these pancakes after a 20-mile run in a northern Minnesota winter, and the experience taught me two things: first, that I could create a creamy, sweet texture without eggs or milk, and second, that there were an awful lot of grains in the world that I had never heard of. Whole-grain flours can be found in health food stores, or, if you have a high-powered blender like a Vitamix, you can make fresh whole-grain flour like I do. Grind together any combination of whole grains to make a total of 2 cups of flour.

The ground chia and flax act as a binder to replace eggs. In addition to tasting great, the pancakes contain plenty of carbs and protein. It's the perfect food for a long morning run, both before and during. I often carry leftovers on the trail.

    ¼ cup spelt flour

    ¼ cup buckwheat flour

    ¼ cup whole wheat flour

    ¼ cup oat flour

    ¼ cup millet flour

    ¼ cup rye flour

    ¼ cup barley flour

    ¼ cup corn meal

    ¼ cup ground flax seed or chia seed

2 teaspoons baking powder

½ teaspoon sea salt

2 cups non-dairy milk (see recipe for rice milk, page 17)

3 tablespoons olive oil

2 tablespoons agave nectar or maple syrup

1 teaspoon vanilla extract

1½ cups frozen or fresh strawberries, chopped

1 teaspoon coconut oil

Maple syrup or fruit sauce, for serving

Combine the flours, ground seeds, baking powder, and salt in a mixing bowl. Add the milk, olive oil, sweetener, and vanilla and mix thoroughly. Fold in the strawberries. Grease a skillet with the coconut oil and heat over medium-low heat for 3 to 5 minutes, or until a drop of water sizzles when it hits the pan. Pour ½ to ¾ cup of the batter onto the skillet for each pancake. Cook until the bottom is golden brown and bubbles appear on top of the pancake, then flip to cook the other side. Repeat with the remaining batter. Serve topped with maple syrup or your favorite fruit sauce.   MAKES 10–12 6-INCH PANCAKES

10

Dangerous Tune

> Snow. Sun. Sandstone. Sky. He was doing what he
> liked and knew. It was now. And this now had no
> pressure, just permission.
>
> — JAMES GALVIN

THERE WERE NO manuals on how to be a 100-mile champion. I knew because I looked. And the Internet was just being born. So I developed my own plan. First, in late April Leah and I moved to Seattle. I had been offered a job at a place called the FootZone by the owner, Scott McCoubrey, another long-distance runner I met at the Cle Elum Ridge 50K in 1997 during my internship in Seattle. I had learned what I could from the snowy trails and the cold nights. For the Western States, I needed mountains.

Second, I turned to coaches from another age.

When Arthur F. H. Newton decided to enter South Africa's Comrades Marathon (which is actually 55 miles) in 1922, he was thirty-eight years old, not particularly fit, and well aware he would be competing against younger, faster runners. Whether out of wisdom or desperation, he trained at the then-radical and unheard-of distance of 10 and more miles a day. In addition to winning that Comrades Marathon, as well as five more, he set world records at 30, 35, 40, 45, 50, and 100 miles. If anyone can lay claim to being the father of LSD

(Long Slow Distance) training, it is Newton. He was also a nutritional pioneer; he swore by a concoction people called his "secret elixir." (It was made from lemonade and salt.)

Lemonade and long distance, though, wouldn't be enough. So I studied the wisdom of the Australian Percy Cerutty, a former women's clothing shop manager, an advocate of whole foods, and one of the strangest characters in the oft-strange pantheon of ultrarunners.

In 1939, when he was forty-three, Cerutty (he said it was pronounced "just like 'sincerity,' without the sin") suffered a nervous breakdown. After doctors told him he would be dead within two years, he embarked on a regimen of diet, exercise, and a philosophy of living that he called "Stotan," which he explained as a combination of Stoic and Spartan. He wrote that an athlete needed "hardness, toughness, and unswerving devotion to an ideal," but he also needed to embrace "diet, philosophy, cultivation of the intellect, and openness to artistic endeavors."

According to Cerutty, "You only ever grow as a human being if you're outside your comfort zone."

Cerutty recovered (he would live to be eighty years old) and, among other training innovations, eschewed stopwatches in favor of an intuitive approach that relied on an athlete's innate intelligence. He had his runners sprint over sand dunes, lift heavy weights, practice yoga, and keep to a strict diet rich in raw foods and whole grains. He studied the way animals ran to see what human runners could learn. He also warned against drinking (any liquid) with meals and socializing after midnight. His most famous protégé, Herb Elliot, the premier mid-distance runner of the late 1950s, called the Stotan sessions "beautiful and painful . . . underneath it all there was a sort of sound philosophy based on 'Let's improve ourselves as human beings, let's become more compassionate, let's become bigger, let's become stronger, let's become nicer people.'"

Both coaches operated outside the norms of conventional athletics — Newton in his emphasis on long-distance training, Cerutty in his admonishments about almost every other aspect of a runner's life — while including training and exertion. Though my childhood was unusual by most standards, my behavior had been ferociously conventional. I had spent my life being the Good Son. I had lived not just inches but yards within the lines etched by parents and teachers, bosses and coaches.

That's why I was drawn to outliers like Newton and Cerutty, men who pushed themselves far beyond the lines that others set.

It was runners like Dusty who stirred me. It was men from other eras — crashing through barriers others had deemed inviolable — who taught me. But the one who pushed me most of all was Chuck Jones. He became my Western States idol.

Jones started running 50-milers in 1985 and in 1986 surprised the (then tiny) ultrarunning community by winning the Western States, upsetting the former champion, pistachio farmer and Church of God preacher Jim King. Jones trained for the race with 200-plus mileage running weeks. (The standard at the time was about 120 to 140 miles.) When an ABC reporter pulled up next to Jones on a particularly punishing ascent late in the Western States and said, "You've been smiling since we started filming you," Jones, without breaking stride, replied, "Well, I like runnin'."

He was the thirteenth of fourteen children. He avoided team sports because his mother couldn't afford uniforms or offer transportation. (His father had committed suicide when Chuck was four and a half.) A drummer and a practitioner of transcendental meditation since he was sixteen, he took up speed walking in his early twenties. To lessen the recovery time, Jones eliminated caffeine, tobacco, and meat — at the same time. It helped.

A difficult childhood. An unconventional and difficult training regimen. A simultaneously cerebral and primitive approach to running that brought childlike joy. It seemed familiar.

It was the same way I felt about Dusty, who since I had left Minnesota had kayaked the entire circumference of Lake Superior, tossed pizzas, won races, built houses, romanced women, waxed skis, lived in five states, and had generally been, well, the "Dust Ball." A few years earlier, the night before Grandma's Marathon, Dusty was drinking at the Anchor Bar, near the finish line. Worried that he might oversleep and miss the morning bus to the start of the race and being at least slightly intoxicated, he took what seemed the most sensible course of action. He ran to the nearby finish line, then ran the course in reverse to the starting line. He then took a nap on a none-the-wiser Minnesotan's lawn until the gun went off, after which he ran the race in the intended direction, finishing in just over 3 hours. If I was always asking why and considering all the options, Dusty was taking what he wanted when he wanted. Dusty, Jones, Newton, and Cerutty had all bumped against the limits of their bodies and their minds, then created new limits. Running wasn't just exercise or a hobby, or even necessarily competition, for them. Basically, they were existentialists in shorts. I wanted to be one, too.

In Seattle, I ran to work, 6 miles each way. After I got home, I ran through the streets of the city, letting the moist air cool me as I felt my muscles loosen and learned about my new home.

My serious training, though, happened on weekends.

That's when I looked for my limits. I found them in the Pacific Northwest at a place called Mount Si.

Serious climbers planning assaults on Mount Rainier and Mount McKinley climb Mount Si with packs to get a taste of the struggle that awaits them. Some families make an annual tradition of a Mount Si climb. Some very serious Seattle mountain runners will run the route. Some very, very serious ultrarunners will run back-to-backs: up and down, and up and down again.

I had my path. It had started in the flatlands, but now it was about to crest mountains. I needed the mountains. On my first Saturday in Seattle, I drove out to the trailhead. I was going to do a back-to-back-to-back.

The mountain rises 3,400 feet, which doesn't sound like much until you realize that it does it in 4 miles. That's over 800 feet per mile. My steepest climb in Minnesota covered a route from Lake Superior

My mom, Lynn, taught me to cook. My dad, Gordy, taught me to hunt and fish. Though I suspect they didn't know it at the time, they both taught me, in word and deed, to endure.

I was four years old and had just finished digging potatoes with my dad. I already knew that the best food in the world was the food you grew yourself.

In 1984, finishing (but not winning) the Park Point Kids' Mile along the shores of Lake Superior, I discovered two things: I wasn't particularly fast, but I seemed to get stronger as the race got longer.

As an 18-year-old high school senior, I started placing near the top in open ski events. Skiing was my passion. Running was a means to stay in shape for that.

"Hippie Dan" Proctor was a local running legend when I met him in 1992, and he taught me about the joys of living a simple, attentive life. When I returned to Duluth in 2010, to visit him in his solar-powered house, I found he hadn't changed much.

The first time I beat my best friend and running mentor, Dusty Olson, was the 1994 Minnesota Voyaguer 50-miler. When I finished, I fell to the ground, convinced this was the hardest thing I would ever do. If only I had known.

I heard about the Western States 100 the way Little Leaguers hear about Babe Ruth. When I first ran it, in 1999, I decided if I didn't win, it wasn't going to be because I didn't give everything I had.

My dog taught me a lot about running. For four years, Tonto trained with me on the mountain trails of Washington and Northern California, preparing for the Western States 100.

Run an event enough times and you'll identify the spot where *your* race really begins. For me and the Western States 100, it's the Rucky Chucky river crossing, mile 78, a final chance to cool down before grinding out the last 20 miles.

Every summer, I loved living dirtbag style with the king of the dirtbags, the Dust Ball. We'd camp at Robinson Flat, just off the Western States Trail, and I'd whip up gourmet meals in my VW Westfalia.

Eating while running is a critical skill for any ultramarathoner. Here I am at mile 50 of the 2003 Western States, chowing down on a homemade burrito.

JASON LEE

Running can be lonely, and ultrarunning can be lonelier, so when you can connect, you do. At the finish of my record-setting Western States 100, I soaked up energy from the cheering crowd in Auburn, California.

PATITUCCIPHOTO

Finishing a 100-miler was great. Winning was greater. Setting a course record was greatest of all. At the 2004 Western States 100, I did all three. Notice the sky. It was the first time I finished the course in daylight.

In 2005, two weeks after my seventh consecutive Western States 100 victory, I set out to conquer the Badwater Ultramarathon, a 135-mile endurance slog through Death Valley. Mile 12, 120 degrees, and I'm leading. What could go wrong?

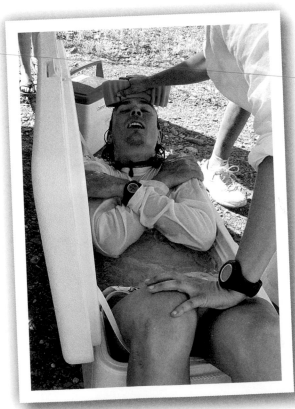

At 48 miles in, I was over 5 miles behind, ready to quit. Those who described the insanity of the Badwater were right.

to the highest ridge. It was 600 feet, but it took 2 miles on a smooth, paved road.

Boulders big as RVs lined the path. Gnarly old roots extended from towering hemlocks and Douglas firs and laid claim to the floor of the trail. Three-foot-long, two-foot-wide leaves from Devil's Club plants brushed me as I climbed. I passed hikers struggling up and others coming down. I was the only runner. From the base of the mountain, it seemed like the ascent would be straight up, but I knew that was impossible; there had to be at least one level patch. And there was, exactly one, halfway. It went 100 yards, and I thought of it as Si Flats. Every half mile, just to remind me that I was in for a day of hurt, there was a moss-covered, wooden signpost. That first day, it took me 14 minutes to cover the first mile.

The mountain reminded me that races are not run all at once, that the only way to survive an ultra was piece by piece. So I ran Mount Si piece by piece. The snowmobile trails in Minnesota with their foot-grabbing snow had taught me the pangs of a single step. Mount Si taught me how to climb as fast as I could when I couldn't see my destination, then to run hard down — not amble — the way I had come up. I didn't jog up Mount Si, and I didn't pick my way down. That first day, I made three trips up and three trips down as fast as I could. Then I drove home and put in a full shift at work.

But the next morning I didn't want to get out of bed. I could hear music. It was the siren song of a warm bed, a cozy couch, a few hours of reading, or listening to music, or just being. No one was forcing me to run. No one said I had to. No one was going to die if I just relaxed a little. Those were the lyrics of the song. It was the catchy, terrible tune that had seduced so many runners to drop out of races. It was a melody I could not afford to listen to. The song was calling: *Rest. You just ran one mountain. No need to do another.*

So much for my improved recovery times, my new über-resilient self, thanks to my diet. Had I pushed myself too far? Most coaches suggest reaching a training peak 80 percent of the distance you're going to be racing. Most coaches, of course, do not run ultras. No one could consistently do 80-mile training runs. So I had decided I would do the next best thing. I would re-create the stress — physical, emotional, and mental — that an ultra would present.

The day after Mount Si, when all I wanted to do was stay prone, I blocked out the perilous tune. I tackled another course just as tough — some would say tougher.

There was no trail map for the Twelve Peaks run, a 35-mile course created by a Seattle runner in his fifties named Ron Nicholl, invariably referred to as "the legendary Ron Nicholl." He was also known as "the trail masochist of Seattle." While many ultrarunners (myself included) look to improve efficiency in their stride and maximize the ratio of the distance traveled to the effort, Ron was known as a guy who did things the hard way until they got easy, which is when he tried to make them harder.

The Twelve Peaks climbs weren't quite as long as those of Mount Si, but they boasted other attractions. They covered 35 miles, compared to the 24 of three trips of Mount Si. They contained an ascent of 10,500 feet and the same descent. And they curled and climbed and plunged over slimy, moss-covered boulders, through mud, straight into a salmonberry-infested jungle known to those who survived it as "'Nam." Thick, wild ferns and sinister hemlock sprouted from impossibly green foliage. Douglas firs loomed, made a cathedral of wood and needles for me, turned midday into eternal night. I ran them in sleet and in snow and in 85-degree heat that turned the forest as clammy as a pressure cooker.

The moss and muck delivered the pain I sought, but I wanted more.

My hero Chuck Jones had granted interviews (and confused interviewers) where he spoke of vibrations and wavelengths and signs from the hidden world, and while I knew what he meant — the sensation of losing oneself, of entering a zone at once connected to the earth and separated from earthly concerns — I wasn't sure how to achieve it on a regular, predictable basis.

I had improved myself as a skier by reading, so I read. And what I discovered was bushido, the culture of ancient Japanese warriors, who espoused courage, simplicity, honor, and self-sacrifice.

According to bushido, the best mind for the battlefield — or the race — is that of emptiness, or an empty mind. This doesn't mean sleepiness or inattention; the bushido concept of emptiness is more like that rush of surprise and expansiveness you get under an ice-cold waterfall. The empty mind is a dominant mind. It can draw other minds into its rhythm, the way a vacuum sucks up dirt or the way the person on the bottom of a seesaw controls the person on the top. When I hear a runner say he "runs his own race," what I hear is bushido.

Bushido is letting go of the past and the future and focusing on the moment. As Thoreau, an American practitioner (though he probably didn't realize it) of bushido and a pretty good distance walker himself, wrote, "Our life is frittered away by detail. An honest man has hardly need to count more than his ten fingers . . simplicity, simplicity, simplicity." I created my own bushido exercises. I stood in icy rivers to strengthen my mind's control over my body. I sat cross-legged and meditated, visualizing my breath, focusing.

Another part of bushido is mastery of the martial arts, an intensely concentrated study of one's craft. My craft was running, and as I climbed those northwest mountains, I tried to do so with extreme focus. It's easy to shut your brain off when you're running long distances, and sometimes it's necessary, but I stayed plugged in. I concentrated on running a particular section harder, on picking up speed downhill while I rested my heart and lungs.

In my two months training in Seattle, my endurance improved all by itself. Dusty and all the other tough guys were right about that. Just do the distance, and that will (usually) save you. But my joints and muscles were memorizing new movements, too. My mind was becoming easier to empty and easier to fill with determination. Sometimes I even felt as if I was floating over the mossy trails.

On my final back-to-back-to-back, before I left for the Western States, I hit Mount Si's first mile marker in 12 minutes. I made it downhill in 30 minutes. I had taught myself to speed up even more than I usually did. My first ascent that last weekend took 49 minutes, and my third took 48 minutes. When I had first crashed through 'Nam, the Twelve Peaks had taken me 6 hours and 40 minutes. My last time there, I ran it in 6:15.

Best of all was what happened to my mind. In the predawn darkness before my final trip through the swamps and peaks of the Issaquah Alps, I heard something. I had made my three trips up Mount Si the day before. It was a familiar sound, but it took a few seconds before I recognized it. I almost laughed. It was the siren song that had beckoned with such urgency two months earlier. *Rest, come back to bed.* That morning, though, it was just a faint little ditty. It was background noise. The Western States would be easy.

MAKING PROGRESS

Regular running is satisfying in itself. If you're the competitive type, even greater satisfaction lies in running faster and longer, in challenging yourself. Progress can be a great motivator and a great incentive to keep exercising.

If you want to improve as a runner, you can (and should) do supplemental training, which involves strengthening, flexibility, and technique work. But the simplest way to improve is to run faster. And the way to do that is to train yourself to run harder, the way I did during my long climbs at Mount Si.

Here's how: After you've been running for 30 to 45 minutes at least three times a week for six to eight weeks, you're ready to start running occasionally at 85 to 90 percent of your physical capacity, or the point where lactate is building up in your muscles but your body is still able to clear and process it. Build to where you can maintain that lactate threshold level for 5 minutes. Then take 1 minute of easy running to give the body time to recover, then repeat. As you progress, increase the number of the intervals and their length while maintaining a 5:1 ratio between work and rest. So you would do 10 minute intervals of hard running followed by 2-minute breaks, or 15 minutes of hard running followed by 3 minutes of rest, and so on.

After four to six weeks, you'll be able to maintain this effort level for 45 to 50 minutes. And you'll be faster. ⚍

Chocolate Adzuki Bars

If you're going to eat a moist, dense dessert on the run, this one is ideal. Made from the most digestible of beans, along with banana, rice flour, and vanilla, these lightly sweetened bars taste even better than their ingredients suggest. Plus, they are an excellent source of carbohydrates and protein.

- ½ teaspoon coconut oil
- 1 15-ounce can adzuki beans, drained
- 1 medium overripe banana
- ½ cup almond or rice milk
- ½ cup light coconut milk
- ½ cup barley flour
- ¼ cup rice flour
- 6 tablespoons cocoa powder
- 3 tablespoons maple syrup
- 1 teaspoon vanilla extract
- 1 teaspoon miso or ½ teaspoon sea salt
- ⅓ cup goji berries, currants, or raisins (optional)
- ½ cup vegan chocolate chips

Preheat the oven to 400°F. Grease a 9-inch square cake pan with the coconut oil. Using a blender or food processor, puree the beans and banana with the almond milk and coconut milk until smooth and creamy. Add the flours, cocoa powder, maple syrup, vanilla, and miso, processing until they are thoroughly mixed. Stir in the dried fruit. Pour the mixture into the cake pan and sprinkle the chocolate chips on top. Bake for 35 to 45 minutes, until firm.

When the bars have cooled, they can be cut into squares, placed in small plastic bags, and refrigerated overnight for the next long day on the road or trail.   MAKES 16 2-INCH-SQUARE BROWNIES

11

"Are You Peeing?"

WESTERN STATES 100, 1999

> If you are not on the edge, you are taking up too
> much room.
>
> — RANDY "MACHO MAN" SAVAGE

THE WEEK BEFORE the 1999 Western States, I spent a lot of time worrying. I worried that my vegan diet might fail me. I worried that I'd run out of energy. I worried that the heat might prove too much.

True, I wasn't as sore as I had been before going to a plant-based diet, and my recovery time was faster than ever. True, I almost never got congested, and whenever a cold or flu swept through Seattle, sending a lot of other runners to bed, I stayed healthy. And of course, I had battled Mount Si and prevailed, if a man could be said to prevail. I had also gone to California a week earlier and trained every day in the 100-degree canyons.

But if you can imagine running 100 miles, you can imagine almost anything. I tried to ignore my darkest visions. I reminded myself how hard I had worked, of my gasping, aching labor. I told myself that the work would protect me at my most trying moments. I didn't need to remind myself of how much I wanted to win. That hunger burned. Did it burn as fiercely in my competitors? I had no reason to think otherwise, and I doubted that I could dim their zeal, at least directly.

So I did something else. I tried to stoke their doubt. The morning of the race I shaved my head, and I let people know that I didn't plan to cut my hair again until I lost the race, and I told myself that it would be a few years. And I said to my pacer, Ian Torrence (Dusty had to attend a wedding), loud enough so people could overhear, "When I take the lead, when I come through in front at Dusty Corners, at 42 miles in . . . ," just so they would know I was planning to win.

If the other runners saw someone so confident, maybe their courage would melt a little bit. That was the plan, anyway. It didn't quite work out that way.

When Ian and I had shown up at the prerace meeting the day before, all we heard was talk of Twietmeyer's sixth victory, which almost everyone agreed was imminent. When Ian had asked one of the organizers if he could tell him the splits for the record time (set by Mike Morton in 1997), people had snickered. Twietmeyer had raised his eyebrows.

Here's what those eyebrows said to me: Who did Ian think he was? And the tall, bald guy? He was from Minnesota! This was a race for mountain men. What did he think he was doing here?

Ian got the splits, though. He wrote on his right forearm (he was left-handed) the time Morton had arrived at each of the fifteen aid stations. On my left forearm I scrawled the same times. Those were the numbers I would need to set a Western States record.

When I got to the starting line at Squaw Valley, I heard comments from people. "Flatlander," people muttered, "second in the Angeles Crest and he thinks he belongs here?" I think I heard some people snicker, "The Minnesota VoyaWHAT?"

Fifteen years evaporated. Suddenly, I was a teenager again.

"Hey, Pee-Wee!"

"Sometimes you just do things!"

"I don't want you around here anymore."

When the gun sounded, I unleashed a guttural, almost barbaric, rebel yell, one that seemed to begin at my ankles. People thought I screamed because I loved running so much, and that was true. But that yell embodied the exhilaration I felt now that I was finally competing in the most storied race against the best ultrarunners in the United States. I had trained as hard as I could imagine. Now I would learn if it had been enough. Could I go the distance against the best in the sport or would the mountain men send me squealing back to the flatlands? I was in first place the first mile, and I was in first place after 10 miles. I was in first place at 20 miles and 30 miles and 40 miles. I ran through snowfields and alpine forests, down wide canyons, over dusty, sun-baked ridges, through the heavy, sweet scent of manzanita, through air so hot it singed my nose hairs, so dry that red dust puffed from the ground with each step, with each rare breeze.

What I heard from the volunteers in the aid stations and spectators wasn't "Wow, the dude from Minnesota is showing us something today" or "Maybe we shouldn't have underestimated him."

What I heard was something else.

He went out way too fast, he'll bonk any minute.

Dumb rookie mistake.

He'll implode by mile 50.

Twietmeyer is going to reel him in, Twietmeyer is going to catch him soon.

He's going to learn that the Sierra Nevadas aren't the same as Minnesota.

The guy's only a 2:38 marathoner, why should we give him credit?

Douglas firs and snow-packed mountains loomed above, rocky canyons yawned below. Yellow sunflowers rioted all over. It was high noon and at least 100 degrees. I was in front, alone with my imagination and my questions.

Why didn't people realize how hard I had trained, how much I wanted to win?

Why was my mom sick? Why had my dad thrown me out of the house? Why did no one, including me, think I would ever beat Dusty—until I did? Asking why was fine, and even if it wasn't, it's what I did. It had led me to link what I ate to how I ran, to link what *anyone* ate to how they lived.

Two o'clock in the afternoon, and I was out of the canyons, into cool 95-degree foothills, still physically strong, still asking why. Asking why had somehow led me to the thing that I loved — the feeling of moving over the earth, with the earth, the sensation of being in the present, free from chores and expectations and disappointment and worry. Asking why had given me the answer, too. I don't think my dad intended it that way, but what he said — *Sometimes you just do things* — carried the weight of hard-earned wisdom.

"There's the flatlander dude," someone whispered — loud enough for me to hear — at the 55-mile Michigan Bluff aid station. "He's in front now, but he won't be for long. That guy's going way too fast. He's gonna crash. Wait until Twietmeyer gets warmed up. That guy's toast."

The naysayers' doubts were whispers compared to the screaming in my head: Did you train too hard? Did you train enough? Can you really run 100 miles on only plants? Did you go out too fast, too early? Are you doomed? But — and this is what I had learned — the screaming in my head could be reduced to faint hissing. All I had to do was remember why I was here, what I wanted — how bad I had wanted it. I had faced difficulties before. You work through them. The lung-burning climbs and quad-pounding descents? A small price to pay for entry into the promised land I had dreamt about. Part of me felt the scalding air. Part of me didn't care. Part of me winced at each painful, jolting step. Part of me didn't care. I was running toward that region where my body couldn't go on, to see if I could will it to do so. It was exactly the place I wanted to be. And there was only one way to get there.

You could carry your burdens lightly or with great effort. You could worry about tomorrow or not. You could imagine horrible fates or garland-filled tomorrows. None of it mattered as long as you moved, as long as you did something. Asking why was fine, but it wasn't action. Nothing brought the rewards of moving, of running.

Sometimes you just do things.

I jogged into the Foresthill aid station at 62 miles, bare-chested, my wet shirt wrapped around my smooth skull. I screamed and hooted — to celebrate that I was still in first place, to express gratitude that I had made it this far, to remind myself that I was alive and on the journey of my choosing. This was the first aid station where a runner could pick up his pacer. I looked for mine.

"Have you been drinking? Are you peeing?"

I told Ian I'd been drinking and peeing plenty, that I felt fine. And it was true, though "fine" is a relative concept for anyone who has just traveled the equivalent of an hour's drive on an interstate highway by foot. Other than normal soreness and fatigue, I felt great. I felt delighted, in fact. My consumption of bananas, potatoes, bean and rice burritos, with the occasional energy gel and Clif Bar, had me running exactly as I wanted to.

Ian shoved two 20-ounce water bottles into my hands, two more into his.

"Before the next checkpoint, I want you to have finished those," he said.

But the next checkpoint was only 3 miles away. If I had been dehydrated, it would have made sense. If I hadn't been peeing, I would have sucked the water down as fast as I could. I started to protest, then thought better of it. The whole idea of having a pacer is that your brain can shut off a little bit. And Ian wasn't just any pacer. In 1999, he would run sixteen ultramarathons and win twelve of them. He had run this course the previous year and knew its challenges. We left the little town on Main Street, then made a quick left onto California, both easy, slightly downhill jogs. Then we plunged down a trail. We would be going mostly downhill for 16 miles. I knew I was supposed to be slugging back the water, but I didn't. It would have made sense to drink before a steep climb. I would have needed the extra fluids. But now?

The air got warmer as we descended 1,000 feet through a crimson dust trail, fine as cake flour. I smelled ancient rock and rich soil.

Run for 20 minutes and you'll feel better. Run another 20 and you might tire. Add on 3 hours and you'll hurt, but keep going and you'll see — and hear and smell and taste — the world with a vividness that will make your former life pale. That's what was happening now.

"How do your feet feel? How are your legs? Are you still drinking?"

It was Ian, behind me, checking, worrying, doing what pacers often do.

I had to think for a second. How did my feet feel? Now that he mentioned it, they hurt. I had a few blisters. My legs? Yeah, come to think of it, they were kind of shot through with invisible knives.

"Fine," I said. "I'm fine."

"Are you drinking?"

I hadn't been, but I did now, drank till a bottle was drained and kept running.

We ran for a few minutes, and Ian didn't say much. Finally, after a twisty descent, there was a climb. It felt good. I felt good. I checked my left forearm. We were way behind on the record splits, but we were still leading. I was doing what I had dreamed and visualized on those snowmobile trails in northern Minnesota and on the mossy trails of the Cascade foothills.

"How we doing?"

We were doing fine, I thought. We were doing great.

Then I felt the weight of my full water bottle. It felt like a particularly heavy cookie I had snuck out of a cookie jar. Ian saw me glance down.

"I want that entire bottle gone by the time we reach the next station."

I chugged it down. We had crested the hill, rounded a bend, and there in front of us was a wooden platform no bigger than 10 by 10 feet, built into the side of a hill. There were three people under an awning — volunteers — and they stared at us.

"Who's this guy?" one of them asked, and before I could say anything, Ian said, "This is the guy who's going to win the race."

We filled our empty bottles, and Ian handed me an inch-long

transparent electrolyte capsule with salt crystals inside, which I swallowed. And just as we were bounding away it hit me. Uh-oh, my stomach felt funny.

We cruised out of the station, about 100 yards through that fine red cake powder, around a bend. That's when I started spewing.

First came liquid, and there — still intact — the electrolyte capsule. Then more liquid. And then — when it started coming out my nose — more liquid. Some chunks of banana. Some green, stinging bile. Just when I thought there couldn't be another wave, there was.

My body was fighting a battle on two fronts: inside, against the heat generated by my muscular exertion, and outside, against the sun-baked canyon air. A rise of more than 4 degrees in core temperature would cause my body systems to begin to malfunction. Fortunately, the last week of training in the heat had helped my cooling systems adapt. The increased blood flow in the surface of my body was allowing extra heat to escape through my skin. I had started sweating earlier and would keep sweating longer and with less sodium (or electrolytes) in my sweat than non–heat acclimatized runners.

The increased perspiration had its downside, though: dehydration. Depending on my pace, I was losing about a liter of water every hour along with a half-teaspoon of salt. My hypothalamus was pumping out antidiuretic hormones, which told my kidneys to mitigate fluid loss by concentrating my urine. Still, even with my body performing its miraculous adjustments, without enough water, dehydration would thicken my blood, increasing the workload of my already-taxed heart. That's what Ian was worried about. That's why he was pushing the water.

He was also worried about another danger: hyponatremia, in which overdrinking, combined with the kidneys' failure to compensate, leads to plummeting blood sodium levels. Runners with hyponatremia will actually gain weight over the course of a race, as the cells in their body swell with retained fluid. Temporary swelling in the extremities isn't so bad, but when brain cells swell, they press against the skull, causing disorientation and confusion. In severe cases, hypona-tremia can even be fatal. Hence Ian's pushing the salt.

Making sure you take in enough water and salt during a long pe-riod of intense effort sounds simple. Tell that to your stomach. A race is a "fight or flight" situation, so my sympathetic nervous system was fired up, shunting blood away from my digestive organs and toward the muscles, lungs, heart, and brain. The pounding of my feet against the ground raised the pressure in my abdomen to two to three times its normal level. Under those conditions, it's hard to keep anything down. Some runners take Prilosec before a race to avoid the inevitable gastric upset, but if I was committing to plant-based, non-processed foods, I wasn't about to do that.

I aimed the puke into the grass off the trail.

Ian patted me on the back. He told me it would be okay, that I would be okay, I would feel better in a minute. I thought he was lying or delusional. Neither option seemed attractive.

I had never thrown up in a race before. Whether it was my cast-iron stomach or because I'd eaten well and taken care of my body, I didn't know. But now, at what should have been one of the crowning points of my life, I was bent over, head turned to the right so I would puke into the grassy hill rather than the other direction, which might alert any competitors who happened upon us and, worse, might lead me to fall down a steep embankment.

Was it the vegan diet? I totaled up my intake since the race be-gan. A bowl of thick rolled oats with banana, walnuts, soy yogurt, en-ergy gel as sweetener, a plum, an apricot, and kiwi. I had awakened at 3 A.M. to eat it so it would have two hours to digest. Two slices of sprouted-grain bread with almond butter. A bean burrito (with rice) at 42 miles. Bananas and cooked potatoes dipped in salt along the way. Clif Shot energy gels, electrolyte drink, and an occasional Clif Bar. I'd been consuming about 300 calories an hour.

Other ultrarunners I had seen gorged on pizza and cookies, bagels and candy. As late as 1999, a lot of conventional thinking in the ultra community was that it didn't really matter what you ate as long as you got lots of carbs and sugar. I was sure my vegan diet was better. I had been sure it was going to help me.

Had it been a mistake? Were Twietmeyer and the others right? Had I let my ego and my wounded pride get the best of me? Or was it simply too much water too fast?

I wasn't just worrying about my mistakes. I was worried what would happen if I kept puking. I knew the horror stories. Some runners get dehydrated, and they puke, and that gets them more dehydrated, which causes more nausea, and then they can't drink or eat anything, and that's when you're in trouble, when you're up the creek without a paddle. Because that's when the medical personnel at one of the stations will make you take an IV. And once you get an IV, you're out. Disqualified.

"It'll be fine," Ian said. "Everything's going to be okay."

Later in my career I would depend more on a growing knowledge of race strategy and tactics to guide me. I would eat and drink at the exact places where my body demanded, because I would become an expert at reading every twitch and cramp and surge of energy. I would know when to rest and when to go. But doubled over at that first Western States, I didn't depend on strategy or knowledge. I couldn't. I was twenty-five, a young buck determined to become king of the mountain. I wanted something, so I moved. Simple. It's something we all have inside us. My body wasn't ready to go, but it didn't matter. That's the moment I learned the power of will. That's the instant I found what I had been looking for.

I straightened up, and Ian removed his hand. I looked at him.

"Good to go," I said, and we went.

I had 32 miles to go — 6 miles longer than a marathon. Ian tried to scare me a few times. "Tim is right behind you," he shouted whenever I slowed, "and he's laughing at you." If I dared to hike — rather than run — up a hill, Ian would crack, "Tim isn't walking up this little hill right now, he's running."

Twietmeyer was 20 minutes behind when we crossed the American River, and as we climbed the 3 miles to the Green Gate aid station, we heard cheering. *"Twietmeyer is closing, the Minnesota dude is about to bonk, Twietmeyer is a real champion."* Neither one of us said anything, but we picked up the pace. We looked at each other, and Ian said, "This is our chance to say to all of them, 'Go screw yourselves.'"

I didn't need any extra motivation. The last 10 miles we ran at an 8:30 pace. The people watching—the Californians, the fans who knew what "real" mountain racing was all about—weren't saying anything, they were just looking. And Ian was cursing the naysayers, saying, "Fuck them." I was angry, too.

The bushido code as I understood it espoused serenity, even in the midst of slaying one's enemies. But I made no attempt to empty my mind of rage. I used it. Maybe it wasn't bushido, but it felt good. I could aspire to peace in the next race. I crossed the finish line at 10:34 P.M., not a record, but 27 minutes faster than Twietmeyer, who came in second. I led the race from start to finish. When I neared the end, I rolled across the finish line in honor of Dust Ball (he liked to crawl and roll across finish lines when he won), and I yelled, "Minnesota!"

I had focused so completely on winning that I'd neglected a few other details—such as where I would stay afterward. I couldn't afford a hotel room, and by the time I realized I might need a place to stay when I was done, they were all booked, anyway. I figured I'd lay my sleeping bag right by the finish line.

Even though I set up there out of economic necessity, I stayed—that night and the next morning and many others—because of something deeper. Camping out at a finish line gave me a chance to cheer on my buddies and to make new friends. More important, it gave me a chance to acknowledge what every single person who completed the race had endured. I had lived in my in-laws' basement, trained when I wanted to sleep, puked, moved numerous times, and gone into debt. The other runners must have endured privations, too. Every single one of us possesses the strength to attempt something he isn't sure he can accomplish. It can be running a mile, or a 10K race, or 100 miles. It can be changing a career, losing 5 pounds, or telling someone you love her (or him). I can guarantee that no one at the Western States *knew* they were going to finish, much less win (including me). A lot of people never do something great with their lives. A lot of people never attempt it. Everyone here had done both. Staying at the finish line and greeting those runners, I could pay tribute to the pain and doubt, fatigue and hopelessness, that I imagined they had pushed through. Staying there allowed me to acknowledge the strength they had needed to summon, to congratulate them on setting their sights on an important goal and achieving it. I didn't realize it till later, but it allowed me to give back something to the sport that had already given me purpose and a measure of peace, that had granted me some answers — however fleeting and ephemeral — to the question why.

I lay down on my sleeping bag and got up to cheer whenever a runner finished. I fell asleep at 1 A.M., and I'm sure I missed a few (I'd been up for 22 hours), but I tried not to. In the morning I got a lift to Latitudes, in Auburn, for some mushroom and sunflower seed tacos and then returned. I stayed there till 11 A.M., the official cutoff time. A lot of the top finishers stayed around for a while, because in those days, while there was certainly a hierarchy among runners, the only place it mattered was on the course. If you were an ultrarunner, you were an ultrarunner. In that moniker everyone was on the same level. We paid the same price and garnered the same joy. And staying at the finish line, I got to remind myself of our collective struggle, to experience that joy over and over again.

COUNTING CALORIES

My biggest challenge in plant-based eating isn't taking in enough protein but taking in enough calories to replace those I burn on my training runs. I make a big effort to include enough calorie-dense foods in my diet — nuts and nut butters, seeds, avocados, starchy root vegetables, coconut milk, and oils such as olive oil, coconut oil, flaxseed oil, and sesame oil. When you're eliminating so many foods in your diet, you need to be careful to include enough new ones to compensate. If you're new to plant-based eating, that's my biggest piece of advice for you: Think about what high-quality foods you can bring into your diet to replace the calories from animal products you're excluding. And make sure you get enough. ⟨⟨

Western States Trail "Cheese" Spread

When I drove to Auburn every summer, I would leave the blender at home, so I'd make this side dish before I left. Spread on Ezekiel 4:9 Bread (made with sprouted grains and no yeast), it provides a great source of carbohydrates and protein. Tahini gives the "cheese" a bite, as well as providing beneficial fatty acids.

1 16-ounce package firm tofu (see note), drained
3 tablespoons white or yellow miso
3 tablespoons lemon juice
¼ cup tahini
2 tablespoons olive oil
¼ cup nutritional yeast
3 teaspoons paprika
1 tablespoon water
½ teaspoon garlic powder
1 teaspoon onion powder
1 teaspoon Dijon mustard

Place all the ingredients in a blender or food processor and process for 2 to 3 minutes, until a smooth consistency is reached. Spread a layer on whole grain bread (my favorite is Ezekiel 4:9 sprouted) with sliced tomato and lettuce for a "cheese" sandwich, or serve with crackers or raw veggies to dip. Keeps about a week in the refrigerator or freeze for up to 2 months. MAKES 3 CUPS, 10–12 SERVINGS

Note: If using a low-powered blender, silken tofu provides better re-sults. Be sure to drain the water first.

12

Battling Bug Boy

WESTERN STATES 100, 2000 AND 2001

> If you could walk a mile in my shoes you'd be
> crazy too.
>
> — TUPAC SHAKUR

WINNING FELT GREAT. Kicking ass — especially the asses of so many who had said I was doomed — was a sensation that all but the most spiritually evolved or brain-fried would enjoy. I had set a goal and achieved it. I had pushed myself to what I thought were the outer limits of my capabilities and then pushed farther — on a vegan diet. Being crowned a champion was good for both my mind and my soul. But it wasn't enough.

I wanted to know more about that space between exhaustion and breaking. I wanted to know more about my body and my will. And I craved the joy and the peace that had filled me when I ran the game trails with Dusty, the quiet, sublime warmth that had enveloped me as the snow settled on the lonely snowmobile trails of the Great North. Besting competitors in a footrace was a thrill, and it was the goal toward which I had been bending the arc of my life. Winning had done wonders for my ego. But I wanted to lose myself, to connect with something larger. I had read enough Buddhist writings by then to realize that chasing a concrete goal was good, but it wasn't the point. And the nuns taught us that blind ambition provided a clear path to dubious behavior, so I knew the answer to Jesus' question, "For what profit is it to a man if he gains the whole world, and loses his soul?" The point was living with grace, decency, and attention to the world, and breaking free of the artificial constructs in your own life. I know all that now. I sensed it then.

But I was twenty-five years old, and I had just won *the oldest and most prestigious trail ultramarathon in the world!* I would continue to push myself, to study the limits of endurance, to seek transcendence. But for at least a little while, I would enjoy my status as champion.

It was a short little while. It lasted until I showed up for work at the Seattle Running Company. The store was the epicenter of the local (and later the entire Northwest and national) ultra scene. It was like the corner bar where all the punk rockers or skateboarders or cops hung out, except the people hanging out at the shop wore running shoes and swapped stories about electrolyte consumption.

"Congratulations," a regular named Jeff Dean greeted me when I showed up after my victory. "You're now officially a one-hit wonder."

Jeff was 5'8", stocky, with a beer belly. He wore thick glasses and talked with a little bit of a lisp. He must have been in his late forties or early fifties, but no one knew. He shuffled when he walked and he shuffled when he ran. He had such weird posture, he looked almost like a hunchback. He ran — or shuffled — 7 miles downtown, and on the way he always looked for loose change. "It was a twenty-cent day," he'd say. Or "It was a buck-thirty day."

Jeff had run a 2:38 marathon years earlier, and that, plus his incredible knowledge about the history and legends of the sport, made him kind of a whacked-out sage in the running community. He was also the unofficial historian of ultras. He gave me two books by James Shapiro, *Ultramarathon* and *Meditations from the Breakdown Lane,* classics on not only the physical and mental dimensions of ultrarunning but the spiritual dimensions as well. Shapiro says, "If your mind is dirty you can run 10,000 miles, but where have you gotten? If you go for a 1-mile run and you're passionately engaged with the world, who cares about the other 9,999?"

When Jeff said I was a "one-hit wonder," I don't think he meant it as a compliment.

I decided I was going to be far more than that. I wanted to win the Western States again, and not only for myself. Mike Morton, the navy diver who had inspired me, didn't get to defend his title in '98 because of an injury. He had broken the Californians' stranglehold on the race and set a record. I wanted to show everyone that my victory hadn't been a fluke, and I wanted to run as a tribute to the diver. Also, I wanted to break Morton's record.

While I was preparing for another victory, I planned to make myself a more complete, mindful human being, more aware of the world around me, of myself, and even of the world I couldn't see. That might sound weird, coming from a kid who grew up hunting and fishing and hating vegetables, but it was true.

First, I refined my training. Even though I didn't exactly enjoy my earlier speed workouts, I added interval training to my program. Once a week I ran to the University of Washington's Husky Stadium. I ran a mile — four laps — at 5K race pace on the state-of-the-art, rubberized track. Then I jogged easy for 3 minutes. Then I ran another hard mile. Then I rested again. I did 5 miles total.

Sometimes I ran in the early morning, between ROTC drills and cheerleader workouts. Sometimes I ran when the football team was practicing; other times in the early evening, when some track team members and other athletes were out. The stadium, which seated 70,000 people, was kind of surreal. I was running as fast as I could, and I was one of the slower people. A lot of them were college track stars. Others were local marathon hotshots.

The interval training not only built my confidence that I could, if necessary, pull away from my competitors, but it helped me focus on what was important. As the nineteen-year-old speed demons and the marathoning champs raced by me, I resisted chasing them. I knew that I wanted to defeat other runners, but in order to do so, I needed to measure my progress only against myself, not others.

When I started, I was clocking 5:25 to 5:30 miles. After two months, I was running them at 5:10. The last mile was always the most difficult. I would always run it the fastest.

I also refined my uphill running. Months of gutting it out on Mount Si and the Twelve Peaks route had helped, but Twietmeyer and Tough Tommy Nielson lived near mountains, too, and I suspected they would all be logging some mega distances for next year's Western States.

So I focused on technique, and I refined the practice that Lance Armstrong and other cyclists had mastered. The trick to uphill racing wasn't so much sheer force as it was turnover. In cycling, the smart (and fast) racer shifts into an easier gear when he hits inclines but maintains his pedal revolutions per minute. Mocked in mountain biking as a "granny gear," that faster gear turned out to be the key to championships. So I looked for my own running "granny gear." I found that by shortening my stride I could "spin," maintaining the ideal turnover of 180 foot strikes a minute. Downhill, I lengthened my stride but stayed light on my feet, and I kept the same 180-footfalls-a-minute pace.

I loved the trails most of all — running away from civilization toward the natural world — but during the early season I started spending more time on the roads with Ian, who eventually moved to Seattle. He and I would go out twice a week for 20 to 30 miles, and we'd focus on hitting miles at a 6:20- to 6:45-minute-mile pace. There was something metric and reassuring about it. Although Ian couldn't stand the fact that my heart rate was always five beats or more lower than his, we helped each other through those tough road miles. It felt so good to be running free and fast, pushing each other to hit that next mile on target. And when we finally made it back to my place, we reveled in the accomplishment of an honest morning's work. I'd celebrate by making us a stack of my eight-grain blueberry pancakes with freshly ground grains or a gigantic skillet of tofu veggie scramble and Ezekiel 4:9 sprouted-grain toast — the perfect recovery food. Life was good and it was simple: hard-earned miles and delicious nourishment.

Running smarter and with more quality, I didn't run as far. A lot of marathoners log 120 to 140 miles. I was doing 90 to 110.

I was used to attacking race courses, regarding steep ascents as obstacles to vanquish, endless trails as journeys to endure. In Seattle, I began taking a more holistic approach. I was reading more about posture and stabilization and core strength and about movement integration from the book *Running with the Whole Body,* one of the few books I could find on running technique. I hit the gym, working on my upper body, because I was beginning to realize how much a strong torso and arms could propel tired legs. I experimented with Pilates. I took up yoga for flexibility, body awareness, and centered focus.

I even tinkered with my breathing. I knew from reading *Spontaneous Healing* that mindful, deep breathing could help the body repair itself. And in yoga (which I struggled with until I understood that it was a practice, not a competition), I learned the concept of Pranayama (literally, "extension of the life force" breathing), which would help, not just my body, but my mind and emotions as well. I picked up a book called *Body, Mind, and Sport,* by John Douillard, and learned that breathing through the nose rather than the mouth lowers one's heart rate and helps brain activity. A yogi announced in class that "the nose is for breathing, the mouth is for eating."

I experimented. I took easy, loping hour runs along Lake Washington. It was flat and damp, and the wind was blowing me sideways. I didn't worry about speed or form. I focused only on breathing in and out through my nose. It was like when I was a kid, teaching myself to relax. I tried doing the same thing on runs that required more effort, and found it very difficult, especially climbing. But from my experimenting, I trained myself to breathe from my diaphragm, to "belly breathe," rather than to breathe from my chest.

Finally, I tweaked my diet. Of all my stabs at self-improvement, this was the easiest, the most joyous.

I'd been vegan for a year, and Seattle was a perfect place to explore and expand the food I was eating. I made smoothies, searched the farmer's markets and my local co-op for more fruits and vegetables. Even though I bought grains, beans, and seeds in bulk and attended member appreciation night once a month at Madison Market Co-op so I could save an additional 10 percent, I was spending more than I ever had on food. And I was fairly deep in credit card debt. While many people freaked out about the year 2000, I was secretly hoping for a Y2K crash to wipe out my debt. There are a lot of ways to live frugally. I know that better than anyone. But the fuel and medicine — the food — I put in my body was not the place to scrimp. My never-better vigor and well-being made the extra investment a no-brainer.

When I raced, I stuck with the usual healthy fare — bananas, potatoes, energy gels — and I added more rice burritos and occasional hummus wraps. I avoided the melons and the oranges often present at aid stations, because I realized that the acidity wasn't so great for my stomach. And I hardly even looked at the junk food that was ubiquitous at those same stations — the M&M's and jelly beans, the potato chips and cookies.

The better I ate, the better I felt. The better I felt, the more I ate. Since going vegan, I had lost a layer of fat — the layer that came with eating the cookies and cakes and Twinkies and cheese pizza that so many omnivores and even vegetarians gulp down. I learned that I could eat more, enjoy it more, and still get leaner than I had ever been in my life. When I went vegan, I started eating more whole grains and legumes, fruits and vegetables. My cheekbones seemed more pronounced, my face more chiseled. Muscles I didn't even know I had popped out. I was eating more, losing weight, and gaining muscle — all on a vegan diet. My recovery times between workouts and races got even shorter. I wasn't even sore the day after 50-mile races. I woke up with more energy every day. Fruit tasted sweeter, vegetables crunchier and more flavorful. I was doing short runs in the morning, working 8- to 10-hour days, then running 10 to 20 miles in the evening. I felt as if my concentration was improving every day.

To refine my approach to running — and eating and living — I read about and attempted to feel what was healthy and natural. I had the enormous advantage of Seattle's vibe of organic and natural everything. I also had access to great experts and technology. In addition to working at the Seattle Running Company, I was working for Dr. Emily Cooper at Seattle Performance Medicine. Athletes would come to us, and we would analyze things like VO_2 max levels and lactate thresholds, as well as discuss their dietary and nutritional habits.

The subject I was most interested in was myself.

In Dr. Cooper's lab, I wore a mask and ran on a treadmill to measure my VO_2 max levels and to estimate my lactate threshold. Sometimes I would take a mask and a portable machine to measure the same factors on trail runs and during intervals. Going hard up a climb, I'd hit 165, 170. On my interval workouts, going all out on the track, it would get up to 180, or about 95 percent, almost as hard as my body could work.

Dr. Cooper had me log foods, too, writing down everything I ate during the day and during a race. She entered all the food into her computer and did all kinds of calculations, and she was blown away.

"Wow," she said after she checked and rechecked the numbers. "You've been doing things right the last few years." She recognized immediately just how in tune with my body I was, how I had learned to listen to what it needed to run on "the edge."

My targeted training made me a more efficient runner. My expanded diet made food taste better and my body work better. Together, they helped change my approach to life. Running with abandon and animal freedom was essential if I wanted to lose myself, to break into another dimension. But science was a way to get in touch with that animal freedom. My dog, Tonto, didn't need to study to find his true nature. I did.

Dusty derided "the fast roadies" or road runners as "people who got up in the morning and counted all their teeth to make sure they were all there." They were anal, he said, so compulsively worried about splits and pace and turnover that they forgot the exuberance of movement. But what I learned in Seattle was that technology and knowledge could help me get even closer to that exuberance, could help me get in touch with my intuition. I was trying to sense what was best for my body and mind — what I craved. But I didn't have to rely on only my feeling. I could cross-check my progress against some hard metrics.

The most important metric to me was how I finished in the Western States 100. I'm not superstitious, but I do believe in developing good habits and the power of repetition. So every year in late June, a week and a half before the race, I would pack my sleeping bag, my race kit, and my canine training partner, Tonto, into my faded, off-white VW Westfalia.

I would also stuff the van with jars of bulgur wheat, cans of lentils and beans, containers bulging with homemade pressed almond butter, tofu cheese spread and carob tofu pudding, and my Ezekiel 4:9 sprouted-grain bread, so named because this Bible verse talks about bread made from a combination of six grains and beans.

Packed, with my buddy Tonto sitting in the passenger seat, I'd drive south to the Sacramento airport, to pick up that scourge of cops and friend to young women worldwide. Ian was a terrific pacer and my friend, and he had helped me win my first bronze cougar, but Dusty was . . . Dusty. Since that first Western States victory in 1999, whether Dusty was working construction in Oregon, waxing skis in Colorado, or tossing pizzas in Duluth, he was the guy I wanted next to me on that last 38-mile stretch of the revered Western States Trail.

He has paced me at the Vermont 100 and the Leadville 100 in 2004 and at countless other races through the years. I've paid his travel expenses, but he's paid for just about everything else, not to mention the time he had to train and the time he took away from his life. He owns a house in Duluth, and as much as he likes everyone to believe otherwise, he has commitments. To his mortgage. To various bosses. To girlfriends.

I always knew Dusty had more natural talent than I did. I suspect he thought so too. Whether I worked harder or wanted to win more or whether Dusty just wasn't interested in the life of a top ultrarunner,

I didn't know. And we never talked about it until much later. I don't know if I could have had as much fun or accomplished what I did without Dusty. Luckily, back then I didn't have to find out.

Other runners paid for hotel rooms in Squaw Valley. Dusty and I camped out high in the conifer-forested foothills 50 miles outside the finish line in Auburn. We pitched my tent in my favorite spot, a rocky overlook surrounded by rodents and lizards, deer and bear (and cougars, whose tracks we would occasionally stumble over). For water we drank from my favorite well at nearby Robinson Flat. Other runners jogged in the relatively cool morning hours. We lazed around camp until the afternoon, when the California sun was beating hardest. That's when Dusty, Tonto, and I made our way to "the Canyons" and ran with the rattlesnakes.

A lot of people gave me grief for the food I ate, and none more so than Dusty. I would make a huge kale salad and tempeh tacos and fresh guacamole and salsa and warm, fresh corn tortillas. I'd heat it all up on the gas stove in my VW bus, and Dusty would say, "Oh, gerbil food again? We're going to run out of toilet paper, with all that roughage!" His postmeal critique: "Better than a kick in the balls, dude."

The truth is, Dusty is a closet vegetarian. He eats healthier than just about anyone I know, but he likes to pretend he doesn't, and he used to call himself a certified Dumpster diver. My other friends and family from Minnesota are another matter. When I would return home for holidays and big meals and someone asked why I'm not having the ham, I would just say I already had some or I'm full. I don't like making anyone feel uncomfortable.

We didn't bring computers or cell phones. I read a lot — Eckhart Tolle's The Power of Now and Dan Millman's Way of the Peaceful Warrior and Bone Games by Rob Schultheis. Dusty spent his time making fun of me and scouring the surrounding area for women. One year we were approached by a couple of girls who turned out to be Mormon. One of them asked Dusty if he believed in anything, and he said, "Oh, yeah, most certainly. I believe in the almighty butt."

On another trip, we stopped near the Sacramento airport to buy a blow-up sex doll, which we mailed to an older accomplished ultrarunner buddy named David Horton — a devout, supercompetitive guy — who was chasing the speed record on the Pacific Crest Trail. We sent it to a P.O. box in Sierra City, California, where we knew he'd be picking up supplies. "We heard you might be lonely," we wrote.

In Seattle, I continued to run with abandon, but I measured the results. The more I measured and adjusted, the more I trusted my instincts. Running as we were born to run is great, and I believe in it. But we live in the twenty-first century, and we have tools our ancestors never did. I wouldn't ignore those tools any more than I would ignore my impulse to get outside on a sunny morning and just run for the sheer joy of it. What I learned during those years in Seattle was that I could run — and eat — with wild, primitive abandon, the way our ancestors had, and that by checking the results of my natural impulses, I could hone those impulses even more. By combining instinct and technique, I searched for that small zone where I could push myself as hard as possible without injury and the unraveling of the body's systems. Accessing and staying in that small zone is the key to success.

In my second Western States, in 2000, I thought I had identified the edge between pushing my body to the limit and going over it. I thought I knew exactly how hard to push, exactly when and how to refuel, and what moments I could, as my once and future pacer Dusty said, "fuck technique." But I learned what every marathoner learns: When you're searching for the edge separating your best and breakdown, it's easy to step over.

In 2000 it happened to me on the same 16-mile stretch of trail where I had gotten so sick the previous year. This time I had monitored my water intake more closely, had eaten a few potatoes and half of a banana and a Clif Shot. But at mile 70, halfway down the American River canyon, I started puking again. This time, my stomach was pumping so violently that I fell to my knees. (While certainly a sign of distress, vomiting in an ultramarathon is not entirely novel, either. A friend of mine and a top runner himself, Dave Terry often said, "Not all pain is significant." He was known for projectile vomiting without breaking stride while running downhill at a 7-minute-mile pace.)

Dusty was pacing me at the time, and he looked back. There was no gentle pat on the back, no promise that everything would be okay.

"Do that shit standing up," the Dust Ball yelled. "C'mon, let's get running." Later, when Dusty thought I had more speed in me, he told me that two women were in the top ten, approaching fast. "They're gonna chick you, Jurker! Do you want to get chicked?" (Dusty had coined the term when he was in high school. It's now part of the ultra-running lexicon).

I won that race in 17 hours and 15 minutes, almost 20 minutes faster than my previous effort. When I returned to Seattle, Jeff Dean told me I was now a "cult figure." He knew about the Californians' fierce tribalism, about their running prowess, and as eccentric as he sometimes was, I think he was delighted that a fellow Northwesterner (even if born in Minnesota) had defended the title.

I wanted more — more victories, more speed, more spiritual development. I wanted more answers, and I thought ultrarunning could provide them. I pored over texts, exploring the link between endurance sports, altered states of consciousness, and wisdom — books like *Running Wild: An Extraordinary Adventure of the Human Spirit*, by John Annerino; *Running and Being: The Total Experience*, by George Sheehan; and *The Marathon Monks of Mount Hiei*, by John Stevens. The monks call their practice of Tendai Buddhism *kaihogyo*, an extensive daily pilgrimage through the mountainous terrain that encompasses hundreds of remote shrines, sacred peaks, stones, forests, glades, and waterfalls. To these monks, the sacred is everywhere.

The most devoted complete a 25-mile run every day for a thousand consecutive days. They wear straw sandals and carry a knife at their waist, to be used to kill themselves should they fail to continue. After five years, they conduct a nine-day fast, after which their senses are heightened to such a degree that they can hear ash fall from an incense stick. In the seventh year of their pilgrimage, the monks undertake the "Great Marathon" of 52.5 miles a day every day for a year. This extended circuit includes not only the rarified holy sites on Mount Hiei but also the crowded streets of downtown Kyoto. Each monk, as he runs past noodle bars and strip clubs, stops to give his blessing to the people in the city hurrying about their business. Each of the writers spoke of rewards beyond speed, beyond endurance, beyond victory.

While I was changing from Minnesota outlier to two-time West ern States champion and fledgling ultrascholar, a massage therapist who often came into the store told me that a vegan diet was nice, but if I really wanted prime performance and maximum health, I should go raw. Gideon was in her forties but looked twenty-five, and her eyes shone with intensity and vitality. She once lived on a commune, and every time I saw her, she would tell me that as good as I had felt af- ter cutting out meat, I'd feel even better cutting out cooking. She gave me a book called *Raw Power,* and as daunting as it seemed, the salad recipes intrigued me. I'd already won two Western States as a vegan. Maybe I could win even more going raw.

So I tried it. I made salads with walnuts, I ate a lot of almond sauce and young coconuts. I made raw tacos, with "meat" made from sunflower seeds and tomato and fresh guacamole wrapped in cabbage leaves. And that's when I perfected smoothies, which I still always have for breakfast.

Eating raw, I discovered that cooking, steaming, and roasting weren't the only ways to prepare or to radically transform foods. I had never thought of black kale (aka Lacinato or dinosaur kale) as some- thing I'd want to eat, especially uncooked. It has a scaly, almost black, bubbly texture, like dinosaur skin. I thought I was doing pretty well chowing down on raw romaine lettuce and spinach. But this fibrous stuff? Uh-uh. That's until I discovered that when you add salt and vin- egar and lemon juice, almost pound it into the thick leaves, and slice a little avocado and tomato in and massage that, what you have are ten- der, delicate leaves with wildly intense flavor. Raw food taught me how bland much of my cooked diet had been.

There were challenges. I had to plan how I was going to get enough calories. Eating at restaurants became tricky. Potlucks weren't easy, either. But food had never tasted so vibrant. Going raw helped me get more in tune with freshness: I could tell from one taste when a carrot had been picked.

At my third Western States, other runners were coming after me. That's what happens when you win a race, especially twice in a row. You become a target.

There was a strong competitor, Chad Ricklefs, who was using his road speed to tear up the ultra circuit. He had talked about how he was going to stay with me, then outkick me at the end. I couldn't hold his bragging against him. I had been confident when I was a rookie, too.

Ricklefs held to at least part of his plan. He stayed with me. He stuck with me. When I sped up, he sped up. When I slowed down, he slowed down. When a black bear lumbered onto the path in front of me, and I stopped in my tracks, so did Ricklefs. (Though when I yelled and waved my arms at the beast until it slouched away, Ricklefs remained still; there were apparently limits to his mimicry). I couldn't believe it, but when I stopped to piss, Ricklefs stopped to piss. He was a small guy, and he wore gigantic sunglasses. According to Dusty, who greeted us at the Robinson Flat aid station, at mile 33, my shadow resembled an insect.

"Hey, Bug Boy," the Dust Ball shouted, "run your own fucking race." And, "Hey, Bug Boy, what are you going to do when we drop your bug ass?"

I don't know if it was Dusty's insults, my pace, the bear, or just the manzanita-scented brutality of the Western States, but shortly thereafter Ricklefs dropped back and then out.

I was in third place, pumping up dusty trails to snow-packed ridgelines where I could hear the snowmelt-engorged river below but not see it.

It was almost exactly the race I had visualized. Then came another Western States body blow, this time a literal one. I had just left the mining encampment called Last Chance and was descending into

Deadwood Canyon, alone on a sandy trail dotted with rocks. I was lengthening my stride, making up time, when I stepped through a gap in two rocks that was covered with small oak leaves. I heard a pop and ripping, like paper being shredded or clothes being torn, and then I felt it. Beyond the jolt of pain was the awful knowledge. I knew I was screwed. This wasn't a roll or even a sprain. This was torn ligaments. It was mile 44, 56 miles to go.

Two years earlier I might have just gritted my teeth and gutted it out. But I was smarter now. I knew my body better. I knew ultras better. Most important, I knew that will wasn't just a matter of strength but a matter of focus. The health of my body was critical to running an ultra. But to run it well, my mind was what mattered.

My first step was to allow myself to feel hurt, and bad, and sad, and all those emotions that unexpected loss — whether in an ultramarathon or a relationship or a job — inspire. So that's what I did while I continued running a mile downhill, then 1,800 feet uphill to the Devil's Thumb aid station 4 miles away. I felt bad, but I kept going.

My next step was to take stock. Was I going to die? Could I put weight on the foot? Did I break it? The answers were no (at least not immediately), yes (at least some), and no. Sometimes you need a doctor or nurse to help you determine whether you'll be doing permanent damage if you continue with an injury. But I'd had some experience. I knew it was bad, but I didn't think it was dangerous.

Step three: What can I do to remedy or improve the situation? Stopping and putting ice on it was not a good option. That was partly because it would cost time. More critical, I knew that the swelling would make the ankle more stable. The inflammation would create a natural cast. I thought it would be extremely painful but that I could get through.

Then the final step: mentally separate all my alarmed and distressed thoughts and emotions — "Why did this happen?" "This is going to really hurt," "How will I continue?" — and plop them someplace where I wouldn't dwell on them. One way to do that was to focus on the tasks at hand and on the benefits of the situation. The tasks: Keep my stride rate high and my foot landings light. The benefits: The agony in my ankle helped distract me from the garden-variety exhaustion, thirst, and soreness of the Western States 100.

I ticked off my checklist silently and kept running. Eight miles later, I passed Scott St. John and moved into second place. I made sure there wasn't even the faintest limp in my stride. You don't want your competitors to know there's a wounded animal around. The wounded animal gets taken down by wolves.

I arrived at the Michigan Bluff aid station, at mile 55, after the leader, Tom Johnson, had already left. Johnson was a two-time winner of the event and held the American record for running 100 kilometers on road.

I had to turn the switch on. I had to tell myself, "You can do it, you can do it." I still felt bad, so I took stock. I took a breath. I took off. At mile 58 I passed Johnson, and at mile 62, the Forest Hill aid station, I picked up the guy who would have made me run — and win — even if my foot had fallen off.

Dusty knew what had happened — I had told him when I saw him at mile 55 — and he didn't talk about it as we ran. He insulted me, as usual. He told me about all the beer we'd be drinking later that night. He might have mentioned that Tom Johnson was a pussy and made more jokes about Bug Boy. And when I asked who was behind me, he said, "Chicks, Jurker, tough chicks are chasing you!" One thing he didn't do was baby me.

I won my third consecutive Western States in 16:38, my fastest time yet. I beat Tim Twietmeyer by 40 minutes (Johnson dropped out not too long after I passed him). I stayed at the finish line — with my foot elevated — to greet Twietmeyer, St. John, Tough Tommy, and every other finisher.

Ultrarunners train so hard and long and compete so ferociously that the friendships that develop are unusually sticky and tenacious. Otherwise, I'm convinced, no one could tolerate the loneliness. Those friendships have nurtured me, none more so than the one that developed in the late summer of 2001.

That's when, at a trailhead in Sun City, California, near the base of Baldy Peak, I met Rick Miller when he emerged from his camper carrying two footlocker-sized coolers of beer. It was the night after the Baldy Peaks 50K. Rick and his wife, Barb, had driven there from their home in Ridgecrest. I had finished third, and Barb took sixth among the women. Now, Rick wanted us all to celebrate.

They asked what kind of running I did. I told them about the Western States and the Angeles Crest, and Rick said that anyone who ran 100 miles on a regular basis was insane. I asked if he ran, and if not, what did he do besides tote beer to his wife's races. He smiled and said he had just finished a 135-mile road race near his home — it ran straight through Death Valley. I told him he didn't have a lot of room to be calling anyone crazy. (I also made a mental note of the event, which I later came to regret.)

The next morning Rick and I ran together, 6 miles of sunny Southern California trail up toward the Pacific Crest Trail. You can spend your life chitchatting with someone — even a good friend — but spend even an hour moving over a rocky path, breathing in pine-scented air, and I guarantee you the chitchat will turn to something else.

Rick and many others helped teach me the great paradox of distance running. It's a solitary activity, and to be a champion one must block out nearly everything except the next step and the next, and the one after that. Notwithstanding the thick ties that bind runner and pacer, teamwork doesn't enter the strategic or tactical considerations of top ultrarunners.

And yet.

And yet ultrarunners — even the fiercest competitors — grow to love each other because we all love the same exercise in self-sacrifice and pursuit of transcendence. Because that's what we're all chasing — that "zone" where we are performing at the peak of our abilities. That instant when we think we can't go on but do go on. We all know the way that moment feels, how rarely it occurs, and the pain we have to endure to grab it back again. The longer an ultrarunner competes, I believe, the more he grows to love not only the sport, not only his fellow ultrarunners, but people in general. We all struggle to find meaning in a sometimes painful world. Ultrarunners do it in a very distilled version. I had learned that by the time I met Rick.

Rick told me about his military service, how he had disarmed bombs for the Navy, that he had lost friends in Beirut and Panama. I told him about my mom, and he told me his mom was sick, too, that she had cancer. I told him about my dad, and he said his dad was a real roughneck, too, and that the two of them had gone through some tough times.

We talked about everything. At the time, I had been reading Noam Chomsky and listening to Amy Goodman on the radio program *Democracy Now.* Rick and Barb were fifty-two and I was twenty-six. Politically, we were two very different breeds. But he told me that we're all human, that there's so much messed-up stuff going on, we need to hold on to what we love. We ran for 2 hours. Every step of the way, I knew exactly where I was. I was running the Path.

Word had gotten out that I had run the second half of the Western States with a blown ankle, and Jeff Dean told me that the victory there elevated me from "cult figure" to "legend." He said he didn't know if he'd be able to come up with another name if I won a fourth time.

I aimed to find out.

BREATHING

Breathing is critical no matter what you're doing, whether it be meditation, calculus, or boxing (beginning fighters first learn how to breathe so they don't exhaust themselves by panting). One of the most important things you can do as an ultrarunner is to breathe abdominally, and a good way to learn that skill is to practice nasal breathing.

Lying on your back, place a book on your stomach. Breathe in and out through your nose, and try to make your stomach rise and fall with each breath. When you succeed in doing so, you're breathing from your diaphragm rather than your chest (which allows you to breathe more deeply and efficiently). Once you've mastered that, try nasal breathing (in and out through the nose) while you're running easy routes. For more difficult runs, like hills and tempo workouts, breathe in through the nose, then exhale forcefully through the mouth (akin to what yoga practitioners call "breath of fire").

Eventually, you should be able to breathe through your nose for entire easy runs and to inhale nasally during the less strenuous sections of even 100-mile runs. I experimented with nasal breathing when I was training for the Western States 100, and it helped me become more of an abdominal runner. Nasal breathing humidifies and cleans the air. As a bonus, it allows you to eat quickly and breathe at the same time, whether running easy or hard. ▬

Indonesian Cabbage Salad with Red Curry Almond Sauce

I became intrigued by peanut sauce as I ate more and more Thai food. When I learned that almonds are higher in calcium than peanuts and contain monounsaturated fat, as opposed to polyunsaturated fat or processed oils, I decided to substitute almond butter for peanut butter. The ginger and curry paste give the sauce a Thai feel, and the agave (or maple syrup) sweetens the dish. If you, like me, thought you hated cabbage, do what I did: Don't cook it. In this case, the raw food tastes much better.

½   head green cabbage, coarsely shredded

4   stalks bok choy or 1 head baby bok choy, sliced into ¼-inch pieces

1   carrot, peeled and cut into thin rounds

1   red bell pepper, seeded and cut into 2-inch-long thin strips

¼   cup chopped fresh cilantro

½ cup raw sunflower seeds
½–¾ cup Red Curry Almond Sauce (see recipe, below)

Toss all the ingredients to combine and let sit for 10 to 20 minutes or more before serving.   MAKES 6-8 SIDE-DISH PORTIONS

Red Curry Almond Sauce

½ cup almond butter
½ cup water
¼ cup fresh lime juice or rice vinegar
2 tablespoons miso
1 tablespoon minced fresh cilantro
2 tablespoons agave nectar or maple syrup
2 teaspoons Thai red curry paste, or to taste
1 teaspoon onion powder
½ teaspoon garlic powder
½ teaspoon ground ginger

Combine all the ingredients in a small mixing bowl or blender. Mix well until smooth. Keeps refrigerated for 2 weeks or frozen for several months.   MAKES 1½ CUPS

13

Of Bears and Gazelles

> Don't work towards freedom, but allow the work
> itself to be freedom.
>
> — DOGEN ROSHI

KNEW MY FOURTH try was going to be brutal. It was 105 degrees, I had a touch of the flu, and I was sure people were talking about me the way I had talked about Twietmeyer. The world was filled with guys like Ricklefs. I had been a guy like that. Maybe the past year someone had been holed up in a basement apartment on the outskirts of Seattle, emerging at night only to run Mount Si, back to back to back to *back*. Maybe that guy was faster than me, stronger. Maybe he was a better athlete.

If I thought biology was destiny, I would have given up a long time ago. I've got scoliosis, my left foot toes out, I had high blood pressure in elementary school, and my marathon time of 2:38 is nothing special. My height is a mixed blessing — good for stride length, bad for heat and technical trails — which makes my brain that much more important.

In a sprint, if you don't have perfect form, you're doomed. The ultra distance forgives injury, fatigue, bad form, and illness. A bear with determination will defeat a dreamy gazelle every time. I can't count the number of times people have said, "I can't believe he beat me." Distance strips you bare.

So what if other bodies might be stronger? I would use my mind. Bushido.

"I want to make everyone work hard," I told a reporter before the race. "I want to make them hurt."

I loved ultrarunning and I loved ultrarunners, but even a super-polite vegan could be a dick during competition, sometimes even to a friend.

Dave Terry, the world-class projectile vomiter, was running on my shoulder by mile 15 of the Western States. Three years had passed since I'd first rolled to the finish line, and Dave and I had become pals. I had grown to admire his work ethic and the way he went out of the way to show kindness to everyone he met. Dave was a solid runner, often in the top three, but seldom a winner. He never let his frustration boil into anything like rudeness. What was most striking was the way he seemed to understand someone's sadness before it was even mentioned. Dave always had a few wise words of encouragement to share — especially, it seemed, to those who needed them most.

"Hey, Scott," Dave said as he pulled alongside. Such a sweet guy. I smiled.

"Hey, Dave!" I said in the same tone of voice I might have used if we had been sharing a beer at his kitchen table or discussing plans for a Saturday night movie.

And then, before he could answer, I said, "What are *you* doing up here? You must really want to hurt today."

Then I took off.

No one called me flatlander anymore. No one opined (at least in my presence) that I was going out too fast or that Twietmeyer — or anyone else — was going to reel me in. When I wasn't leading, I reeled others in.

It wasn't just competitors who were treating me differently. People came into the store just to ask me questions — about what I ate, how I trained, and what shoes I liked. I had sponsorship deals from various footwear, clothing, and energy bar manufacturers, but that only covered travel expenses (not necessarily lodging or food).

It was all because I could run far, fast. And I could do that, I was convinced, because of what I was eating. I stopped the raw diet right after my 2001 Western States victory — the extra time involved in chewing was too much. I'm serious. That, combined with my concern about getting enough calories, drew me back to cooking. But I kept a lot of what I had learned: the smoothies, a large salad for lunch, paying attention to ingredients and preparation. Eating raw was like getting a Ph.D. in a plant-based diet — hard work, but worth it.

At the same time, due to losing a food sponsor, I started making my own gels. I mixed brown rice syrup with blueberries or cocoa powder and made it in bulk. I also experimented with kalamata olives and hummus on whole wheat tortillas for long runs.

My blood pressure and triglyceride levels dropped to all-time lows; my HDL, "good" cholesterol, shot up to an all-time high. I had virtually no joint inflammation, even after miles of pounding trails and roads, and on the rare occasions I sprained an ankle or fell and whacked my elbow or knee, the soreness left faster than it ever had before.

Was it the fiber that sped food through my digestive tract, minimizing the impact of toxins? Was it the food I was adding — the vitamins and minerals, the lycopene, lutein, and beta carotene? Almost every day a new micronutrient is discovered in plant foods that offers protective effects against disease. Or was it what I *wasn't* eating, the concentrated carcinogens, excess protein, refined carbohydrates, trans fats? Factory-farmed animals are treated with growth hormones and steroids to encourage their rapid transit from birth to slaughterhouse. If we wouldn't take steroids ourselves — or eat a bowl of transgenic, pesticide-soaked soybeans — why would we eat the flesh of an animal that has?

Or was the sum of a plant-based diet greater than its parts? Vegetarians are likely to have healthy habits outside the kitchen as well as more active lifestyles and less smoking. A major study shows that vegetarians watch less television, smoke less, and sleep more per night than meat-eaters.

I wasn't sure of the answer, but my diet seemed to be working. So when I came across naysayers — and there were plenty — I weighed my experience against their theories. When I read *Eat Right 4 Your Type*, by Peter D'Adamo, right before my first Western States and learned that my blood type, O, was the least suited of all types to vegetarianism, I worried a little, but not too much. According to D'Adamo, my ancestral profile made me a "canny, aggressive predator" who preferred baby seal meat to bean burritos. But those burritos had fueled me through that first Western States as well as two others. (I wasn't the only one who didn't go along with matching diet to blood type. Dr. Fredrick Stare, founder of the Nutrition Department at the Harvard School of Public Health, calls this book "not only one of the most preposterous books on the market, but also one of the most frightening. It contains just enough scientific-sounding nonsense, carefully woven into a complex theory, to actually seem convincing to the uninitiated.")

I maintained my smoothie habit. I made more friends at farmer's markets. I soaked beans, baked bread, rolled oats. I entered other races, searched for new training routes. Even though I knew the Western States would be more challenging than ever, I was confident.

Before the race, Dusty had bet an old friend of his in Minnesota, Rod Raymond, one of the standout endurance athletes of Duluth, that I would win a fourth consecutive Western States. Rod took the bet. If Dusty lost, he would have to landscape the Raymonds' front yard, a job worth $2,000. But if Dusty (and I) won, Rod had to give Dusty his 1984 Suzuki Tempter motorcycle.

The race was tough but not close. The last 20 miles, Dusty ran beside me, repeating over and over: "*Vroom, vroom,* c'mon, Jurker, gotta get my motorcycle."

Later, Dusty called Rod and got his voicemail. He yelled into his cell phone. "You owe me a motorcycle, bitch!"

I won a fifth Western States in 2003 in 16:01, another 20 minutes faster, and *UltraRunning* magazine called it "Performance of the Year." During that race, Dusty, behind me, screamed something as we were descending a dried creek drainage, headed to the American River, but

I didn't pay attention. It was 72 miles in and I was gliding, effortlessly. "Dude," he said, "do you realize you just stepped on a rattlesnake back there?"

That was the race when Tonto died. He had been spending the week with Dusty and me, running every day. During the race, Tonto stayed at my friend Shannon Weil's ranch, which was on the course. I saw Tonto at mile 55 when I passed the ranch. The next morning, after I had won, Shannon called to tell me Tonto was gone. After the awards ceremony, Dusty, Scott McCoubrey, and another friend and runner named Brandon Sybrowsky helped me bury Tonto just outside of Michigan Bluff, right next to the Western States Trail.

I won again the next year, in 2004, and set a new record of 15:36 (9:22 per mile pace), earning another "Ultrarunner of the Year" honor and, more importantly, accomplishing what I had set out to do six years earlier. Brooks Sports hired me that year to work with their design team on a new trail shoe called the Cascadia and to do presentations and store appearances. In 2005 I won a seventh consecutive Western States, something no man had done before (or since). I also trimmed off 14 inches of my hair to donate to Locks of Love, for children with cancer. It was no big ceremony, but it felt better than any other haircut I had ever received.

I treasured those races, but just as much I treasured the weeks before the competition. The local press sought out Dusty, and he always had a quote ready. In 2003, the *Auburn Journal* accidentally ran Dusty on the front page with the caption, "Scott Jurek 5-time winner of WS100." We laughed about it and even had him go up at first to accept my award. The WS board wasn't happy. But we loved it.

At night, at the campsite Dusty and I had set up in the Sierra Nevada mountains, the temperature would drop into the 30s, and before turning in we'd look at the sky. Neither of us talked about the way Dusty had inspired me to run or the success that accrued to me because of that running. We didn't talk about how being with each other was in many ways an escape for both of us. For Dusty, those weeks took him away from his peripatetic life, his wanderings in Minnesota and Colorado, chasing snowflakes and trying to eke out a living through odd carpentry jobs. For me, it was a refuge from a life of responsibilities I had never anticipated.

Not even ten years earlier, I had been trudging snowmobile trails, dreaming big and spending big. I had planned on running hard, counted on winning. What I hadn't anticipated were sponsorships with Brooks, Pro-Tec, and Clif Bar, delivering presentations, and attending trade shows in between races. But, as I had discovered, those were flags on the path of ultrarunning, markers on the path Hippie Dan had urged me to find. Or were they warning signs? I didn't know.

I wanted more. I wanted to push myself, to crack myself open and discover something fresh. I wanted a new challenge.

Tamari-Lime Tempeh and Brown Rice

The big concern I hear from people about a plant-based diet is difficulty. It takes too long. It requires too much focus. For those folks I make this dish, which — if you cook the rice beforehand — you can have on the table in less than 20 minutes. The brown rice gives the dish a nutty texture and provides essential amino acids. Tempeh contains 3 grams of protein for every gram of fat, which makes it one of the leanest, most protein-heavy of the soy products (which was invaluable when I was cranking up my training, looking for more protein). Better, it's fermented and easily digestible, even for people who have trouble with most soy products.

4   cups uncooked brown rice

2¾ cups water

1   teaspoon coconut or olive oil

8-12 ounces tempeh, sliced ⅛- to ¼-inch thick

Juice of 1 lime or lemon

1   tablespoon tamari or shoyu mixed with 1 tablespoon water

Red Curry Almond Sauce (see recipe, page 122)

Add the brown rice and water to a pot and bring to a boil. Simmer over low heat for 30 to 40 minutes, until the water evaporates and the rice is tender. Fluff with a fork and cool.

Coat a large skillet with the oil and heat over medium-low heat until a drop of water sizzles when it hits the pan. Saute the tempeh for 3 to 5 minutes on each side, until lightly browned. Remove from the heat. Squeeze the lime or lemon over the tempeh and sprinkle with the tamari or shoyu.

For each serving, place a cup of brown rice on a plate or in a bowl. Crumble several pieces of tempeh on top and drizzle with 1 to 2 tablespoons Red Curry Almond Sauce. Enjoy with a side of Indonesian Cabbage Salad (see recipe, page 121).   MAKES 4 SERVINGS

14

A Hot Mess

BADWATER ULTRAMARATHON, 2005

Fall down seven times, get up eight.

— JAPANESE PROVERB

O N AUGUST 3, 1977, the hottest day of that year, a fifty-year-old named Al Arnold tried to run from Badwater, California, through and across Death Valley to the summit of 14,000-foot Mount Whitney. Six-foot-five and 200 pounds, he had tried the feat twice before, failing both times. This effort would be his last. He succeeded (and thus was born the Badwater Ultramarathon) and said, regarding the last 40 miles or so: "It was like all tranquility that can exist . . . existed for me." He said that photographs taken of him after mile 100 show an unearthly glow coming off his body.

Today, the 135-mile course starts in Death Valley, at 280 feet below sea level, and arrows on a paved road straight to the portal of Mount Whitney, at 8,300 feet. It was the crazy race Rick Miller had told me about four years earlier.

The Badwater Ultramarathon (or simply the Badwater) is big overseas and has been the subject of more than one documentary film. Part of the reason is that the race director, Chris Kostman, is something of a publicity genius. The press material calls it "the world's toughest foot race," which I seriously doubted, as it was on roads and (for ultrarunners) relatively level. Most untough of all, the cutoff time was 60 hours. You could *walk* the thing and finish. I had run in hot weather before, at the Western States. I had climbed (and descended) 10,500 feet on my training runs on the Twelve Peaks. I caused despair in others, not the other way around, so the Badwater didn't scare me, but it did intrigue me. It was not as obviously difficult as other events I had won, but there was something perversely challenging about it. I aimed to find out what. Most serious runners wait at least a month between ultras. But less than a week after winning my seventh Western States, I flew to Las Vegas. A lot of people said I was crazy to enter another race, especially *this* race, especially so soon.

When I arrived in Death Valley, I took a training run that singed my nose hairs. I felt as if a branding iron were pressing on my skull — from the inside. I drove to a Home Depot and purchased an industrial-strength sprayer. I helped Rick and Barb Miller rig up a coffin-sized cooler, which would be filled with ice water. I had, of course, asked Dusty to pace me. (When he felt the heat, he said he would do it only if I promised to take him to Las Vegas for a few days afterward, strippers included.)

My main competition would be last year's second-place finisher, a Canadian baggage handler named Ferg Hawke, who said things like: "The first half of the Badwater is run with the legs, the second half with the heart." He sounded interesting. Not a threat, but interesting. There was another guy, a fifty-year-old named Mike Sweeney. He had brought vests of synthetic ice packets that he had duct-taped together. He had also stored — on dry ice — small Tupperware bowls inside larger Tupperware bowls, anchored by an inch-thick layer of ice between the two. He planned to wear the device (he had three) on his head, duct-taped around his chin. Sweeney dove off cliffs for fun and smacked his head a lot. He said it made him and his skull stronger.

Also competing would be a trio of large German men wearing floppy garden hats, who, recognizing me before the race, chanted, "Vee vill overtake you!"

Ultramarathons tend to attract obsessive people. To undertake a race of over 50 miles requires training that can occupy 3 hours a day, a routine that involves cramps and pain and loneliness, not to mention the inevitable moments of doubt and maybe even a little self-loathing. Ultras seem to attract seekers of all kinds, including recovering addicts and alcoholics, seers, sages, some very wacky engineers and poets, and assorted windmill-tilters. Not to mention the monks and holy men.

Consider Sri Chinmoy, who, after arriving in New York City in 1964, taught meditation and a lifestyle of personal transformation in which athletics featured heavily. He attracted thousands of followers, among them Carlos Santana and Carl Lewis, and maintained a center in Queens. He demanded that his followers practice celibacy and vegetarianism and abstain from drugs, alcohol, and smoking. Many of them worked for Chinmoy in his associated businesses, such as the Smile of the Beyond Luncheonette in Jamaica and the Oneness-Fountain-Heart in Flushing.

The Sri Chinmoy Marathon Team, founded in 1977, has gone on to promote and compete in numerous ultras. The most famous is the 3,100-mile Self-Transcendence Race, the longest footrace in the world, held on a city block in Queens — 164th Place to Abigail Adams (84th) Avenue to 168th Street to Grand Central Parkway. The 3,100-mile distance honors the year ('31) of Sri Chinmoy's birth. Runners must complete 5,649 laps of the .5488-mile course in fifty-two days (extended to fifty-four in 2011 due to extreme heat). It is tantamount to running two marathons a day. Many run for 17 or 18 hours a day. The experience is so grueling and repetitive that few even undertake, much less complete, the race. In 2011, ten runners competed and eight finished.

But the most famous (and infamous) contemporary band of allegedly spiritual long-distance runners is probably the group known as Divine Madness. Members make a monthly financial "commitment" to the group. Its founder and leader, Marc Tizer, aka Yo, encourages communal living, ultrarunning, and free love. He will tack on extra miles in the middle of the group's training runs to keep them "adaptable." He has runners hold out their arm and he presses against it, then diagnoses their problems, what kind of running shoes they need, and who they should sleep with. They eat and sleep on the floor and work at subsistence jobs. Two former members of the group filed a civil lawsuit against Yo in 1996, joined in 1997 by a third, alleging mind control through sleep deprivation, fasting, and isolation. That case was settled out of court. One woman lodged a sexual assault case with the police. Mark Heinemann was an apparently healthy group member who dropped dead of pneumonia after a 48-hour race. He was forty-six.

Mike Sweeney passed me at mile 15, but I wasn't worried. Even if he hadn't been a head-smacking, ice helmet–wearing cliff diver, I wouldn't have been worried. I was looking forward to the uphill at 40 miles — that's when I would reel him in. That's when I would claim the Badwater as mine.

A few miles later I dropped from second to fourth place. Ferg had passed me, and a guy I never heard of named Chris Bergland did, too. I felt as if I might puke. One of my crew members said to slow it down, to take it easy, but I was getting my ass kicked by a bunch of underdogs. I was hearing reports that Sweeney was ahead by 25 minutes.

It was the heat. My training runs had helped, but nothing could have helped me enough for this. Imagine a sun so pitiless that it seemed to want to personally torture you. Imagine that every time you inhaled, the air was so hot that it seared your already parched throat and stung your lungs. Now imagine that a tall, cool, iced bottle of water was waiting for you, along with an aquamarine swimming pool and giant puddles of shade under oversized umbrellas and that fans were wafting cool breezes your way as you lay down on crisp, chilly sheets. Now imagine that all that relief was only another 110 miles away, and you had to run there, through heat every bit as awful as what you had just endured — maybe worse.

I ran (mostly uphill) to the aid station at Stovepipe Wells, 20 miles away, where my crew had prepared the giant coffin cooler. Dusty was jumping up and down in the parking lot, barefoot, wearing a black down expedition jacket, shouting "Hot potato, hot potato!" He was doing it to amuse me, I'm sure, to take my mind off the difficulties ahead. If I hadn't felt like my internal organs were liquefying, I might have chuckled.

I took off my sun pants and long-sleeved sun shirt — both specially designed by Brooks — and wriggled in. I thought I heard my crew discussing Sweeney's lead, and I remember thinking that I should get out, that if *sometimes you just do things*, then that moment would be certainly be an auspicious time to start. My body thought otherwise. I don't think I ever felt so good. Dusty suggested it was time to go, but I demurred.

When — finally — I climbed out, I wanted to immediately climb back in. After 2 miles, I told my crew I needed it again. Two more miles, one of them said, but they drove 3 miles. When I arrived, I told them I was ready, but again they said 2 more miles. And again they drove 3 miles. Rick Miller told me to stop thinking about the giant cooler, and he sprayed me down with the contraption I had bought at Home Depot.

There's something profoundly lonely about any ultra, but the Badwater is the loneliest of all. Ancient sand dunes roll over the valley floor like waves. Huge boulders lounge in the middle of emptiness. The salt flat shimmers and beckons with its treacherous beauty.

The wonderful thing about ultramarathons is that, no matter how awful things get, how searing the pain you're in, there's always a chance to redeem yourself. If you're willing to work, salvation awaits. Sweeney was still a good 5 miles ahead, and I had 10 miles to go before I got to the top of Town's Pass, mile 59 of the race. Those 10 miles — with their choking heat and blowing dust and the murderous incline and altitude — were popular among automakers. They used the stretch to test their latest models for performance under rigorous conditions. It had gotten too hot even for the desert rat Rick Miller, so Dusty joined me and ran me up the next 10 miles. "You da man. Yeah brotha', that's how you do it, Jurker, hell yeah!" the Dust Ball hollered. We crested the pass just as the sun set. Dusty peeled into the twilight to get some rest for the night shift, and my friend Justin Angle took over.

I learned how to run downhill on Mount Si, and I put those les-sons to use on the descent to Panamint Valley. I felt as if I was float-ing. I flew by Ferg and yelled, "Free speed!" I found out later that I was clocking 5:00-minute miles. I blazed into the valley at dark. Night had not just fallen, it had thudded and crashed and the air had cooled — to 105 degrees. But that was all right because out of the blackness jogged the jester of the dark, the rogue prince of the cake eaters. We blazed into the night. We might as well have been back on the game trails of Duluth. What could go wrong?

I found out at mile 70. One minute I was flying, the next I was dy-ing. I started looking for a sidewinder in the desert. If one bit me, I could quit without shame.

Ferg passed me a few miles out of Panamint Springs. I sat by the side of the road. Then I puked. And puked some more. My crew joined me. They told me to put my feet in the air, and my crew moved me to the desert side of the van so Ferg's crew, who were always sneaking up on me or back to me to see where I was and how much Ferg needed to worry, couldn't learn anything. Leah and Barb and Rick huddled over me, telling me I had beat longer odds, that I'd run tougher races. I was dry heaving. I heard a voice say, "I don't think this is gonna happen," and I realized it was my voice.

I had studied enough nutrition and physical therapy to know that what was happening should not have been happening.

In some ways, an ultra isn't even as hard as a marathon. My heart rate was lower and my lungs were less taxed than they would have been during a shorter, faster race. Sure, most marathons don't go through the heart of Death Valley, but I had done my homework on that front, so my body should have been primed. All those runs through the heat at Rick and Barb's had made my sweating and circulation more ef-ficient. The time spent training at altitude had sparked adaptations such as an increased network of capillaries, bigger energy-producing mitochondria, and elevated levels of the enzyme 2,3-diphosphoglyc-erate to help oxygen reach my tissues. The body's ability to adapt is truly astounding. That's why I say that, with the right training and support, anyone can do an ultra.

Yet there's a reason why top marathoners aren't flocking to the sport, and it's not just the lack of cash and prizes. Although the pace of an ultra is slower, maintaining that effort for hours and hours can leave the best of us huddled at the side of the road, dry heaving. For one thing, there's the cumulative loading on the muscles and bones. Every time the foot hits the ground, the quadriceps and calf muscles have to lengthen to absorb the shock of the impact, and that adds up when you go a hundred miles, whether you're barefoot or in Brooks, running or walking, slapping your heel or landing on your toes. Downhills are the worst of all. When you see runners shuffling across the Badwater finish line, it's not because they're too tired to push off, it's because they're too sore to land.

Even if you're able to keep food down under these conditions, you'll eventually hit the famous "wall" where the glycogen energy stores in your liver and muscles are depleted. In a marathon, the wall comes at the tail end of the race, but in an ultra, it's not even at the midpoint and it happens many times. You'll have to spend hours in the catabolic state where your body is forced to burn fat, protein, and even its own muscles to ensure adequate energy reaches the brain.

A cascade of stress-related hormones floods the body in response to the sustained exertion. Blood tests after ultras have shown elevated cardiac enzymes, renal injury, and very high levels of the stress hormone cortisol, the proinflammatory compound interleukin-6, and creatine kinase, a toxic byproduct of muscle breakdown. That's a lot for the immune system to handle. Approximately one in four runners at the Western States gets a cold after the race, and this is in the height of summer!

Most of all, the ultra distance leaves you alone with your thoughts to an excruciating extent. Whatever song you have in your head had better be a good one. Whatever story you are telling yourself had better be a story about going on. There is no room for negativity. The reason most people quit has nothing to do with their body.

Was my mind failing me? Could I have done something differently?

. . .

"You're not gonna win this fucking race lying down in the dirt. C'mon, Jurker, get the fuck up."

I got up, tried to run, and almost fell.

"C'mon, Jurker," Dusty said. "We're just gonna walk. We're just gonna take a little walk in the desert."

We walked, and after a little while, Dusty said, "Let's run 20 feet. It'll be just like Nordic ski training. It'll be like ski walking." He said "valking," imitating our old Russian coach, and I couldn't stop chuckling. But I managed a sip of water.

Sweeney was miles ahead. I couldn't even catch the crazy Canadian. What was I doing? I might have said this to Dusty.

"We'll just take this piece by piece," he said. "Piece by piece."

I forgot about catching anyone. I forgot about finishing. I forgot about everything except making it up the next switchback. Dusty saw the expression on my face. He told me this wasn't life and death, I didn't need to kill myself.

Piece by piece. Switchback by switchback. We crested a lonely hummock freckled with Joshua trees. My stomach felt better. I started to run. Dusty started to run. I picked up speed. So did the Dust Ball. "Rhythm and form, Jurker. Rhythm and form. C'mon, stretch it out! C'mon, you want to fucking be somebody? Let's do this!"

We ran. I had traveled 85 miles. We ran over a rolling plateau on the border of Death Valley National Park. A crew member told us Ferg had passed Sweeney and that the cliff diver was cracking. Dusty and I flew. We ticked off an 8-minute mile, then a 7:30 mile, then another 7:30. I felt as if I could run forever.

If you're an athlete and you're fortunate, you've felt it. Being "in the zone," tasting *satori* — the sudden, Zen-like clarity that comes when you least expect it, often when your body is pushed to the limit. Running backs speak of the game slowing down until all the other players are moving with almost cartoonish sluggishness as the running back in the zone darts among and between them. Basketball players testify that the hoop at which they're shooting not only seems larger but *is* larger. Runners speak of feeling absorbed into the universe, of seeing the story of life in a single weed on the side of the road.

When I've been lucky enough to feel it, the sensation is one of effortlessness. It occurs when the intensity of the race, the pressure to win, the pain, build to a level that's nearly unbearable. Then something opens up inside me. I find the part of me that is bigger than the pain.

Satori can be sought, but it cannot be held. A few strides after an epic feeling of bliss, I'll get an ache in my knees or the urge to pee or I'll start worrying about how the person I'm chasing down is feeling. I can't beat back those feelings or desires, but I know they're not what really matters. What matters is the place of effortlessness, of selflessness. There might be many paths to that magical region — prayer and meditation come to mind. My way leads up to and past the point of absolute, maximal effort. It's only when I get to a place where all my physical and psychological warning lights are flashing red, and then run beyond it, that I hit the sweet spot. I know people who get there on a 5-mile jog or by mindfully chopping a carrot. I've traveled to the zone myself by those activities. In an ultramarathon, though, a trip to the zone isn't a luxury, it's almost a given. At half past midnight, I had stopped floating. Where was Mike? At 1 A.M., surrounded by the stunted Joshua trees under a moonless, starry sky, Dusty and I heard him. He was gasping and moaning. The vest had not only melted but had dragged at Mike with its 20 pounds of dead weight. The ice helmets had been too cold to wear. Mike's pace had been suicidal. He was suffering from hyponatremia, drinking too much water combined with his kidneys' failure to expel enough from his body. He was stumbling, and his face looked swollen. His sodium levels were plummeting.

As we passed, I saw the expression on Mike's face. There's no way he should have been standing, much less moving forward. I gained a lot of respect for Mike that night. I gained a lot of respect for Badwater.

Dusty and I passed Ferg at 90 miles, and he passed us a half-mile later. "Sorry, Scott," he said. "I have to do this for the folks back in Canada."

I hadn't actually *raced* this late in an ultra since dueling Ben Hian and Tommy Nielson at Angeles Crest. For more than five years, when an ultra was 80 miles old, I had already won. Not this time. I added Ferg Hawke to the list of ultrarunners who had earned my respect.

A few minutes later I passed him again, this time for good.

I ran through the dried bed of Owens Lake at sunrise with my best friend, and as the darkness clicked to red and brown, Dusty slowed down and shuffled off to a shadowy pickup truck to do what only the patron saint of wild men knew. I ran to Lone Pine, where the deerflies came out, and toward Mount Whitney, and I ran past the 100-mile mark, farther than I had ever run before. A legend known as Badwater Ben sat in a car and watched me run. Fourteen years earlier he had been running the Badwater when he came upon a body. He had interrupted his race to perform an autopsy. I learned later that when Badwater Ben saw me running and gauged my speed and the distance I had come, he had remarked to his companion in the car that he was worried.

I crossed the finish line, 135 miles from where I had started, after 24 hours and 36 minutes. No one had ever run it faster, nor had anybody won the Western States 100 and the Badwater 135 a mere two weeks apart.

When it was done, I sat in the pine needles, and I thought about my mother, who would never walk, and my father, who had never seen me run. I thought of the coaches who had helped me, the runners and writers who had inspired me. I thought of my wife and my best friend, who even though they seldom spoke to each other anymore had both supported me.

"Hey, Jurker!"

It was Dusty, as usual dragging me from my reveries.

"When're we going to Vegas? When're we going to see the strippers? You fucking promised."

⇒ FINDING THE TIME

If you're going to run regularly, you're going to need to carve out part of your day, even if it's 30 to 60 minutes. If that seems impossible, ask yourself: How much time do I spend watching television? Or surfing the Internet? Or shopping? Take some of that time and devote it to doing something good for yourself. If you're still in a bind, double up on activities. Run to work and back. Many companies have become increasingly helpful to employees who want to exercise, providing showers, changing rooms, and sometimes even incentives; they realize that a fit worker will incur fewer health costs. Run to work and get a ride home. Run to the grocery store and have someone pick you up. Combine errands, running from place to place, and you'll get a workout in while you're taking care of business. And if you're already working out regularly, you'll be that much more fit. ⇒

Coco Rizo Cooler

I learned of this combination while traveling and eating my way through Italy (thus the Italiano name), and it proved invaluable during my Spartathlon training and racing. Rice milk is cooling and tastes great, which is often overlooked but in fact a critical factor in race foods. The coconut adds even more taste, as well as another body-cooling substance and a source of quick energy. Chia seeds deliver yet a third flavor, as well as texture and easily digestible protein. The thick, almost gelatinous liquid slides down the most parched throat. For a sweeter drink with more carbohydrates, add 3 or 4 dates or 2 tablespoons maple syrup.

    1 cup cooked brown or white rice
    ½ cup light coconut milk
    4 cups water

2 tablespoons agave syrup

½ teaspoon sea salt

½ teaspoon coconut extract

2 tablespoons chia seeds

Place the rice, coconut milk, water, agave, salt, and coconut extract in a blender and blend on high for 1 to 2 minutes, until completely smooth. Add the chia seeds and shake. This mixture can be poured into a water bottle for a refreshing drink before, during, or after exercise.   MAKES 5 8-OUNCE SERVINGS

15

These Guys Again?

> When you run on the earth and with the earth,
> you can run forever.
>
> — RARAMURI PROVERB

THE E-MAIL HAD shown up on my screen in mid-2005. It was from someone named Caballo Blanco, which in Spanish means "white horse." I learned later that Caballo had formerly been known as Micah True and that he had been a boxer, itinerant furniture mover, and distance-running sage. But when he e-mailed me, all I knew is that he had been following my career and that he had a proposition.

He lived in an adobe hut dug into the side of a deep, hidden canyon in Mexico. Nearby lived a group of indigenous Indians called the Raramuri ("running people"), also known as the Tarahumara. He said they were the greatest runners on earth. He wanted me to participate in an epic 50-mile race he had set up in the canyon: one of the world's greatest runners (me) against the world's greatest runners, with a prize of 1,000 pounds of corn and $750. I remembered the tribe. The Tarahumara were the middle-aged guys in togas who smoked cigarettes before the Angeles Crest 100 and couldn't run downhill. The greatest runners on earth?

I liked travel, and I liked exploring different cultures, and the guys in the togas had always interested me. But the trip would have messed up my schedule. I was training for the Austin Marathon, and running a 50-miler immediately afterward didn't make sense. I didn't speak Spanish, and I didn't know how I'd get down there. Plus, it's not as if it was a big challenge. I'd already beat the Indians.

Caballo wrote that the Tarahumara he knew were nothing like the ones I had bested at the Angeles Crest 100. He also said that he sensed in me a purity of spirit similar to that of the running Indians. He said that the Tarahumara were struggling to survive under difficult circumstances and that if a runner from the United States visited, it might help.

I wrote back that I'd love to support the plight of the Tarahumara, but I wasn't going to be able to make it. That was a mistake.

A few days later, I got another e-mail from Caballo.

"The plight? The Tarahumara don't have a fucking plight! They don't need your help!"

I thought, "Wow, this guy is really out there," and I forgot about it. But I kept getting e-mails from him, talking about the mystical running Indians of the hidden Copper Canyon and how they knew things the rest of the world didn't.

If I could figure out a way to get down there, I might go. Then the universe figured it out for me.

I got another e-mail invitation, this one from a writer named Chris McDougall. He said he was working on a book about the Indian runners, and that he was fluent in Spanish. He, too, promised that these Tarahumara would give me a good race.

I agreed, but not because I needed another good race. I found plenty of those. I raced the White River 50-miler, the Miwok 100K, the Way Too Cool 50K, the grueling Wasatch Front 100, and — on the East Coast — the Mountain Masochist 50-miler and the Vermont 100. I was on the winning teams in Japan's Hasegawa Cup and in the Hong Kong Trailwalker, where we set a new course record. I had my own physical therapy practice, my own coaching business, was working 50-plus hours a week (and still just scraping by), and had started a running camp a few weeks before the Western States, where I tried to share what I knew about technique and will. At my camp, I served hearty vegan meals. I was making a living doing something I loved. I was teaching others. Had running ever given anyone more? My problem was: I wanted more. My bigger problem: I wasn't exactly sure what more I wanted. I told McDougall I would meet him in El Paso.

There were nine of us: McDougall and his coach, Eric Orton. Caballo. Me. A pair of wild rookie ultrarunners from Virginia, Jenn Shelton and Billy Barnet. A man named Ted McDonald, who called himself Barefoot Ted because he recently started jogging without shoes. My buddy and photographer Luis Escobar and his father.

Caballo told us the race would start from the village of Urique. To get there, we'd have to hike 35 miles, over a series of knife-edged canyon ridges, through land where entrepreneurs with small armies and automatic weapons harvested marijuana, over an invisible route that no one but the guy who lived in the mud hut really knew. Caballo mentioned that a group of Tarahumara might join us.

We hiked for 3 hours, but we didn't see any Raramuri. Caballo, our guide, told us he had heard that a mysterious virus had swept through one village, that maybe it had spread. He said we should be patient. But he said we should also be prepared for the possibility that we'd be making the trek without company. We crashed across rivers and up cacti-lined ridges, over burro trails so faint that without Caballo, we almost certainly would never have found our way out.

At 9 A.M. we arrived at a group of wooden and adobe one-story buildings huddled together at a riverbank. We were at the bottom of the Copper Canyon, 5,000 feet below the rim. The sun was up, and we were sweating profusely. Caballo suggested we wait, that maybe the Tarahumara would join us here. He warned us that they were incredibly shy, that we should not be too loud or aggressive if they showed up. We shouldn't try to shake their hands. Their greeting consisted of lightly touching fingertips, nothing more. He also mentioned that it would be good etiquette to bring gifts. He suggested Coca-Cola and Fanta sodas.

I was appalled. I hadn't traveled the length of a country in order to bestow on an indigenous group of athletes plastic containers filled with high-fructose corn syrup. Why not just bring some blankets infested with smallpox? But Caballo insisted.

We huddled in the shade of the little store, trying to stay cool as the sun beat down the deep canyon, holding on to our sweating bottles of Coke. Caballo suggested we start hiking up the trail, that maybe — or maybe not — our hosts would join us on the trail. No one saw them step out of the woods or around the bend. One minute the trail was empty, the next, a group of five men in skirts and bright blouses were approaching. They had popped up like a herd of wild deer.

We touched fingers and, without a word, started climbing 5,000 feet to the top of the canyon; once we reached it, we would leave to descend again. Somewhere between 10 and 40 minutes later — no one was sure — there were six more Tarahumara with us. They appeared out of the woods, like smoke.

One of the tribe seemed to be watching me with special interest. I was watching him, too. He looked stronger than the others, and there was something in his eyes — pride, confidence, maybe even a little wariness — that I recognized. I had it, too. His hair was jet black, and he had a movie cop's powerful jawline and muscles like climbing rope. It was Arnulfo, the great Tarahumara champion, the swiftest of "the running people." McDougall had told me about him. And Caballo had told Arnulfo about me, that I was a great champion, too.

We climbed in clusters of gringos and Indians, with Caballo leading us. We climbed through cacti and small brush, through desert oak and onto patches of arid, open land dotted with agave plants. During our brief stops, while Jenn, Billy, Ted, and I took pulls from our water bottles, the Tarahumara fell to the ground, almost as if their calf tendons had been cut. The first time I was shocked. Then I realized that they were resting, that it was a highly efficient way of conserving energy. I watched their feet as they climbed and saw that there, too, the Tarahumara moved without wasted motion. I was beginning to learn one of secrets of this ancient tribe. It was the secret of efficiency.

• • •

They carried no water bottles but seemed to know every hidden seep in the wilderness. Whenever they were near one, they would quickly move toward it, bend down, take a few quick sips of water, then return to the trail. When we offered our gifts of Coke, they accepted the bottles without a word, guzzled the entire contents, then flung the empty containers to the side of the trail. (It wasn't that they didn't care about the environment, they just didn't understand the notion of nonbiodegradable.)

At the end of our canyon trek we landed at a road, 5 miles from the village. There was the sheriff and his pickup truck. We Americans stood and looked — we didn't want to sully our spiritual day with a car. The Tarahumara immediately jumped in. It was efficient. The next five days, we got to know the Tarahumara. When we pulled out energy gels and bars, they laughed and chattered among themselves. Then they reached into their capes and pulled out pinole, roasted corn ground into a powder and mixed with water. It's their corn Gatorade. For food, they would carry tortillas with beans. Everything they ate was whole and pure. It was on that trip that I began to appreciate how much energy was packed into a single avocado. When we sat down to share meals, I also learned to sit at the end of the table where the guacamole would be set down. I would advise no one to get between a Tarahumaran and a bowl of guacamole. I watched Arnulfo. He watched me.

I had traveled here because the Tarahumara fascinated me, and I had some time. I looked at the trip as a learning vacation. But I was starting to get the idea that there was going to be nothing leisurely or just-for-fun about this race, especially not to the Tarahumara. I knew that I would go all out. It would be disrespectful to do anything less.

The race started five days later at 8 A.M. As soon it began, I realized what I had been suspecting ever since the Indians appeared from nowhere on the road by the river. The guys I had raced at the Angeles Crest 100 were the Tarahumara B-team. Three of these guys launched themselves from the starting line as if we were running a 5K. They were in their twenties, and none of them were smoking. They carried no water, and if they had food, it was in the folds of their capes.

I started out at a comfortable, winning pace. I knew that no one could keep up the pace they were setting, especially in this 100-degree heat. Ten miles later, they were still keeping it up, but I wasn't worried. I knew what distance did to a man's body. I kept up my pace and ate — as usual — 200 to 300 calories per hour. I carried two bottles of water. I ate oranges and bananas. I also tried pinole at one of the aid stations.

After 20 miles, I had passed a dozen Tarahumara and was slightly surprised that there were still a few in front of me. Ten miles later I was even more surprised. After 35 miles, hot, tired, and thirsty, when I realized there were two Tarahumara in front of me, wearing robes and rubber sandals, I was not only surprised, I was amazed. And worried. The leader was Arnulfo, wearing a deep crimson running shirt.

I ran faster, until I was ticking off 7-minute miles. I have passed other ultrarunners late in a race doing 7-minute miles. I have seen the looks in opponents' eyes when I sped past. I knew a move like that could break a man. But they were still ahead.

I was a professional racer, trained almost year-round. I was at the height of my career. These guys had never heard of "tempo runs" or interval training. That's when it hit me, the real secret of the Tarahumara. They didn't prepare for runs. They didn't run to win or for medals. And they didn't eat so they could run. They ate, and they ran, to survive. To get someplace, they used their legs. To use their legs, they had to be healthy. The first great secret to the Tarahumara's endurance and speed and vigorous health was that running and eating were essential parts of their lives. The second great secret — one I try to remember every day — is that while the Tarahumara run to get from point to point, in the process they travel into a zone beyond geography and beyond even the five senses.

They run — and live — with great efficiency, without a lot of needless thought. They don't reject technology in order to be fashionable or to make a political point. If technology is available and helps them lead a more efficient life, they embrace it. They'll jump into a pickup truck for transportation. They'll improve their huaraches with the rubber from discarded tires. It's exactly what I had been trying to do — to blend intuition with technology.

Maybe it's presumptuous of me to describe what the Tarahumara probably don't articulate themselves, but when I was with them I couldn't help but feel that they were experiencing a peace and a serenity, that they — through running and through living with great simplicity — were able to access a state of being, a zone, a "sixth sense," where they were in touch with the world in its purest form. It's the zone I had been seeking for so long.

The Raramuri moved through their world with form that could have come from a textbook. Their gait was fluid and economical. They took short strides, landing almost daintily on their mid-to-fore-foot. There was no wasted side-to-side energy, and their posture was open in the shoulders, relaxed.

The Tarahumara were later immortalized in McDougall's book *Born to Run,* where he called them "super athletes." I would quibble with that. I would say they were super efficient. They were just much, much more in tune with their bodies and their surroundings. They knew things we had forgotten, with all of our stopwatches and sports foods and fancy running shoes.

Spending a week with the Indians in Copper Canyon helped crystallize ideas that I had been thinking about since my first week at Team Birkie ski camp as a teenager. After my race against the Tarahumara, "born to run" became a catch phrase and a credo for hundreds of thousands of people. As humans, we were meant to move swiftly over the earth. We *knew* how to run. If we could just return to that state of instinctive bliss, the theory went, we could re-embrace the form and ease we had abandoned and run free from pain, fatigue, and injury. Getting rid of our modern shoes was the suggested first step in this return to jogging Eden.

It wasn't barefoot running that made the Tarahumara great runners, though. (They wore huaraches.) Form is what matters in running. Barefoot running can help you develop great form, but it's merely a means to an end. If you like running without shoes, great. If you prefer something on your feet, that's great too. I agree that modernity has brought with it a host of bad habits and disastrous unintended consequences, not only in running (an overdependence on heavily cushioned shoes being chief among them, and the sense that running is reserved for only a select few), but in eating, too. Fast foods, mass production, grotesquely large servings — those by themselves have made us sick. Modernity has also brought us electricity, penicillin, and open heart surgery, of course. Altogether, our modern inclination toward sloth, the easy availability of processed food, and the prevalence of life-saving medical treatments have made us a long-lived, unhealthy people.

What I saw in the Tarahumara was a group of people who ran — and ate — the way their ancestors had run and eaten. They depended on food that was grown locally and obtained with some difficulty. They ran with abandon and un-self-consciousness. They ate meat, but they ate it the way generations past ate it — on the rare occasions they could get it. It was a precious commodity, not a staple.

I'm healthier and I can run longer and faster because I eat a plant-based diet. But I don't preach to my carnivorous friends or lambaste anyone who eats a baked potato slathered with butter and sour cream. Anyone who pays attention to what they eat and how it affects them will naturally move toward plants — and toward health.

Exercise is simpler and more complicated. We need to move. But should training be an intuitive, free-form affair or a structured science? I try to let science steer my training while staying open to the animal joy of running. I take days off when I feel I need them, even if my training plan doesn't call for it. Ultrarunners need to bring all the knowledge we can bear to our training, but we can't afford to be rigid. If there's one thing I can count on in a 100-mile race, it's that I will encounter things I didn't count on.

Dealing with physical uncertainty used to be part of life. So did training. We ran toward food and away from predators. We feasted and fasted according to the season. We spent a lot of time walking and napping.

Now we sit. We drive and surf on the Internet and watch television. And, naturally, we suffer. A recent study in the *American Journal of Epidemiology* followed 123,216 subjects over fourteen years and found that men who spent more than 6 hours a day sitting were 17 percent more likely to die during that time than men who sat for less than 3 hours. For women, the increased risk of death was 34 percent. This increased mortality persisted regardless of whether the participants smoked, were overweight, and — this shocked me — regardless of how much they exercised.

Humans aren't built to sit all day. Nor are we built for the kinds of repetitive, small movements that so much of today's specialized work demands. Our bodies crave big, varied movements that originate at the core of our body. Imbalance comes when we spend all day doing small, repetitive actions like typing, scanning groceries, flipping burgers, or operating a computer mouse.

Much of the purpose of structured training, therefore, is compensatory. It's not so much that we need to learn to run per se, as we need to unlearn bad habits and correct imbalances wrought by the modern lifestyle.

The race in Copper Canyon consisted of a few loops along dry, dusty roads at the bottom of the canyon, up 2,000-foot climbs studded with grapefruit and papaya trees, past towering rock formations. We ran through town three times, past locals drinking and laughing, and through the happy, tinny sounds of a mariachi band.

I hadn't planned on racing so hard — I was on vacation. I kept up my 7-minute pace. I had trained, but these guys had spent their whole lives training, even though they wouldn't have called it that. I wanted to blend my running and my diet as seamlessly into my day-to-day life as the Tarahumara did. I also wanted to win this race. And I knew they did, too. A victory for me would be a great honor. For them, it would represent enough corn to feed an entire village for a year.

I increased my pace, and there, around a bend, I caught a flash of electric blue. It was Silvino, in his traditional Tarahumara attire. I closed. I breathed in the sweet scent of flowering cacti. I ran past the thorny ocotillo plants with their garish red buds. At 40 miles I pulled up to Silvino, motioned for him to follow. We didn't exchange words, but I wanted the two of us to catch Arnulfo. I wanted the three of us to duke it out at the finish line together. Silvino was done, though.

I saw Arnulfo at the last turnaround, and he looked spent. We exchanged a glance, and I could see the fatigue and dehydration in his eyes. I knew the look. But I saw something else, too. I saw the fighter in him. I knew he wasn't going to let up. We had 5 miles, and he had 7, 8 minutes on me, and I thought I could do it. I made the turn, and pure competitive, animal instinct kicked in. This time it wasn't enough. Arnulfo had it, too.

He beat me by 6 minutes. Less than a mile.

I didn't hug him or anything like that. I told him in English (which he didn't understand) that I was very impressed and that he was very strong. In Spanish I said "*muy fuerte*" over and over.

Then I bowed to him. Out of respect.

People asked me later if I had let him triumph in the interest of cross-cultural understanding or as a gesture of kindness. Those people didn't know how important competing was to me. Arnulfo beat me fair and square. But I returned the next year and got him by 18 minutes. I gave the corn and the $750 to the Raramuri.

⇒ THE NAKED TRUTH

The beautiful thing about running barefoot or in minimal footwear is that you are working with your body's natural *proprioception,* the ability to sense your own position in space. With nothing between you and the ground, you get immediate sensory feedback with every step, which encourages you to stay light on your feet and run with proper form. Some people who are recovering from injuries or who have structural anomalies or who just like their shoes will keep lacing up. But whether you wear shoes or go barefoot, what's important is that you pay attention to your form. If running barefoot helps with that, it's beneficial.

You want to try barefoot running? Before you toss the

shoes and enter a 10K, remember: slow and easy. When runners do too much too soon, injuries often result.

First, find an area of grass or sand and take easy 5- to
10-minute runs once or twice a week. Remember, easy. Don't
worry about speed at all. You're working on your running
form. As long as it feels good, increase the length of one of
the runs until you're up to a 20- to 45-minute barefoot run
once a week. I like to do 2 to 3 miles on the infield of a track
or in a park after an easy run day or for a cooldown run after
a track workout.

Two important things to remember—other than starting slow and easy—are that you don't need to run barefoot
all the time to get the benefits. And you don't need to run
completely barefoot. Lighter weight, minimal running shoes
and racing flats will give you a similar type of feel as running barefoot. It will all help you with form. I have been running most of my long training runs and ultra races in Brooks
racing flats for almost a decade, even Badwater and Spartathlon. Racing flats and minimal shoes provide the best of
both worlds: comfort and performance.

Holy Moly Guacamole

*Avocados are a great source of healthy, monounsaturated fat, and the
jalapeño adds a nice jolt of spice (scrape the seeds out before mincing
and use half of the pepper if you can't take the heat). Noble foods on
their own, they combine to create one of mankind's greatest inventions.
It's certainly one of my favorites. I can't think of many dinners—and
not a single Mexican one—that aren't improved with a serving of guac.
Take a spoonful of this mixture and you'll agree. For a quick and healthy
snack, enjoy on warm corn tortillas.*

> 2 ripe avocados
>   Juice of 2 small limes
> 1 medium tomato, diced

 1 garlic clove, minced

 1 jalapeño pepper, seeds left in, minced

10 sprigs fresh cilantro, minced

 1 teaspoon sea salt

Halve the avocados and scoop out the flesh into a mixing bowl. Squeeze in the lime juice and add the remaining ingredients. Mash with a potato masher or a spoon until semi-smooth and let rest at room temperature for 10 to 20 minutes.

MAKES 2½ CUPS, 6-8 SERVINGS

16

The Central Governor

All it takes is all you got.

— MARC DAVIS

N O ONE WANTS to win more than I do. What I've learned in ultras, though, is that where I finish is merely an outcome — even though I reach for it with every sinew and tendon and muscle of my being. What matters more than victory is what I do to reach it and how. Have I prepared? Am I focused? Have I have been treating my body with attentiveness, eating healthfully and with care? Have I been training properly? Have I pushed myself as far, and as hard, as possible? Those are the types of questions that have guided me in my career and that can guide anyone who seeks something (which is to say, everyone). You *want* to get the promotion at work, or the girl, or the guy, or the personal best in the 5K race, of course. But whether you get what you want isn't what defines you. It's how you go about your business.

Ultras teach that lesson with unforgiving precision. Never did I see it more clearly than in the Western States 2006. And I wasn't even competing.

A month before the race, a friend and running partner asked if I would pace him at the event.

I had known Brian Morrison for a year or so. We ran together in the winter and spring of 2006, before I made my trek to Mexico. He was twenty-seven, a manager at Seattle Running Company, and he and I would catch the bus to Green Lake, where we did tempo runs — 50 to 60 minutes at 85 percent effort — on the 3-mile loop. We ran the wooded trails at Cougar Mountain, and I showed him the Twelve Peaks and the new 40-mile Rattlesnake-to-Cougar training route I devised. He asked about the Western States canyons, about the heat, about the hill work we should be doing. He asked me everything and I told him everything. I don't believe in secrets. It's not a bit of arcane knowledge that will allow me to beat someone or someone to beat me. Winning at an elite level demands technique and strategy, to be sure, but mostly it's heart. Brian had plenty. He had drive and powerful ambition. In many ways he reminded me of me.

It was strange at the starting line, not screaming, not sprinting to the head of the pack. To keep busy, and because I felt as though I owed so much to the race that had in a way defined me, I handed out race bibs and volunteered the way I had at many ultras I didn't run. It was weird following the progress of other runners and visiting with aid station volunteers who helped me out over the past seven years. But it was pleasant. That's a mild word, but compared to the intense highs and lows I experienced during my previous Western States, the extremes to which the event had pushed me, it was exactly right. It was pleasant. What made it more than pleasant was Brian. I had told him before the race that he had what it took to win. For 55 miles I kept track of his progress from different points on the course — pacers weren't allowed to run until mile 62 — and he did nothing to disabuse me of my confidence. He was moving well, in fifth place, looking fresh and relaxed. But at mile 55 things got less pleasant. That's when Brian started to have a hard time. It was 105 degrees, Western States weather, and I could tell it was affecting him. He was slowing down. I knew that when I joined him we'd have work to do. I knew we'd have to pick up the pace. I had been up since three o'clock in the morning, and I was worried about whether I had it in me. I knew that

I could race an ultra myself and win. Being responsible for someone else's success, though, scared me a little. I hadn't anticipated the doubt. I would have to deal with that before I took my first step.

I dealt with my anxiety the same way I had dealt with my bum ankle in the 2001 Western States. Four simple steps: First, I let myself worry. Second, I took stock. I would be doing the equivalent of a 38-mile training run with someone who had been running for the better part of a day—not a huge deal. Third, I asked myself what I could do to remedy the situation. That was easy. All I had to do was be a good pacer. The fourth and final step: Separate my negative feelings from the issue at hand. Realizing that my negative feelings had little to do with reality made this step the easiest of all.

When I joined Brian, the announcer blared over the speakers, "Scott Jurek is about to pace!" I was merely there to help someone else, but hearing my name out loud like that unleashed a surge of adrenaline into my blood. Then it was time for business.

At mile 62, Brian was in fourth place. I told him that by the time we got to the Rucky Chucky river crossing—16 miles away—we were going to have passed everyone. I told him we'd be leading then, and we would lead all the way to the finish line.

He turned it on. He became a different runner. He didn't say anything, because runners don't talk much. They want to conserve all their energy for the race. But I talked. I turned into Dusty. I became Brian's second brain, cajoling, sweet-talking, demanding when I needed to demand. Within 12 miles we had passed everyone. By the time we came to the river crossing, he was hooting and hollering. He was super pumped even though we were both boiling. I did what I knew how to do, which was to push him as hard as I could, but making sure it wasn't too hard. I made him lie down in creeks, and I shoveled water over him. I remember once having to lie down in a puddle that I immediately realized was half horse manure, but I didn't move. I knew how overheated we both were. I had him drink at aid stations. There was never a point where I thought he wasn't getting enough water or was getting too much. By mile 78, when we turned to look behind us, there was no one there. We weren't running scared, but when you're in front, you want to send a message to your competitors: "Don't even try."

I told Brian, "Let's crank it up. As long as we keep running 8-minute miles, if we throw a 7:30 in every so often, you've got this."

We got to Highway 49, over 93 miles in, and I told Brian's crew chief (and fiancée), Andrea, that I was going to need someone else to take over. With all my attention to Brian's drinking enough water and eating, I hadn't drunk or eaten enough myself. I was sick to my stomach. I was fatigued. I was dehydrated and bonking. I thought I might slow him down. Andrea asked if I could keep going, to stay with him for another 3 miles until No Hands Bridge, which was 3 miles from the finish. At that point, Brian's victory wouldn't be in question. I could stop then.

So I dug in, and we ran another 3 miles through choking dust and heat. Brian told me the downhills hurt, but I told him pain was temporary, to get through it. Otherwise, we didn't say much. There was no need. Three miles from the finish line, I had pushed him as hard as he needed to be pushed, and when another pacer, Jason Davis, appeared, I told Brian he was in good hands and I'd meet him at Robie Point, a mile from the finish line. I said I'd follow him to his first Western States victory.

Brian and Jason climbed another 2 miles on dirt. I caught a ride and met them on the road in Auburn. Brian hadn't seen pavement in some time. There were cars and houses and people having parties in their yards, waiting for the top finishers. Physically, he looked fine. As far as I was concerned, this race was over. All we had to do was jog along city streets to the finish line. All Brian had to do was get there. But when he spoke, I knew he wasn't feeling quite so confident. "How far back are they?" he asked, and he looked over his shoulder. He was scared. I laughed and told him to relax, that he didn't need to worry. We were running slightly uphill and he was *hammering*. He was going at an 8-minute-mile pace, and I told him he didn't have to run that fast, but if he wanted to finish strong, that was cool.

"How far back are they?" he asked again. "How far back?"

I had suffered late race hallucinations myself, and I did my best to not freak out, and especially to make sure he didn't freak out.

Luis Escobar, my photographer friend, was running with us now, and so was Jason Davis. We were motoring down the last downhill and we could hear the crowd, we could see the lights. Brian was yelling, "Where is it? Where is it?" The race ends in Auburn at the Placerville High School track, and we were all yelling back, "It's there. You got this! You got this!"

It was ten at night when we rounded a corner and stepped through the small opening in the fence and onto the track. People were cheering, but not as loud as Luis, Jason, and I were yelling, "You did this, Brian! You're the Western States champion!"

About seven strides onto the track, our cheers went from "Brian, *you did this*," to dead silence. Twenty feet in, 300 yards from the finish, Brian collapsed.

"What's the matter, Brian?" I asked.

He said, "I can't get up."

I had noticed him weaving on the final downhill, but I had weaved a lot myself in races. The ultra is a brutal thing.

"You gotta get up, Brian. You *gotta* get up!"

Jason and I helped him stand, but he wouldn't walk. I said, "You *gotta* keep moving." I was Dusty again, but this time nothing seemed to work.

Maybe we should have let him stay on the track. He couldn't stand on his own, and now he was babbling, not making sense.

It was a really stupid mistake when I look back on it. Jason and I put Brian's arms around our shoulders, and we walked him toward the finish line. We didn't cut across the infield, toward the medical tent. We took him around the track. It was instinct. I was in survival mode, taking care of someone who was in really bad shape, but I was in pacer mode, too, and racer mode. I was in runner mode. I wanted Brian to get what he wanted. I wanted to help him get to the finish line. And I did.

We got him to the finish line, and from there the medical staff took over. One of the doctors asked him if he knew who won the race.

"Scott Jurek," he said.

"No," the doctor said, with a thin smile, "you won. You won the race."

Within 15 minutes, he was in an ambulance. And as they were lifting him in, I was standing next to him, and he looked at me and said, "Scott, I did it. I won the Western States."

I was hanging out at the finish line, greeting the next finishers as I always did, and they were happy to see me, but I started hearing other people, onlookers and race board members, saying things. I heard that Brian was going to be disqualified. I heard people saying it was my fault for helping him around the track. And then finally a board member walked up to me and said Brian didn't win and he would be disqualified for accepting help.

I told him the board didn't need to do that, that being disqualified was a black mark for a runner, and if anyone deserved sanction, it should be me. I told them if they weren't going to award Brian the victory, the very least they could do was to give him a DNF, Did Not Finish.

Nope, it would have to be a DQ. I thought the board members were just doing it to bolster their egos and make a statement about the sanctity of the race. I walked to the Auburn hospital the next day — no one from the Western States board had been there. When I entered Brian's room, he spoke first.

"Hey, Scott, it doesn't look like I'm going to be out of here in time for the awards ceremony. I want you to accept it for me."

I got straight to the point. I said I'd been at the track all night and that the board had made a big to-do about his not making it to the finish line and DQ'd him. They had awarded the win to a runner named Graham Cooper, who finished *12 minutes* after him. I told him I was sorry and that I wished I could do something to change the board's decision. I told him I was sorry I didn't take him across the infield. I said I knew how hard he had worked and how close he was to winning. I said I knew what being close felt like (I had only recently failed to catch Arnulfo) but that I could only imagine his pain. It was one of the most difficult things I've ever had to do.

When I got back to Seattle, there was already chatter about the race all over the Internet. Some of it was unbelievable. I read that I had pushed Brian too hard, that I was his "coach." I read that I had not given him enough water and that I had given him too much. I read that I sabotaged his race because I didn't want anyone taking the spotlight off of me.

I learned more than one lesson at the 2006 Western States. One I hadn't been expecting: No matter what you do, there are going to be haters out there. My Zen self tells me they're no worse than people who idolize you for the wrong reasons. What people think about you doesn't really matter. The trick is to be true to yourself.

People still ask me about what happened to Brian. The short answer is, I don't know. The longer answer is, it could have been one of many things. I don't believe it was really a medical issue, at least not in the traditional sense. I think Brian stopped because his brain saw the finish line and told his body, "Hey, dude, you're done, you did it, you can rest now," and his body shut down. As powerful as our legs are, as magnificent as our lungs and arms and muscles are, nothing matters more than the mind.

The Western States doctors identified a number of reasons that might have explained why Brian couldn't make it that one last time around the track. They said that his disorientation and lack of coordination were consistent with hyponatremia. They said he might have been dehydrated, had low blood sugar, that there may have been something wrong with his heart. They suggested, finally, that it was total muscular fatigue. He had pushed himself too hard those final miles leading up to the high school track, and his leg muscles were simply too tired to go on. From a medical perspective, the proximity of the finish line was not an issue. Conventional wisdom holds that our ability to push ourselves and keep pushing is limited by peripheral measures of fitness such as VO_2 max, the amount of oxygen we can use for aerobic respiration, and lactate threshold, the point at which our muscles accumulate lactic acid faster than they can clear it. Efficiency comes into play in determining how well we can exploit our body's fitness level, as does the resilience of our muscles and bones. In an ultra, there are the additional issues of maintaining hydration and nutrition. From this perspective, Brian's body had just had enough, and it could have been any of a number of factors that caused it to happen to him.

Science is about objective measurement, so it's understandable that it has an innate bias for things that can be measured. It's easy to put someone on a treadmill and read their VO_2 max or take their blood sugar reading and say it's low. It's not possible to measure the mysterious workings of will. In *Lore of Running*, Dr. Tim Noakes promotes an alternate theory about how our bodies endure exercise. He believes that a central governor in the brain evaluates the athletic task and determines how many muscle fibers should be recruited. In the case of a run, the brain judges how far away the finish line is, compares it to past training runs, and sets a pace that, barring accidents, the body can maintain without injury. Push too hard, and the brain ramps up sensations of fatigue and pain, trying to fool you into slowing down. Once you understand this, you can reprogram yourself to go much faster. Noakes teaches us to stop giving credence to negative thoughts that are only related to how close we are to the finish line.

The central governor theory is controversial, but it squares with my experience of the sport. I have always run better than I should have, given my physical gifts and my marathon time. I have always said that the ultra is a mental game. Consequently, I don't believe it was necessarily an accident that Brian stopped so dramatically right when he did. I think it's possible Brian's central governor, under tremendous physiological stress, caught sight of the finish line, believed the race was over, and pulled the plug. In the context of a 100-mile race, one lap around a high school track doesn't seem that long, but once Brian's brain had made that decision, it was impossibly far. When the captain jumps ship, you can't help but sink.

Brian's collapse was dramatic, and from a medical point of view, provocative. But — and this is the lesson known by anyone who has ever tried with all his will to attain something and fallen short — how Brian finished wasn't what defined him. Collapsing 300 yards from glory made him a fascinating footnote in Western States 100 history, but it didn't make *him*.

Brian put everything he had into an ultra. He was a champion. That year, to me and many others, he was *the* champion.

POSTURE

To run far, fast, or efficiently, you have to run with proper posture. Keep your shoulders back and your arms bent 45 degrees at the elbow. Allow your arms to swing freely, but don't let them cross the imaginary vertical line bisecting your body. This will create openness in the chest, better breathing, and more balance.

Lean forward, but not at the hips. Imagine a rod running through your body from the head to the toes. Keep the rod at a slight forward angle to the ground, with a neutral pelvis. When the entire body participates, you're using gravity to your advantage. Remember, running is controlled falling.

Incan Quin-Wow!

Quinoa (pronounced KEEN-wah) is one of the first grains (technically a seed) humans ever cultivated and used in cooking. It has a dense, earthy flavor and is one of the few grains with all nine essential amino acids, so it's perfect for a dish like porridge — hearty, basic, and satisfying in an almost primal way. When I learned about quinoa, it helped me appreciate the many ancient foods and cultures that could enrich my life, if only I made room for them. Make it the night before, so you can warm it up to eat before a long morning run. A great mixture of carbs, protein, and fat, this porridge is sweetened with fruit and cinnamon. Replace the vanilla with almond or hazelnut extract for a nutty variation.

1 cup dried quinoa, rinsed and drained

2 cups water

1 cup almond milk or your favorite nondairy milk

1 ripe pear, cored, quartered, and finely sliced,
  or 1 banana, sliced

¼ cup dried coconut flakes

3 tablespoons Flora Oil 3-6-9 Blend

½ teaspoon sea salt or light miso

½ teaspoon vanilla extract

1½ teaspoons ground cinnamon

Garnish: Raisins, apple slices, and chia seeds
or your favorite nuts

Add the quinoa and water to a medium saucepan. Bring to a boil, reduce the heat to low, and simmer for 15 to 20 minutes, until the water is absorbed and the quinoa turns translucent. Fluff the quinoa with a fork and cool for 5 minutes.

Place the quinoa and the remaining ingredients in a blender or food processor and mix for 1 to 2 minutes, until smooth.

This porridge can be made the night before and refrigerated so it is ready before a morning workout. For a warm porridge, pour the porridge into a small pot and warm on very low heat for 5 minutes (you may omit the Flora Oil from the mixture and stir it in after the porridge is warmed). Garnish with raisins, apples, and chia seeds or your favorite nuts. MAKES 4 SERVINGS

17

Hunted by the Wasatch Speedgoat

HARDROCK 100, JULY 2007

> The world breaks everyone, and afterward,
> some are strong at the broken places.
>
> — ERNEST HEMINGWAY

DON'T THINK ABOUT your ankle!"

Dusty was yelling at me again. Would he be yelling at me when we had white hair and canes?

"C'mon, Jurker, don't think about your ankle! Climb!"

I didn't answer. I was too busy sliding backward down a glassy snowfield, trying to stop my descent with three good limbs. We had just hammered through a steady downpour, up a ridiculously steep 4,400-foot incline through an opening in the Colorado Rockies called Oscar's Pass. The rain had glazed the snow, turned it to ice. We had turned off our headlamps so the record holder who had been stalking me for 70 miles couldn't gauge the distance he had to make up. It was 2 A.M., black except for every few minutes when lightning bolts strobed the scene: Dusty standing on a mountain, looking down, yelling (of course); me, crawling, sliding, then crawling some more, dragging what I hoped wasn't a broken ankle.

Forty miles earlier, at a cold, windswept little valley, Dusty had taunted a forty-year-old named Karl Meltzer.

"You're getting beat by a guy with an ankle the size of a grapefruit," Dusty jeered.

Meltzer had just smiled. He had won the Wasatch 100 six times and was known as "the Wasatch Speedgoat." He had also won this event—the Hardrock Hundred-Mile Endurance Run, or Hardrock 100, four times. In fact, he held the course record. One of his other nicknames: "King of the Hardrock."

"The race doesn't start until Telluride," Meltzer said. Dusty and I had begun our climb to the snowfield from Telluride. I looked back over my shoulder.

"Climb! C'mon. It's just snow. You're a Nordic skier, you can do this. You've dug deeper before."

I wasn't so sure. I had dropped out of the Hardrock 100 in 2000 after only 42 miles. At the time, I blamed the effort I had expended in my second Western States victory. I had also blamed the altitude. And I blamed the naiveté and youthful optimism of two certain Minnesotans. Dusty picked me up at the Denver airport the day before the 2000 race. We drove eight hours to Silverton, Dusty behind the wheel, me pretzeled on top of plastic bins filled with his construction tools, where the back seats used to be. We arrived at 6 P.M., ate and tried to sleep, then stepped to the starting line at 6 A.M.

After winning my seventh Western States I had decided that, with the proper acclimatization and training, I could conquer the Hardrock. In June 2007 I had arrived in Silverton, Colorado, a month before the race.

Then, two nights before the event, I had sprained my ankle.

I had been camping at Molas Lake, at 11,000 feet, sucking in the thin air, almost feeling my marrow pumping out more oxygen carrying red blood cells. Mornings, I lingered with locals and other runners at the Avalanche Café on unpaved Blair Street. To save money I made my own breakfast and brewed my yerba mate. Late morning, I headed into the mountains to learn the secrets of the course. My guide and companion was Kyle Skaggs, a twenty-two-year-old emerging ultrarunner who was spending the summer as a research assistant at the Mountain Studies Institute, a nonprofit organization dedicated to examining the ecology and climate of high-altitude locations.

Kyle, along with his older brother, Erik, would go on to become the best known — and in certain quarters the most idolized — siblings on the ultra scene. Lean, ruggedly handsome, and irrepressible, the pair were referred to as "the Young Guns" and "the Jonas Brothers of trail running" on the running forums. They have doubtlessly increased the recent female interest in the sport. (When he worked at Oregon's Rogue Valley Runners shop, Kyle was famous for drawing huge numbers of women who asked him to analyze their gait but never bought shoes.) The brothers had been born and raised in rural New Mexico, and along with a dedication to mountain living and environmentalism, they would go on to approach races with a blithe aggressiveness that shocked racing veterans.

Kyle would not be running the Hardrock in 2007, but he knew the mountains and knew racing strategy. Together we explored some of the trickier portions of the course, climbing endless switchbacks, sprinting ridges, descending boulder fields, and crossing a number of snowfields, including a few 50-degree slopes where, if we had slipped, we almost certainly would have died.

Even though the Hardrock contained as many perils as I had ever seen on a course, the dangers fit into a majesty I had never encountered. In many ways, it was not only the toughest course I had ever explored but the most beautiful. We ran past turquoise lakes, brushed purple columbine and crimson Indian paintbrush. There was the shocking green of the tundra and the blinding white of the snowfields, gold rock and red rock, ascents that seemed as if they would never finish, endless vistas, deep, cozy valleys, and sharp, cloudscraping peaks.

Many evenings we spent with Kyle's Mountain Studies Institute colleague, a thirty-something from India named Imtiaz. We cooked meals together in the organization's kitchen. Kyle made mushroom quesadillas and Imtiaz made eggplant curry and dal with basmati rice. The kitchen was full of mouthwatering aromas as we sautéed tomatoes and zucchini with ginger, cumin, and mustard seeds. We discussed the subtleties of spices in Indian cuisine and the benefits of Ay-urvedic medicine.

Years of eating plants had convinced me that the best way to get well and to stay well was to eat simply and to avoid processed foods whenever possible. After my epiphany in my first internship with an old man and his hospital food, I tried to treat injuries and illness with natural remedies whenever possible. Food was my medicine. I even avoided anti inflammatories like ibuprofen, which other long-dis-tance runners gobbled by the handful. I thought it masked pain so much that I might risk serious injury by running when I shouldn't. I had also heard too many stories of runners taking so much ibuprofen that they damaged their kidneys. It was a classic case of treating symp-toms, of wanting the quick fix. It was, in many ways, typical Western medicine.

By the week of the race, after nearly a month of workouts, simple living, and a lot of new vegan food, I was devouring 13,000 foot peaks and 30-mile journeys without the sensation of breathing through a cocktail straw. Even Kyle, with his fresh, twenty-two-year-old muscles and two months of altitude training, was surprised I was pushing the pace on our weekly ascents of Kendall Mountain. High altitude? I was ready.

I had to be. The Hardrock includes eleven mountain passes, six of them over an elevation of 13,000 feet, and also climbing a 14er (a 14,000-foot peak) — a total vertical climb and descent of 66,000 feet, more than would be involved in climbing and descending Mount Everest from sea level, as the race organizers like to point out.

Two nights before the race, I joined a youth DARE program soc-cer game on a grassy field not far from the town's hundred-year-old cemetery. That's where I tore my ankle ligaments when trying to steal the ball from a seven-year-old.

I gulped glass after glass of tumeric soy milk and lay for hours with my leg elevated with a bag of ice wrapped around my bulging ankle. I dosed myself with the homeopathic remedy arnica montana and with pineapple enzyme, bromelain. It wasn't enough. The pain electric-eeled my synapses. There was no way I could run the race. Imtiaz watched me limp into the Mountain Studies kitchen and asked if he could take a look. He ground a scoop of black pepper and added tumeric, flour, and water until it was a thick, heavy paste. He pressed the paste onto paper towels, then wrapped them around my ankle.

I dragged myself into my tent that night, and Dusty saw the compress.

"Jurker, you might want to consider some Vitamin I [ibuprofen] this time," he said.

By the time I was scrambling up the snowfield, I had covered 79 miles on that ankle. The toughest section was yet to come. The race course dubbed as "Wild 'n Tough" was not a course you wanted to run on a freshly sprained ankle. At times it followed animal paths and other times there was no trail, only trail markers to navigate scree slopes and snowfields. Nineteen and a half hours earlier, in the gymnasium of the Silverton High School, I had applied a new Imtiaz special compress, then clamped a Pro-Tec ankle sleeve and aircast over it. Over that I wrapped so many layers of duct tape that it was 2 inches thick. The last time I had seen the ankle, even after two days of treatment, it shined, purple as the inside of a thundercloud. It was so swollen I couldn't see my anklebones.

My injury provided a great excuse to lose. But I didn't want an excuse. The truth is, in this race, even on a good ankle, I would have been running if not scared then at least supremely wary. Anyone who knew the San Juan Mountains would be doing the same. A man named Joel Zucker had died of a brain aneurysm after running the 1998 Hardrock, and scores of people had been injured over the years. Hardrockers knew that, but they kept running. Hardrockers had run until blood leaked from their capillaries into their flesh, which made their hands turn into catcher's mitts and their feet into clown shoes.

But they kept running. Some veteran Hardrockers even chuckled at the sight. On the other hand, pulmonary edema, where the blood seeps into the lungs, could be fatal. Still, past runners had heard moist wheezing deep in their chests, finished the race, and *then* been driven over Molas Pass to the Durango Hospital with fluid in their lungs.

Dozens of runners' guts milkshaked during the course. There was always plenty of puking, not to mention an abundance of hallucinations. Racers watched boulders turn into Subarus, trees morph into masses of laughing worms. They mistook stumps for severed elk heads. The slowest runners had the most visions, probably because their sleep deprivation was more extreme. The Hardrock has a 48-hour time limit. Dawdlers could pretty much count on phantom hikers joining them the last few miles of the course. Some of the poltergeists told jokes.

The first year of the race, 1992, only eighteen of the forty-two entrants finished. Racers had to cut down tree limbs that were blocking the course; the winner knocked on the door of a trailer at the finish line to alert the race officials that he was done.

Nowadays, the organizers set up aid stations at intervals on the course. But they set up many fewer than other 100-mile mountain races. Hardrockers speak with a disdain that sometimes approaches contempt of races like the Leadville Trail 100, which is more famous and more popular, has more corporate sponsors, and which, compared to the Hardrock, "is running over some hills." The Western States is an interesting and famous event, but those Californians who speak of it as the most grueling of ultras? To Hardrockers, they're amusingly provincial.

Some Hardrock highlights: at least one sleepless night and usually two waist-deep river crossings. Harrowing exposure to heights, fixed ropes, and steps cut into snowfields, tundra, and rock, hopping cross-country where no trail exists. Another feature of the race: scree fields that crumble under your feet as you spin in place.

You might think that an event that taxes the human body so mercilessly would have inspired a history of healthy eating. You would be wrong. Next to a typical old-school Hardrocker, the most ravenous catfish in the world is a finicky gourmet eater. For breakfast, especially in the 1990s, the race pioneers tended to scarf doughnuts and slug back multiple helpings of bacon and sausage links. Lunches and dinners often included pepperoni pizzas and greasy cheeseburgers. Not until the race itself, though, did the early Hardrockers make the bewhiskered bottom feeders look prissy. The legendary ultramarathoner and mountain racer Rick Trujillo, who lives just over the mountain from Silverton, in Ouray, Colorado, won the Hardrock in 1996 on a diet of Mountain Dew and Oreos. (He continued his promiscuous diet until 2007, when at age fifty-nine he was rushed to the hospital with chest pains. He eats more salads nowadays.)

Only about half the Hardrock entrants make it to the finish line. If a racer doesn't make it out of each station by a prescribed time (based on the 48-hour maximum), he or she is told the race is over. Getting "timed out," especially after 60 or 70 or 80 miles, is such a bitter experience that many racers have pleaded to go on (some have actually threatened the aid station crews), and empathic but firm organizers have had to address the issue in the race handbook: "You are all experienced ultra runners. . . . Do not debate cutoff times with the aid station personnel!"

"This is a *dangerous* course!" according to that handbook, a fantastic compendium of arcane statistics, numbingly detailed course descriptions, hair-raising terrors, and chilling understatement.

When it comes to the temptation to scale peaks during storms, for example, the manual advises: "You can hunker down in a valley for 2–4 hours and still finish; but if you get fried by lightning your running career may end on the spot."

Regarding "Minor Problems," the manual advises crew members: "You may also see, in the later stages of the run, runners who are extremely depleted in sugar and dehydrated. They usually will be extremely fatigued and may be nauseated and vomiting."

"In addition to trail running," the manual says, "you will do some mild rock climbing (hands required), wade ice cold streams, struggle through snow which at night and in the early morning will be rock hard and slick and during the heat of the day will be so soft you can sink to your knees and above, cross cliffs where a fall could send you 300 feet straight down, use fixed ropes as handrails, and be expected to be able to follow the course with a map." (Volunteers placed plastic flags along the course every year until marmots started gobbling them. Now they use reflective metal markers.)

By the time I had made it through the snow to join Dusty, we stood at Oscar's Pass. We had just climbed 4,400 feet, and if I had not known better, I might have felt an instant of lightning-lit, semicrippled relief. But I did know better. I followed D-Ball as he ran down the back side of the mountain toward a hellish crevasse called Chapman Gulch. I bounded down a series of boulder-strewn switchbacks. Dusty claimed later that he looked back and saw me using the brace to wedge my foot between rocks. I didn't realize it at the time, though, probably because my neurosynapses were sizzling from a massive overload of "AIEEE" impulses. It would have been painful on two good feet.

I had survived descents as rocky and steep before, though. What I had not survived was what I encountered when we reached the bottom: the awesomely awful genesis of the most difficult climb of the course, a treacherous, hope-suckingly steep scramble over boulders, gravel, and loose scree to Grant's Swamp Pass.

In 1998, as the two-time Hardrock champion David Horton was ascending this section of the race, a melon-sized rock dislodged by a runner above fell and struck his right hand. "A little later," Horton wrote in his account of that race, "I noticed that my glove was soaked through with blood." After finishing (of course), he realized that it was a compound fracture.

Horton's story was shocking but not singular. Just as the Hardrock is the toughest ultra around, it tends to draw the toughest ultrarunners.

Laura Vaughan, who set a women's record at the Hardrock in 1997, the only year she ran it, also was the first person to finish the Wasatch Front 100 for ten consecutive years and the first woman to break 24 hours. That makes her fast. What makes her tough, though — what makes her a bona fide Hardrocker — is that in 1996, nine weeks after giving birth to a son, she ran the Wasatch and breastfed her baby at the aid stations. Her ten-year ring from the event is engraved "Lactating Laura."

Tough?

Carolyn Erdman entered the Hardrock for the first time in 1997, when she was forty-eight years old. She made it 85 miles before the race organizers told her that she was moving too slowly and that she was done.

In 1998, she entered again. Four weeks before the event she ran a 50-mile warm-up race in Orem, Utah. Three miles into it, she fell and scraped her left knee. There was blood and a little pain, but she thought it was no big deal. By the time she finished, she could see her patella; she was shocked at how white it was. The doctor in the emergency room told her she was lucky he didn't amputate the limb. She spent a week in the hospital with intravenous antibiotics. Surgeons operated on her twice.

The next year she ran again and was timed out at mile 92. The next year, on her fourth and final attempt, she timed out at mile 77.

Tough?

Kirk Apt started vomiting at mile 67 the first time he ran Hardrock, and 3 hours later he was still vomiting. On his next race attempt, his quadriceps cramped at mile 75, so he hobbled the last quarter of the course. (He won the race in 2000, the year I dropped out.) He's finished the race sixteen times and counting.

The rock was worse than the snow. The climb was crueler. I had been racing for 22 hours. I had been racing for what seemed like my whole life. *The race doesn't start till Telluride?* I wolverined the rocky ground and willed my good leg to keep pushing. For each step I took forward I would gain only half a step, as the loose scree crumbled from underfoot. I was climbing hard but hardly moving. Where was Meltzer? Had he turned his headlamp off? He couldn't have won four Hardrocks without being ruthless.

Tough? *Sometimes you just do things!*

Somehow we made it over. We crested the pass and bounced down the other side. My ankle didn't hurt anymore. I couldn't feel it at all. At 4 A.M., after another climb and another descent, the land took shape around us, the blackness turned into mere dark, then into gray, and finally a pale, wonderful dawn. Watching the glow of a new day in those mountains was almost a religious experience. Some people wonder if a Hardrocker-ultrarunner in the throes of exhaustion and near-agony can enjoy the scenery. As I navigated my way down the final gnarly descent, I didn't just enjoy it, I reveled in it. I wallowed. We heard the sound of a running stream, and we both knew what that meant. We were 2 miles from Silverton and the finish line.

"Let's get this bad boy done," Dusty said. "I need a nap."

We crossed the finish line at 8:08 A.M., in 26 hours and 8 minutes. It was 31 minutes faster than Meltzer's record. I sat down and removed my elaborate ankle protection — still purple and swollen to twice its normal size. I made occasional trips to the high school, to use the bathroom, shower, get something to eat, and take a short nap. But for the next 21 hours, 52 minutes, and 29 seconds, I spent most of my time in the dirt at the finish line. I wanted to greet the other ninety-six finishers, especially my sea-level compatriot, ultra-studette Krissy Moehl, who finished third place overall setting a new women's course record a mere 25 minutes behind Meltzer. In ultrarunning, the mountains and willpower equalize the genders.

Strawburst Anti-Inflammatory Smoothie

I have always shied away from using pharmaceutical agents like ibuprofen to treat pain and swelling, so it's natural that I have experimented with natural anti-inflammatories. When I sprained my ankle days before the 2007 Hardrock, my experiments took on a new urgency.

This smoothie combines the anti-inflammatory ingredients of pineapple (bromelaine), ginger, turmeric, and Flora Oil (omega-3 fatty acids). It's a great daily postworkout drink, soothing aching muscles, and a terrific addition to your regular meals before your run on a long training day. It has a fruity, sweet taste like Starburst candy and is loaded with healthy fats as well as carbohydrates and protein.

The miso replaces the salt and electrolytes lost in sweat. In Japan, miso is viewed as an endurance-booster. Edamame provides an extra whole-food protein boost. Fresh turmeric root can be found in the produce section of natural foods stores. You will need a high-powered blender to process the roots. If you don't have one, opt for the dried turmeric and ginger.

  2 cups water

  1 banana

  1 cup frozen or fresh strawberries

  ½ cup frozen mango

  ½ cup frozen pineapple

  ½ cup frozen shelled edamame

  ¼ cup dried coconut flakes

  3 tablespoons Flora Oil 3-6-9 Blend

  1 tablespoon plant protein powder (brown rice, pea, etc.)

  1½ teaspoons miso

  1 1-inch piece turmeric root, chopped, or teaspoon ground turmeric

  1 1-inch piece ginger root, peeled and minced, or ¼ teaspoon ground ginger

Place all the ingredients in a blender and blend on high for 1 to 2 minutes, until smooth.   MAKES 3 8-OUNCE SERVINGS

18

In the Footsteps of Pheidippides

SPARTATHLON, SEPTEMBER 2007

> Let food be thy medicine and medicine be thy food.
>
> — HIPPOCRATES

TWO MONTHS LATER, my sprain was healed, and I was filled with the optimism and joy that only winning a 100-mile mountain race on a bum ankle can bring. All that good stuff was very fortunate, because I was about to begin a 152-mile race with a broken toe.

It was called the Spartathlon, and even though I had won it the year before, a few months after my second Badwater victory, I knew that this year would be more difficult. It's always easier to sneak up on someone than to defend a title.

The Spartathlon begins at the base of the Acropolis in Athens and ends in front of the statue of King Leonidas in Sparta, a distance of 245.3 km (152.4 miles). The course is predominantly road racing (95 percent) with some improved dirt roads (4 percent) and a small section of mountainous trail (1 percent). The elevation ranges from sea level to 3,937 feet, climbing a few mountain ranges for a total elevation gain of over 8,000 feet. In addition to the sheer length of the course, runners are challenged by the potent Greek sun and coastal humidity. In the heat of the day, temperatures can reach 90 to 100 degrees Fahrenheit.

The total overall time limit for the course is set at 36 hours, but there are seventy-five race control points, each with its own time cut-off. Approximately half of the 300 or so starters finish each year. Volunteers at the aid stations offer water, nectar juices, sodas, bread, yogurt, as well as other items, and runners are allowed to leave drop bags at any of the stations, so it is theoretically possible to run this race without a crew. No pacers are allowed.

I ran the Spartathlon in 2006 because of its reputation. I returned in 2007 because of my experience that first year and because of what I had learned of the history of the race.

The most famous long-distance race with a Greek origin is the marathon, which celebrates the arduous journey of the messenger who ran from Marathon to Athens, a distance of 26.2 miles, to announce Greece's victory over the Persians in 490 B.C.; he then dropped dead from exhaustion. Though Pheidippides is the messenger most often credited with the noble and fatal trip, the runner was probably named Eucles, according to the ancient writer Plutarch.

The real story of Pheidippides, according to those same historians, is much better and has a happier ending. It also inspired the modern Spartathlon.

The Persian fleet was on a roll. They had plundered their way through the Greek islands, sacked the city-state of Eretria, and then had their sights set on Athens. The Athenians sent a small force, commanded by General Miltiades, to seal off the exits from the Bay of Marathon, named after the ancient Greek word for the fennel that probably grew wild there. The ancient historian Herodotus writes that the Athenian generals dispatched Pheidippides to the great city of Sparta to ask for reinforcements in holding off the much larger invading force.

Pheidippides reached Sparta the day after he left Athens, but his plea fell on deaf ears. Although sympathetic to their fellow Greeks' plight, the religious Spartans were in the middle of a festival to Apollo and could not wage war until the full moon. It must have been a long 152.4 miles back home with the bad news, but luckily Pheidippides had something else to report.

While running through the mountains above the ancient city of Tegea (checkpoint 60 of the modern Spartathlon), he had a vision of the nature god, Pan. The son of Hermes, the divine messenger, Pan ruled over shepherds, nymphs, and rustic places. He was a great guy to have on your side in a big battle, because he could induce a wild fear in mortals called "panic." This god called Pheidippides by name "and bade him ask the Athenians why they paid him no attention, though he was of goodwill to the Athenians, had often been of service to them, and would be in the future."

If we read it closely, everything we need to know about running is in Pheidippides' story. He ran over 300 miles — the first half in a little over one day — and he didn't even get what he wanted! If you run long enough, that tends to happen. Whatever quantitative measure of success you set out to achieve becomes either unattainable or meaningless. The reward of running — of anything — lies within us. As I sought bigger rewards and more victories in my sport, it was a lesson I learned over and over again. We focus on something external to motivate us, but we need to remember that it's the process of reaching for that prize — not the prize itself — that can bring us peace and joy. Life, as countless posters and bumper stickers rightly attest, is a journey, not a destination. Pheidippides kept going, and he ended up getting something even better, something outside the normal realm of human experience. Nature itself called out his name — Pan is nature incarnate — and it gave the great runner a sacred message to bring home to his people. The message was pretty much what nature's message always is: Pay more attention to me, and I will help you the way I've always helped you in the past.

Pheidippides recounted his vision to the Athenian generals, who took it seriously and erected a new temple to Pan after the war. Unable to wait until the Spartans arrived, the Athenians charged the Persians. The Athenians fought with legendary courage, dividing and conquering the Persian force. Their underdog victory at Marathon is considered the tipping point in the Persian Wars, heralding the golden age of Greece.

The Spartathlon, first run in 1983, was the brainchild of Wing Commander John Foden, a native Australian on the verge of retirement from the British Royal Air Force. Foden's forty-year military career included service in the Korean War, the Suez Crisis, the Brunei Revolt, and the Turkish invasion of Cyprus, but he was also an avid amateur athlete and a student of the classics. One day, while rereading Herodotus, he started wondering if Pheidippides' legendary run was something within a modern runner's power.

John and four buddies from the RAF decided to make the attempt. In the words of the Irishman John McCarthy, "We established a credible and historically correct route using ancient military roads, pilgrim ways, dry river beds and goat tracks, taking into consideration the ancient political alignments and enemy states to be skirted." The five runners set off from Athens on October 8, 1982, and the "three Johns" succeeded, arriving in Sparta in front of the statue of Leonidas on October 9: John Scholten in 35.5 hours, John Foden in 36 hours, and John McCarthy in just under 40 hours.

They decided to establish a yearly run that, in the Olympic vein, would offer no prize money or commercial gain but would instead promote a spirit of international cooperation and fellowship. Indeed, the Spartathlon is one of the best values in the world of ultrarunning. The entry fee of $525 gets you lodging and meals for six days as well as two of the best awards ceremonies you'll ever attend, museum tours, bus transportation, and ample food and water at the aid stations.

In 1983, 45 runners from 11 countries competed. In 1984, the International Spartathlon Association was founded to manage the race.

After he retired, Foden stayed active in the ultra community, promoting races all over the world. I found his booklet, "Preparing for & Competing in Your First Spartathlon," very helpful my first year. He continued to break age group records into his seventies, and in 2005 he was the oldest participant in the 300-km Haervejsvandring Walk from Schleswig in Germany to Viborg in North Denmark in seven days.

In the Western States and other ultras, I had battled the best long-distance runners the United States had to offer. The Spartathlon attracted the finest in the world. When I showed up in 2007, I faced the 2001 champion, Valmir Nunes from Brazil. He had just broken my Badwater course record and held the third fastest 100-km time in the world. There was an impressive number of other former champions: the 2000 champion, Otaki Masayuki, and the 2002 (and eventual 2009) champion, Sekiya Ryoichi, from Japan. Markus Thalmann, the 2003 champion from Austria, was there, too, as well as Jens Lukas from Germany, who had won in 2004 and 2005. When I had won the previous year, I was the first North American to do so. The greatest Spartathlon champion was — and probably always will be — homegrown. Twenty-six-year-old Yiannis Kouros was living a Spartan lifestyle as a groundskeeper near Tripoli when the Johns undertook the first Spartathlon test run in 1982. Hearing of their mission to resurrect Pheidippides, the literary-minded Kouros was entranced. He had run twenty-five marathons at that point, with some modest successes and a personal record of 2:25; he was about to find his niche. In 1983, Kouros burst onto the ultramarathon scene with a Spartathlon and ultramarathon debut in an astounding 21:53. His margin of victory was so great — more than 3 hours ahead of the runner-up — that the race director refused to award him the trophy for two days — until it could be proven that he had not cheated.

He went on to win the Spartathlon three more times, and these remain the four fastest times ever for the course, ranging from 20:25 to 21:57. Pheidippides couldn't have done better. I've chased many a record, but my best times are in fifth, sixth, and seventh place overall, 23 minutes behind his slowest time.

Now semi-retired from ultras, Kouros is undefeated in any continuous world-class road ultramarathon competition beyond 100 miles, and he still holds world records on the road and track for almost all distances and durations beyond the 12-hour event.

Kouros is a philosopher-athlete in the ancient Greek tradition. His results seem to stem from an overflowing energy of spirit. He paints, writes poetry, records songs, played the role of Pheidippides in the movie *A Hero's Journey,* and delivers motivational talks "to get people inspired and alert, so they can discover and utilize the unconditional abilities of human beings, in order to bring (beyond personal improvement) unity, friendship and harmony to the world."

He has certainly inspired me to push beyond the limits of form. Kouros is not much to look at as a runner, with his boxy build and choppy gait, although little is wasted on his runs, and he keeps moving even while he eats and drinks. His upper body is remarkably muscled. When you look at sprinters, you see those developed upper bodies, too. I think Kouros has found an extra energy source up there in those powerful pectorals and deltoids. Many runners have learned that a strong upper body helps with technique and speed. Kouros, though, seems to have discovered a secret about transferring propulsive power from the arms to the legs.

Ultimately, Kouros teaches us that the ultra is an exercise in transcendence. He explicitly defines it as a test of "metaphysical characteristics," as opposed to inborn athletic gifts or level of conditioning. Only a continuous run of 24-plus hours will do, "as a runner has to face the whole spectrum of the daytime and nighttime and be able to continue. Doing so, he/she will prove that he/she can run beyond the effectiveness of genetic gifts and fitness level, as these elements will have gone from the duration of time and the muscular exhaustion." While respecting the athleticism of such events, he disqualifies 50-milers and stage runs from the category of ultra, as they will favor athletes who are well trained and gifted. The true ultrarunner must endure sleep deprivation and complete muscular fatigue. Only then can he or she "find energy after the fuel is gone."

Reflecting on Kouros's message and thinking about the bliss that awaited those who could push through an ultramarathon's pain helped me when, nine days before the event, I woke in the middle of the night and, on my way to the bathroom, stubbed my pinkie toe. The next morning it was black and blue and just hanging there. I was pretty sure it was broken. Over the next week, I tried to tape it against the toe next to it. I tried walking on the beach, bracing the toe with taped

At my second Badwater Ultramarathon, in 2006, I experienced the most grueling finish of my running career. I'm grateful that Dusty was with me, making me realize that yes, I could go on.

LUIS ESCOBAR

Before heading into the depths of Mexico's Copper Canyon, in 2006, to race the Indians known as the "running people," I met the mysterious race organizer, Caballo Blanco (White Horse). Here we discuss the wondrous properties of pinole.

The Tarahumara are known for their grace and speed. The fastest and most graceful of them all is Arnulfo Quimare, and to this day I consider him one of my noblest competitors.

I stay at the finish line to show respect to fellow runners, and because it's a blast. At the conclusion of the 2006 Copper Canyon Ultramarathon, I'm with (L to R) Arnulfo, Manuel Luna, Silvino, Herbalisto, and a local child.

The Hardrock 100 takes runners up 33,000 feet and over eleven mountain passes. In 2007, two nights before the event, I tore the ligaments in my right ankle. The Hardrock suddenly got harder.

At the Hardrock 100, runners encounter snow, ice, rain, sleet, and lightning. I'm not sure I ever felt quite as small, or as humbled. If you're an ultrarunner, you can fight nature or embrace it. I suggest the latter.

In 2007, in my second Spartathalon victory, as I passed the ruins of
Corinth I imagined Pheidippides at my side. Running has taken me places.

Most times, sunrise in the Italian Alps would cheer me. In August 2008, though,
I was in third place in the Ultra-Trail du Mont-Blanc, nursing a bloody knee.

JENNY UEHISA

In 2010, *New York Times* columnist Mark Bittman interviewed me. Before any questions, he opened his fridge and asked me to prepare a meal. I whipped up a veggie and tofu stir-fry with homemade Indonesian almond sauce and quinoa.

My mother struggled with Multiple Sclerosis most of her adult life, and her last few years were filled with pain. Her response to my concern was always the same and it still inspires me: "Don't worry about me. I'm tough."

Mountains, deserts, and canyons bring with them fiendish challenges, but nothing compares to the monotony and mental strain of a 24-hour race. In 2010, I traveled to Brive la Gaillarde, France, to see if I could set a national record.

I met Jenny Uehisa in 2001 through the Seattle running community, and I was taken with her kindness, adventurous spirit, and infectious smile. Today, there's no one I depend upon more.

In September 2010, I went on a USO tour in Kuwait, where I ran alongside 1,400 soldiers in a 9/11 memorial event, signed autographs, and swapped stories. I consider the trip one of my greatest honors.

I love eating healthy food, but like my grandma Jurek, I find preparing it for others is almost as gratifying. In 2010, I cooked Thai curry and brown rice for fifty in Chamonix, France, a few days before the Ultra-Trail du Mont-Blanc.

Popsicle sticks. I tried a stiffer insole. I told myself that I had almost nine days, that the body could do miraculous things.

Finally, I reminded myself to be grateful for my latest injury. It helped me remember why I ran ultras in the first place. It wasn't for the chance to best a record. It wasn't for simple physical pleasure. It was for something more profound, something deeper. To run 100 miles and more is to bring the body to the point of breaking, to bring the mind to the point of destruction, to arrive at that place where you can alter your consciousness. It was to see more clearly. As my yoga teacher would say, "Injuries are our best teachers."

I'm convinced that a lot of people run ultramarathons for the same reason they take mood-altering drugs. I don't mean to minimize the gifts of friendship, achievement, and closeness to nature that I've received in my running career. But the longer and farther I ran, the more I realized that what I was often chasing was a state of mind — a place where worries that seemed monumental melted away, where the beauty and timelessness of the universe, of the present moment, came into sharp focus. I don't think anyone starts running distances to obtain that kind of vision. I certainly didn't. But I don't think anyone who runs ultra distances with regularity fails to get there. The trick is to recognize the vision when it comes over you. My broken toe helped me do that.

By the time of the race, my toe still hurt with every step, but I was trying to ignore the pain. I had other things to think about — Nunes, for example. Masayuki and Ryoichi from Japan, Austria's Thalmann. The only other runner I paid some attention to was Polish, and he had run to Greece from his country, pushing a modified baby buggy that he had rigged to carry his goods and gear. Piotr Korylo had stopped in Rome to see the pope. I admired his single-mindedness, but figured he had to be exhausted. I didn't see him as serious competition.

The Spartathlon course is hilly but not steep, which presents problems of its own. Even the fastest ultrarunners in the world are forced to walk steep sections of the Hardrock, for example, but in the Spartathlon the only excuse for walking is weakness. So I ran. Thalmann and Nunes went out first, as I expected. The Pole overtook Nunes after a mere 20K and was building a huge lead.

With no pacers, the first time you see your crew is 50 miles in. I kept a steady pace, occasionally downing some gels, potatoes, bananas, and energy drinks, willing myself to stay in the moment, to concentrate on the next step and the step after that. It was about five o'clock in the afternoon, the temperature was in the mid-90s, and I had climbed away from the sea, had woven in and out of orchards of orange trees and through the ancient, column-filled city of Corinth. I was running toward the sun, which was setting behind a great hill in front of me, turning everything a misty, thick red. I tried to not think too much; in a race this long, at a moment this hot, with lips this parched, thinking could be dangerous. It too easily led to a calm, rational assessment of where I was, how far I had to go. Rational assessments too often led to rational surrenders. I tried to go to that place beyond thinking, that place that can bring an ultramarathoner such happiness.

People always ask me what I think about when running so far for so many hours. Random thinking is the enemy of the ultramarathoner. Thinking is best used for the primitive essentials: when I ate last, the distance to the next aid station, the location of the competition, my pace. Other than those considerations, the key is to become immersed in the present moment where nothing else matters.

But I was struggling to hold on to third place, and I was *so* thirsty. Every time I saw someone — a villager, a vintner, an old lady sitting in a patch of shade — I yelled, "*Paghos nero parakalo,*" which means "ice and water, please," but no one seemed to understand. Finally, emerging from a chalky, lonely taverna, a bent old woman in a long, navy blue dress shuffled toward me. "*Paghos nero parakalo,*" I called, and miraculously she seemed to understand. She yelled something to a man standing in the doorway as she mimed drinking.

She had thick arms, thick ankles, and a rough, weather-beaten face. Her husband handed her a large glass of water filled with chunks of ice, and she gave it to me. The ice could have come from keeping freshly caught fish cold. I could not have cared less. To me, the chunks were more valuable than glittering diamonds. She also picked a handful of basil leaves from the garden at her feet and thrust them into my hands. I was trying to drink and thank her at the same time when I saw her motioning to the basil leaves and then to my small waistpack, where I carried my gels and food. She was telling me to put the basil in there. When I took the pack off, though, she pulled one of the leaves out and stuck it behind my ear. Then she kissed me on the cheek.

Suddenly I felt a lightness and a strength. Whether it was her kindness, the water, or the basil (which I discovered later is the king of herbs, the word *basil* deriving from the Greek word *basileus,* which means *king*; it is revered as a symbol of strength and good luck in Greece), my mind shifted. It was the moment in an ultramarathon that I have learned to live for, to love. It was that time when everything seems hopeless, when to go on seems futile, and when a small act of kindness, another step, a sip of water, can make you realize that *nothing* is futile, that going on — especially when going on seems so foolish — is the most meaningful thing in the world. Many runners have encountered that type of crystalline vision at the end of a race, or training run, that brings with it utter fatigue and blessed exhaustion. For ultrarunners, the vision is a given.

I was the same person, mildly dehydrated, hobbled with a broken toe, hot, fatigued, with quads and calves that felt as if they had been beaten by baseball bats. But I was a different person.

I picked up my pace. Nunes and Thalmann had fallen behind, and the Polish guy was in front. An inexperienced runner who took the lead in a race like this after 10 miles was self-destructive. One in front after 25 miles was self-destructive but very, very determined. The same man leading after 50 miles was insane — or he wasn't as inexperienced as I had thought. Either way, he was dangerous.

I ran through more vineyards, but I knew Korylo was still leading. He was so far ahead I couldn't see him.

I had to beat him, but I couldn't obsess about him. In the same way, I had to claw my way to the finish line with everything I had, but I couldn't think too much about that line. When I got to the 50-mile mark I couldn't think that I had 100 miles to go. I had to remember and forget. We move forward, but we must stay in the present. I tried to do so by breaking races into small, digestible parts. Sometimes I focused on the next aid station, three miles ahead. Sometimes I pictured the next shady spot down the road, or the next step.

Did "*Sometimes you just do things*" really mean "*Try not to think about consequences, just trust in your body and yourself and the universe*"? Was my dad not just a hardass Minnesotan but a mystic? It made me smile to think so. At 70 miles, Nunes pulled up to me and I gestured toward the front, raised my shoulders. Who *was* that buggy-pusher?

Nunes didn't speak much English and I didn't speak any Portuguese, but he said, "Scotch, you strong," and took a few steps in front of me, waving with me to keep up. We ran together for 30 miles, chasing the Polish guy. We ran over dry, baked earth and past ruins and through dusty villages where little kids materialized from dark passages and ancient doors and ran after us, shouting and laughing. I didn't know if they were making fun of us or exhorting us to go faster. I thought of my days on that dead-end dirt road and wondered what I would have done if a bunch of men ran past my house. I wondered if any of these Greek children climbed the hills nearby and wondered why things were.

At 100 miles, a man gave me a flower. He was crying as he handed it to me. Almost every person I met in Greece seemed to radiate a passion for life. I think it was inextricably linked to the land, the water, and the plants. There's a myth that when Athens was founded, the gods argued over who would get to be the patron of the beautiful new city. It came down to Athena, goddess of wisdom, and Poseidon, god of the sea. Zeus declared that the two should each create a gift to give to the mortals of the city, and whoever gave the better gift would be its patron. Poseidon made water gush out of the Acropolis, but it was salty and so not of much use. Athena invented the olive tree, which could give the people fruit, oil, and wood. As a plant-based athlete, it was moving to see a culture where plants retain symbolic power and where people still use herbs to heal. It's in their history, after all. Greece was the homeland of Hippocrates, the founder of modern medicine, who singled out diet and exercise as important components of health and wrote "let food be thy medicine." In *On Ancient Medicine,* he wrote: "It appears to me necessary to every physician to be skilled in the ways of nature, and strive to know, if he would wish to perform his duties, what man is in relation to the articles of food and drink . . . And it is not enough to know simply that cheese is a bad article of food, as disagreeing with whoever eats to satiety. One must know what sort of disturbance it creates, and why, and with what principle in man it disagrees." To be fair, Hippocrates wasn't advocating giving up cheese entirely; he goes on to say that some people tolerate it better than others. Maybe he knew about lactose intolerance.

In Greece, I filled up on pomegranates and figs, wild greens from the mountains called *horta,* and lots of olives. It was a foraging paradise. On almost every training run I passed through vineyards of grapes and almond and citrus and quince trees (often grabbing fruit and eating it as I went). The Greeks had a simple diet — and an exceedingly healthy one.

At 107 miles, I churned over the pass where Pheidippides saw an apparition. Scientists today might say it was a hallucination brought on by sleep deprivation and fatigue, but there was something haunted about the rocky mountaintop. Bonfires glowed at the pass, and dozens of villagers cheered as I crested the top and descended to the town below. I had a little less than 50 miles to go. I had never felt better.

I didn't notice my broken toe anymore. The rest of my body ached, but I didn't care. That's one of the many great pleasures of an ultramarathon. You can hurt more than you ever thought possible, then continue until you discover that hurting isn't that big a deal. Forget a second wind. In an ultra you can get a third, a fourth, a fifth even. I still had more than 40 miles to go, but that's a second wonderful thing about 100- (and plus) milers. You can trail, and despair, and screw up, and despair more, and there's almost always another chance. Salvation is always within reach. You can't reach it by thinking or by figuring it out. *Sometimes you just do things.*

At 120 miles, I passed through Tegea. Someone there said that the

Polish guy had left just a minute earlier. I grabbed an energy drink and several Clif Shot energy gels. I saw a pulsing red beam ahead of me. It was the police escort that stays with the leader throughout the race. Salvation smelled like dust and crushed grapes and history. It glowed. I ran toward it. When I passed Korylo, he seemed to barely be moving. I ran as hard as I could.

"Good job," I said, and tried to run even harder. I couldn't keep this pace up for long, but I knew how demoralizing it was to be passed by someone moving at a pace you knew you couldn't match. I was sympathetic to him and admired his courage and tenacity, but when you have a chance to demoralize a competitor, you take it. I took it.

I ran hard for another mile or so and then looked back. Nothing. The escort was with me now. Some 5, 6 miles later, still nothing behind me. Then, from out of nowhere, a headlamp moving fast, swallowing distance. I tried to speed up but couldn't. I looked back again. I thought, *This guy is tough. I've got to put the hammer down, now.* I went all-out, as hard as I could, for 3 miles. I was putting down 7-minute miles. No way anyone could keep up with that. I looked back. The light was closer. I ran harder. I found the inner reserve that most of us never have to look for (another gift of ultramarathons), and I kept pushing until a car pulled up alongside me. It was one of the race officials.

"Scott, do not worry," he said. "This runner is not to be worried about."

I was thinking, "*What are you talking about? That guy behind me is one tough Polack.*" I pushed hard for another 2 miles, and the race official drove up again. This time he said, "Scott, do not worry, this runner is not in the race," and again, my reaction was, "*What do you mean, he's right there!*"

At the next aid station, I learned the truth. The headlamp behind me belonged to a "bandit" runner, a guy who had jumped onto the course at 120 miles. I had just run an intense 15K after 130 miles, and I still had 22 to go. It was time to pull out the four-step checklist. Number one: I was exhausted. I let myself feel that and I acknowledged it. Number two: I took stock. I was slightly pissed off that I had just expended so much energy, all to put distance between myself and someone I needn't have worried about. And I was still exhausted and upset. But it wasn't life-threatening. Three: I asked myself what I could do to remedy the situation. I could stop, but that wasn't an option. The answer: Keep moving. And four: Separate negative thoughts from reality. Don't dwell on feelings that aren't going to help. I kept moving.

Was perseverance that simple? Was will that reducible? Certainly I wasn't the only one with a checklist. What kept me going while others stopped?

Recent research suggests that it's not just the brain that differentiates those who continue from those who stop. It might be the chemicals released by the brain.

Dr. Andy Morgan at Yale Medical School studied the brain chemistry of soldiers subjected to mock interrogation techniques at Fort Bragg's Resistance Training Laboratory. As a group, Special Forces soldiers released a greater amount of a chemical called neuropeptide Y (NPY) than did the regular infantrymen. NPY is an amino acid that helps regulate blood pressure, appetite, and memory. It also buffers the effects of adrenaline, preventing high energy from turning into wasted mania.

Not only did the Special Forces soldiers release more NPY during the interrogation, but, twenty-four hours later, their levels had returned to normal, whereas the regular soldiers showed significant depletion.

Other research has shown different, less chemical variation between the hardy and the truly exceptional. In *Surviving the Extremes,* Dr. Kenneth Kamler studied the factors that separate winners from losers in the world's toughest environments. He examined the cases of Mauro Prosperi, a competitor in the 1994 Marathon des Sables, who survived nine full days in the Sahara, and the Mexican prospector Pablo Valencia, lost for eight days in the Mojave in 1905. When they were found, both Prosperi and Valencia had lost approximately 25 percent of their body weight to dehydration, an amount that would normally prove fatal.

Kamler concluded that four factors contributed to these men's almost inhuman ability to survive: their knowledge; their conditioning, which in effect "inoculated" them against the desert; luck; and — the factor he saw as by far the most important — the will to survive. Prosperi, a highly competitive athlete, had an uncommonly strong survival instinct. Valencia was filled with murderous rage toward his incompetent guide; the intensity of his desire for revenge spurred him on, even through a near-death experience.

I wasn't that angry at the bandit runner. I wasn't sure if I was juiced up with unusually high levels of NPY and DHEA. But I had come this far, I was in front, and I aimed to stay there.

The last 30 miles of the race follows a narrow, two-lane highway straight into Sparta. It climbs for half that distance, then plunges downhill into the city. As I climbed, the police escort was behind me, and in front was absolute blackness. Every so often I'd hear a growling and snapping from a dog or feel the hot wind of a diesel as it roared past. I had never felt so tired. Several times I found myself dozing off as I ran uphill. I slapped my face to make sure I stayed awake. Then I saw the photographer, squatting on the double yellow line in the middle of the highway, snapping pictures of me as I approached. It worried me, because semi-trucks were splitting the night more often, and I thought he'd be killed. I waved at him to move, but he kept clicking. I noticed the two cameras hanging around his neck, the long lens on the one that he kept clicking, and even his stubble. The closer I got, the more clearly I saw and the more he clicked until I was upon him, which is when he disappeared. It took me a moment to realize: He had never been there.

When I crossed the finish line at 23:12, the mayor, surrounded by a group of young women, placed a wreath on my head, and someone draped an American flag around my shoulders. I had finished 20 minutes slower than my victory the year before, but still, no one had ever run the course faster except the great Kouros. No other North American had ever won the race. I hung out in the medical tent for a little while, got some sleep, greeted finishers, and then slept some more.

Later, I went over the race in my mind and thought about the things many ultrarunners think about. Chief among them is how to go on when you feel you can't go on anymore. The Yale study demonstrates that Special Forces soldiers are different than regular ones but not how they got that way. Did they obtain the required stuff of super warriordom through a lucky draw in the genetic lotto, or did it develop through training? Are elite athletes born or can they be made? More to the point: What were my limits? And how could I discover them unless I tried to go beyond them? The last was a question I asked myself each time I ran an ultra. It's a question that every ultrarunner and anyone lucky enough to reach for something outside her comfort zone can ask—and answer—herself. It was a question I had come close to answering in my second, grueling Spartathlon. I planned to keep asking.

WHEN YOU'RE IN A FUNK

Almost every competitive runner I know goes through a period when he or she feels like quitting. I certainly include myself in that category. What's ironic is that the tools that help make an elite athlete—focus, effort, attention to the latest technology—definitely do not provide the answer to getting out of a funk. I find the best way to get your running mojo back is to lose the technology, forget results, and run free. And forget that running needs to be painful or that it's punishment. (Definitely get rid of those echoes of countless coaches ordering you to "take a lap" because you dropped a pass or double-dribbled.) Run for the same reason you ran as a child—for enjoyment. Take your watch off. Run in your jeans. Run with a dog (does *he* seem worried?). Run with someone older or younger, and you'll see running, and the world, differently. I know I have.

Run a trail you have never run before. Pick a new goal, race, or a large loop that keeps you motivated to get out on

those bad-weather days. Do all and any of these things often
enough, and you'll remember why you started running in the
first place—it's *fun*. ≡

Kalamata Hummus Trail Wrap

*This amazingly simple and portable meal and trail snack combines ol-
ives from Greece with Mexican tortillas and Middle Eastern hummus.
I learned about hummus when I first started reading vegetarian cookbooks and studying world cuisine, and I started making these wraps for
my long training runs in the Cascade Mountains. The sesame butter
provides a smooth texture, and combines with the chewy tortilla and
salty olives to create a nuanced, multilayered meal from a decidedly
multinational but very harmonious dish. If you are making this to eat
on the trail, you may wish to omit the garlic.*

3 cups cooked garbanzo beans

3 tablespoons tahini

2 tablespoons tamari, 2 tablespoons miso,
   or 2 teaspoons sea salt

¼ cup freshly squeezed lemon or lime juice

½ garlic clove, chopped (optional)

1 teaspoon ground cumin

   Black pepper

⅛ teaspoon cayenne pepper (optional)

8 flour tortillas

   Chopped kalamata olives

Place the beans, tahini, tamari, lemon juice, garlic, and cumin in a
food processor or blender. Process until smooth. Add a small amount
of water to keep the mixture moving if needed. Season to taste with
black and cayenne pepper.

For each wrap, spread a thin layer of hummus on a tortilla and
sprinkle some of the olives in a line down the center of the tortilla.

Roll the tortilla into a tight wrap and cut into two or three pieces, depending upon the size of the tortillas.

Pack the rolls in a small plastic bag and refrigerate overnight so they are ready for the next morning's long run. For a more substantial lunch, add lettuce, red bell pepper, and tomato before rolling the wraps. Hummus keeps refrigerated for 5 to 6 days or freezes well for several months.   MAKES 8-10 SERVINGS

19

Lost

DULUTH, MINNESOTA, 2008-10

There is a crack, a crack in everything.
That's how the light gets in.

— LEONARD COHEN

TOLD MY MOTHER about my first victory in the Western States, how I had screamed "Minnesota!" when I crossed the finish line. I described the rain on Mount Si and the blistering heat of Death Valley. She hadn't opened her eyes for three days.

I flew to Duluth's Chris Jensen Nursing Home after a staff member called and told me my mom didn't have much time. The first day, she tried to talk to me, but her disease had ravaged her vocal cords — nothing came from her lips but a faint whisper. When she looked at me I could feel her love, but I could also see her fear and her pain. The first day, I sat next to her and held her hand in mine. I told her that I loved her. The second day, she closed her eyes.

I told her that my brother and sister were there, and her sister, that we would always be there, that we loved her. To cool her fever, I put a cold, wet washcloth on her forehead. I moistened her mouth with a foam swab, adjusted the oxygen tubes feeding into her nose. Her skin was smooth, glowing. She had spent most of her life unable to do things most of us take for granted. She was fifty-eight years old. I stroked her hair, pulled back in a braid.

She always encouraged us to be grateful for the things we had — for life itself. She always expressed joy. Yet I knew she would be relieved to escape the pain.

I wondered — not for the first time — whether she would have been happier if I had stayed close to home, if I had taken care of her. I wondered how I would live without her. She gave me confidence and support, taught me about real strength and acceptance. And yet I, too, would feel relief at her deliverance from agony.

I had visited her twice a year. I took her to movies, especially those featuring Julia Roberts, and afterward Red Lobster, where I minced her favorite meal of shrimp scampi so she wouldn't choke. Every time I left, she chided me for worrying, told me to enjoy myself, that she was fine, that she enjoyed watching her television and Julia Roberts movies, that as long as she had her remote control, she would be fine.

When it was time for me to leave, she would say good-bye and that she loved me. But her final parting was always the same. "I'm tough," she said. "Don't worry about me." The words stayed with me as I climbed into my rental car and pulled away.

But for the past five years she couldn't push the buttons anymore, was on a pureed diet, and her voice had grown more faint. With shame, I remembered waiting impatiently as she struggled with my father down the aisle of St. Rose Catholic Church to join me and my little brother and little sister in the front row. I remembered twenty-five years earlier, too, a vital, beautiful young woman who was starting to drop things. She was greeting a friend who had returned from a trip to France. I saw my mother tilt her head back with a lover's ardor, waiting to be bathed in the miraculous healing water from Lourdes.

She had such faith. How could any god let this happen?

Sometimes you just do things. But this time I didn't know what to do. I hadn't known for the past two years.

Leah and I had been in trouble all that time. She told me we married too young. She told me that I wasn't funny, that I wasn't interesting. She told me she was starting to have feelings for other men. I promised that we would work things out. That's what you did when things got hard. You worked them out, you kept going. Especially when you married someone: That's when you didn't give up. Then she told me she was in love with another man, that she wanted a divorce. We separated in February 2008.

I had been with her almost my entire adult life. I called Rick Miller, sobbing, and he told me that everything happens for a reason. I spent weeks at a time in Ashland, Oregon, staying in the basement of my friends Ian Torrence and Hal Koerner. Hal and I raced each other for five or six years at the Western States, and Ian and I went all the way back to the Zane Grey 50-Miler, more than ten years earlier. Rumors started that I was washing dishes to pay the bills and logging hundreds of miles in the foothills of the Siskiyou Mountains. My Hardrock buddy Kyle Skaggs heard the rumors and the real story (the ultra community is small) and told me I should come to Flagstaff for a week and hang out with him and our friend Tony Krupicka, an up-and-coming young runner who in high school viewed me as one of his top three favorite runners. Kyle went further; as a joke he made a votive candle in my likeness and gave it to Jenn Shelton. He said it represented the patron saint of ultrarunners.

We camped outside Grand Canyon National Park that spring and ran along a plateau between the rim and floor of the Grand Canyon. Part of it was called the Tonto Trail, and I had never felt such stunning expansiveness and desolation.

It suited my mood. We camped for four nights. We ran 35 miles one day, then slightly shorter distances the other three days. I made tempeh tacos and fresh guacamole and spent nights huddled near the fire in my lightweight sleeping bag. The temperature dipped to 18 degrees. I told Tony that I didn't believe love was eternal, that people make too big a deal of it. He told me I was wrong, that love was everything. Kyle was living out of his car and said he was headed to Silverton after our trip. He planned to run the Hardrock that year. He had all of his personal belongings in Rubbermaid bins. Some of our friends called him "the Rubbermaid Tramp."

After one of our runs, drinking Tecates, and finishing up some beans and corn tortillas around a campfire, I realized that I envied not just Kyle's freedom but the life that he and Tony lived. We had gotten slightly lost that day, had run 12 miles farther than we had intended, into and out of drainages, through hidden side canyons and back out. We were dehydrated and bonking all the way back on the 3,400-foot climb on the South Kaibab Trail to the South Rim.

When we finished, I could see in the two younger runners' smiles the feeling I had fallen in love with more than a decade earlier. I started racing ultras when they were in grade school. Their joy reminded me how I used to feel, what I used to know.

We had trails and the fresh air and a little water and food and our fit bodies to move through and with the land. That was all we needed. Seeing Kyle and Tony so happy reminded me that that was all I ever needed, all any of us needed.

How had I drifted away from those simple joys? I wanted to regain the purity and gratitude that Kyle and Tony seemed to hold so effortlessly, so lightly. I wanted to run with the wide eyes of a novice again, with the passion and freedom of someone from whom nothing is expected.

I wanted to be a dirt bag. I wanted to camp out, to drive where I wanted. I wanted to not worry about Leah, to not worry about making a living as a physical therapist and coach while building a career as an ultrarunner. I had been working since I was a kid. I wished I had taken some time for myself. I wanted to keep running, to live in the moment, to explore my limits — but I wanted to do so with no obligations.

When I returned to Seattle, I spent a lot of time with one of my few single friends, Walter. I needed an escape. Even running long distances wasn't bringing me the peace it had before. So Walter and I spent some time at the bars, playing pool, drinking a little more beer than I usually did, flirting with women. I needed to figure things out.

I volunteered at a race on Orcas Island. On the course, I noticed a hollowed-out tree, and I thought how wonderful it would feel to sit down inside and stay there forever. I felt hollowed out myself.

Running allowed me to define myself as an athlete. It had honed my discipline and strength and sped my path toward healthier, more joyous eating. Pursuing goals with single-mindedness had ultimately bestowed on me the greatest gift of all: the capacity to forget myself, to be absolutely present in the moment, and to appreciate the perfection of every moment. But now even the thought of running did nothing.

Walter suggested I see a shrink. The shrink suggested six months of psychotherapy. I told her to forget it.

Most of the people who knew me knew how I was feeling. Probably all of them knew. The one to speak it was Dave Terry, who had become not just my competitor but a good friend. Dave was more reflective than a lot of jocks I knew, a deep thinker. He worked as a musculoskeletal radiologist but always had time to talk. He could talk about anything, and he did so with a dry wit. His life seemed as balanced as anyone's I knew. He rode his bike or ran 10 miles to work each way, loved a good meal and good company. He loved women, too, and there often seemed to be one around.

We sat at his kitchen table, each of us with a beer.

"Scott," he said, "sometimes we have to go to dark places. Things will be better off and you'll grow. You just don't know it now."

I kept running, a 50K here, a 50-miler there. I set personal bests at many early-season races, including the Way Too Cool 50K and, the very next weekend, the Chuckanut 50K. Then I went to Europe to attempt the race around the circumference of Mont Blanc but dropped out with a knee injury. I stayed in Europe, road tripped, ran, biked, and partied in the Dolomites of Italy, all with Dusty. Then I traveled to Greece and won my third Spartathlon (my fastest time ever). I was feted as a hero in Athens, Sparta, and all over Greece.

When I finally returned to the States after two months in Europe, I couldn't sit still. I went to Vegas for my thirty-fifth birthday with Hal, Ian, and Jenn Shelton, with whom I became friends after the Copper Canyon, to run a 50K. We partied hard and I finished third. But if the dark place had grown brighter, I barely noticed. Running had always provided answers, solutions. Might it still?

In November I went to Texas to run a type of race I had never tried before. In the vast majority of ultras, distance and terrain provide fixed variables, and time reflects an individual's success (or ignominious failure). In some ultras, though, the measures are reversed. In those races, time is the fixed variable. Runners run around — and around and around — a course often smaller than a mile for 24 hours. Whoever runs farthest wins.

Even the toughest and swiftest ultrarunner finds that the 24-hour contest's monotony provides mental and emotional challenges that can be insurmountable.

In terms of physical demands, muscular stress, and caloric expenditures, a 24-hour race is much like any other ultramarathon. Except there are no mountain passes and wildflowers to imbue the event with beauty, no horizon or distant peak by which to measure your progress, no one ahead or behind you to race against, no lonely dawns or solitary twilights in which you can wrap your thoughts. Most noticeably there is no finish line, just a moment in time to mark the end.

Not all that long ago, weekend joggers would wonder aloud why anyone in the world would ever run a marathon. Many marathoners still raise their eyebrows at the notion of running farther than 26.2 miles. And even among ultramarathoners, there are those who don't see the point of the 24-hour event. I never saw the point myself until I read *Ultramarathon* by James Shapiro in 1999.

Though extreme long-distance running contests have surely been staged longer than anyone has been writing about them, records of 24-hour races extend as far back as 1806, when two English athletes named Abraham Wood and Robert Barclay Allardice faced off on the Newmarket to London Turnpike for a wager of 600 guineas. Enormous crowds, wet weather, and allegations of cheating marred the event, but a new sport was born in the modern era.

The concept of the 24-hour race stretches back much farther, to a time when humans measured their endurance against the cycle of the sun. The ancient Greek historians wrote of day runners who could cover long stretches between one dawn and the next. According to Peter Nabokov's *Indian Running,* Native American ceremonial running was also measured against the sun, "the runners through their exertion strengthening its movement across the sky."

In the 1870s, the 24-hour event branched off into the six-day race, in which competitors would travel as far as they could on foot in that time. The six-day footrace stopped drawing fans, and for the most part stopped altogether, in the 1890s. It's experienced something of a rebirth the last thirty years.

The 24-hour race, though, never went away. In 1953, the great Arthur Newton, the father of Long Slow Distance training, persuaded the British amateur Road Runners Club to stage a 24-hour event. For almost the next thirty years, 24-hour events were staged in Italy, South Africa, New Zealand, and even the United States. The first truly international competition was held at Lausanne, Switzerland, in 1981.

That's when the Frenchman Jean-Gilles Boussiquet ran 272.624 kilometers, or 169.3 miles.

In 1984, Yiannis Kouros of Greece ran 177 miles at a 24-hour event in Queens, New York, in spite of taking nearly 28 minutes to stroll through his last mile. He was just getting started. The next year at the same race, despite Hurricane Gloria's 60-mph winds and driving rain, Kouros made it 178 miles. This time he didn't walk the last mile.

In 1996, Kouros ran a little over 182 miles (around a track), and in 1997 he ran 188 miles, 1,308 yards. His mark was 17 miles farther than anyone else had ever run in 24 hours. It was the equivalent of seven marathons plus 5 more miles. His average pace for those marathons? Some 3 hours and 19 minutes. Upon finishing, he confidently stated, "This record will stand for centuries." I wasn't aiming to break his record. I thought he was right. But I was trying to get as close as I could.

I chose the Ultracentric Experience, held in the Dallas–Fort Worth area. I thought it would be a good test and that I could set a national record. But I also thought the course would be flat, as the race director had promised. It wasn't. I was tired, and I was impressed at the monumental *sameness* of the event, but that's not why I dropped out after 8 hours and 50 miles. I stopped because I knew I had no chance for a record and because running a flat course for 24 hours is difficult enough. A 24-hour race on a 1-mile loop with not one hill but two wasn't just a challenge, it was insane.

I flew to Minnesota to see my mom. From my sister's house, I called a friend in Southern California. Her name was Jenny, and I had known her for eight years, during the time she worked at Montrail, a company that had sponsored me. Jenny and I ran in the same circle of friends and attended the same runner parties. She had long black hair and a big, almost blinding smile. Not afraid to speak her mind, she told me I needed to log some miles in the dating scene, so she set me up with some of her girlfriends. But she and I stayed good friends.

I wasn't ready to settle back into Seattle. I wanted another trip. Jenny had recently moved to Ventura for a design job at Patagonia. She invited me down to visit, and the idea of sunshine and beaches sounded better than November rain in Seattle. I had told my friend Luis Escobar that I would volunteer at his 50K race in Santa Barbara. Now I was thinking of moving there, so I wanted to check it out. I told Jenny I would come to California straight from Minnesota. When she asked if I wasn't burnt out from traveling, whether I wouldn't prefer to stop at home in Seattle first, I told her, "The road feels more like home to me right now."

I stayed at Jenny's. We went for runs along the beach and talked about relationships and life. We picked oranges and pomegranates and cooked together, and I spent a lot of time by myself at the beach while she went to work. I felt peaceful. I felt happy. I flew back to Seattle feeling content.

If I had known the turn things were about to take, maybe I would have tried to hold on to those feelings.

At the beginning of 2009, I developed plantar fasciitis, a painful swelling of the connective tissue that runs across the bottom of the foot. I worked on rehabbing like crazy and adjusted my training, running barefoot on the sand and grass, icing and strengthening. Some days I felt great, other days the irritation in the foot caused me to cut training runs short.

Then Leah called and told me she hired a lawyer. She wanted my coaching business, physical therapy practice, and my professional running career appraised, and she wanted her share of my businesses.

I imagined a life of training, working, and racing, and then writing checks with all the money I had earned and having only enough to pay my room and board — if that. Back to square one in debt. I had just gotten out of debt a few years earlier. I was angry — and frightened of bankruptcy. I contemplated "going guerrilla." I would retire from competitive running, go off the grid, and work on an organic farm for room and board. My plan would give me more time to visit my mother, too.

Before I went underground, I made another trip to Ashland to visit Ian and Hal. We ran and hung out together, and after a 15-mile loop at a place called Applegate Reservoir, just outside Medford, we sat together over beers at a burrito shop.

It hit me that night — as I was contemplating a life alone on a country farm — how important friendship was to me. It also struck me how ironic it was that my most important friendships had come from a sport singular in its isolation and demands on self-reliance. Ultramarathons aren't won by teams, yet the bonds I have forged through this sport of obsessive individualism are stronger than any others in my life.

Ian and Hal were as seasoned and wise as any in the sport. Like me, they were part of the twenty-something ultrarunners from the mid-nineties. We, known as the new "Old Guard" by our younger rivals, knew the purity of the sport, but we knew something that the newbies didn't: how easy it is to lose sight of what really matters. How simple and easy and wrong it is to get caught up in all the hype of winning and reputations. I'm sure we had veterans say the same about us.

Like veterans of any sport, of any age, we drank beer that evening and pondered what the kids coming up didn't know. We talked about the days before the Internet, and Twitter, and cell phones — when to get a reputation or something as precious as a sponsorship you actually had to *do* something, like win a Western States — or more like several (Hal had won it twice). We talked about how anyone could post a blog now saying that so-and-so was washed up (there had been many written about me) or that such-and-such was the guy to watch (even though he hadn't done much more than run a small town ultramarathon or fairly fast marathon). We drank more beer and toasted a time when earning a sponsorship meant a free pair of running shoes and maybe some shorts, and — if you were really amazing and amazingly lucky help with travel expenses. We talked about how the surfers chasing waves and the dirtbag climbers in Yosemite had it right, that even though big money was coming to those sports, the real athletes did it for the love of the sport itself and the love of each other — encouraging one another to explore their limits.

I mentioned something about how it was easy to criticize someone anonymously on the Internet, and Ian — who had heard criticisms personally when he paced me at the Western States in 1999 — said, "You should go back there and win it again, just to shut them up."

Yeah, I said, not a bad idea, but not for me. I told the guys my plan for retiring and going off the grid so I wouldn't have to buy back businesses and my name and racing career.

Ian snorted.

"Hey, dude, just go out there and run hard and pay it off. Settle it."

Shortly after that night my sponsor, Brooks Sports, asked me to run the Western States 100. Whether it was to shut people up or to please Brooks, I'm not sure, but I agreed.

I don't know if it was my flaring plantar fasciitis or lack of training or the virus and fever I fought a few weeks before the race. I don't know if I was physically fine but emotionally and mentally still a wreck. I was in the top five at 40 miles, when I ran down Deadwood Canyon to where the famed swinging bridge crosses a branch of the American River. The trail squirreled 2 miles and 1,500 feet up from there, to the Devil's Thumb aid station. Three aid stations farther on was the town of Foresthill and Dusty. If I made it that far, I could finish. I *would* finish. I was still in the top ten. At Foresthill, Dusty would scream and curse, whisper and cajole. *One piece at a time! Who do you want to be?*

Instead of grunting up the climb, I jumped into the cool water of the American River and went for a swim. Not in a million years could I have imagined myself stopping in the middle of the Western States 100 (or any race, for that matter) to go for a swim. The waters were rejuvenating, and all my worries melted away. I floated on my back, staring at the brilliant blue sky. Dusty wouldn't get to work his dark magic this day. My race was over.

Later, after wandering around the course, urging on runners, thanking volunteers I never had the chance to talk to, trying to enjoy the race as a spectator for once, I returned to the river at the Rucky Chucky river crossing. Dave Terry, who had come to volunteer, was there, too. We sat on the bank, two veterans, and shot the shit. I told him I had quit the race. He said it was no big deal, I had nothing to prove, that sometimes finishing and winning weren't the answer. He said we all went through difficult times, that during the tough times we learned the most, and those lessons made us stronger. He said I'd be okay. Dave was always a top runner, but never *the* top. Maybe that explained his kindness.

Things did work out. Or at least they seemed to. Jenny and I fell in love and managed a long-distance relationship. We'd stay at my apartment in Seattle or hers in Ventura, California. We fastpacked into remote hot springs, went climbing in Joshua Tree, caught live music in L.A. We'd hit the Pacific Crest Trail in early spring, and even though we would spend 4 hours there, a lot of it was taking pictures, smelling flowers (literally), lying in the grass, and looking at the sky, reveling in its beauty. Jenny was turning from vegetarian (since high school) to vegan, and I was cooking Thai pumpkin curry, tofu avocado rolls, and eight-grain strawberry pancakes. Jenny was impressed because she'd never seen anyone mill their own flour before. When we were in Ventura, we'd hang out at the farmer's market, forage the neighborhood for figs, guava, and avocados. We'd run on the beach and squeeze fresh orange juice from her neighbor's tree. It all helped take my mind off the fact that I hadn't won a major race that year.

I decided I would redeem myself in the 105-mile Ultra-Trail du Mont-Blanc (UTMB), in France.

The course circumnavigates Mont Blanc, covering 105 miles in three countries, with more than 30,000 feet of both ascent and descent. It draws more than two thousand participants each year. The equivalent of the Tour de France in the world of trail 100-mile racing, it had defeated me twice already. Or I had defeated myself. In 2007, I dropped out halfway into the race, painfully aware that the ankle I had injured before the Hardrock less than six weeks earlier hadn't healed. The next year, because I had seen only 50 miles of the course, I arrived a few weeks before the race and ran the entire course with Italian friends over three days. Then I figured I should learn it from the French, too. So within 12 hours of finishing the three day tour, I set off to run it in four days with Team Lafuma, including Julien Chorier, Karine Herry, and Antoine Guillon. It was the most mileage and vertical change (200 miles, 60,000 feet of vertical change) I had ever run in seven days. It was too much. On the last day, I developed patello-femoral pain (aka "runner's knee"), which sidelined me for the next ten days. I did everything to rehab it, but on race day, after spending a lot of time in second and third place, the knee hurt so much that I couldn't run downhill. I dropped out at mile 75.

In 2009, I was in good shape and in a good frame of mind. Jenny was running, too, and Dusty was crewing for me (the race doesn't allow pacers). What I hadn't counted on was the rain and, worse, the fog. I ran well early and was in the top ten until I got lost. I found my way back and moved into the top three. And that's when nausea and cramps hit. The last 20 miles I could hardly keep anything down. This time, though, I was determined to finish. And I did, in a little over 26 hours. Eighteenth place.

When the announcer handed me the microphone after I crossed the finish line, the first thing I said was: "I am proud to be in the

UTMB finisher family." Dusty said, "I'm proud of you, Jurker!" The next day Dusty crewed, and we both cheered for Jenny as she finished in her first try.

I finished the race I had vowed to finish. Jenny and I were having fun together. Things were working out. Then, on September 25, Scott McCoubrey called to tell me Dave Terry had killed himself. He had recently gone through foot surgery and was not able to get back to running. None of us knew it, but he battled depression much of his life. He was fifty years old.

After attending Dave's funeral and burial earlier in the afternoon, a group of his friends — mostly runners — gathered at Scott's cabin at Crystal Mountain, near the White River 50-miler race course in Washington. Dave had run in the race more than ten times. We cried and asked one another if Dave had ever let on how sad he was. We laughed, too, and talked about how kind he was, how he brought a richness to all of our lives.

Dusty was there. He gave me shit, as usual (even at a memorial service), but this time it had an edge to it. He kept saying things like "You want to try a real race, try beating my marathon time" and "Don't forget who has the faster 100K time." It was during this period that he made sure I knew how many homes he owned (two) and mocked me for how much money I lost in my divorce. And after the gathering he stopped calling me. When he texted, he would write, "You fucking loser."

I knew that another friend of Dusty's killed himself just a few months earlier. I figured that it was grief talking, so I tried to joke it away.

A month later, I decided to get back on the path in Cleveland. A 24-hour race was being held there. It took place on a concrete loop 1 mile around. I called Dusty to ask him to come with Jenny and me, but he didn't answer, so I left messages. He didn't return my calls, so Jenny called him.

He declined the invitation. "I'm tired of being Jurker's bitch," he said.

Though Dusty had always been the better, and much better

known, athlete in high school, he didn't make a life as a professional athlete. When Jenny told me what he said, I began to rewind the last year or so. *Born to Run* had been published and become a phenomenon—and phenomenally successful. I had been featured in more magazine articles. Meanwhile, Dusty and I hadn't talked as much as usual. Had he been pulling away, chafing at my increased notoriety, me, "the Jurker," the less innately talented of boyhood friends? One of the things I appreciated about running was how it strengthened and deepened friendships. Could it have cost me my most important, closest friend?

I did the only thing I could—I gave him space. I didn't call or write, didn't ask him to help me at races. I didn't visit. And I missed him.

I arrived in Cleveland on a cold, wet October weekend, and I dropped out of the race at 65 miles. My legs were still tired from UTMB. My heart and soul were weary from just about everything else.

Five months later, at the nursing home, I called Jenny, and she flew to Minnesota.

"Mom," I said, "this is Jenny, the girl I've talked about so much." My mother didn't say anything—she couldn't—but I knew she understood. Jenny and I spent my mother's last three days with her. While I took care of my mom, Jenny was taking care of me, making sure I got food, sleep, and fresh air from time to time. We played my mother's favorite Celine Dion CDs and sang along.

I slept in the chair by my mom, and Jenny slept in a makeshift apartment in the nursing home basement.

The first night, I saw how frightened my mother was. She had always told people not to worry. "I'm tough," she always said to anyone who asked if she was feeling all right. "I'm tough." But before she slipped into unconsciousness, it was as if she was reminding herself that she could do this one last thing, that she could move through this, that she could do the thing we all fear.

She died on March 22. Those last hours I didn't stop stroking her hair or telling her, "Don't worry, I'm here." I told her that I was a good cook because of her. I told her I ate fresh fruit and vegetables because of her. I told her I ran because of her. I told her I could still picture the little garden on our dead-end road. I could feel the rough wooden spoon, my hands clutching it, hers covering mine. I told her I remembered that, how warm her hands felt. I told her I loved her and that she would always be with me.

I didn't tell her I was lost.

Carob Chia Pudding

I started making this pudding during my first years at the Western States. I knew I would be camping in the mountains and I wanted to have a ready-made protein source after evening training runs and something sweet to complement my dinner. The sweet, chocolate-like flavor comes from the raw carob (if you think you hate carob, you have probably been eating only the roasted variety). After spending time in the Copper Canyon, I added chia seeds to the recipe, which gave it a tapioca-like texture. When people taste this pudding, they can't believe it contains tofu.

16 ounces silken tofu, drained
 3 tablespoons maple syrup
 3 tablespoons raw carob powder or cocoa powder
 1 teaspoon miso
 1 teaspoon vanilla extract
 2 tablespoons chia seeds
    Mint sprigs, for garnish

Place the tofu, maple syrup, carob, miso, and vanilla in a blender and blend for 1 to 2 minutes, until smooth. Transfer to a serving bowl and stir in the chia seeds. Refrigerate for 10 to 20 minutes, then serve in small cups or bowls, garnished with the mint.   MAKES 4-6 SERVINGS

20

Secrets of the Dark Wizard

YOSEMITE VALLEY, 2010

Empty your mind, be formless. Shapeless, like water.
— BRUCE LEE

TREES AND CLIFFS swayed in front of me, and I knew that one misstep would send me plunging to earth. My arms were out, my right foot a foot in front of my left, and I was trying to balance on an inch-wide piece of climbing webbing, tied to a Ponderosa pine in front of me and, 30 feet behind me, an old gnarled oak.

For most of my life, a misstep preceded a stumble. Here, it would lead to a fall. Here, balance didn't mean improved performance. It meant success or failure.

"One step at a time. One step."

The ground swayed.

My teacher regularly walked over chasms thousands of feet deep. He scaled terminal granite rock faces with no safety equipment. He pioneered the sport of freeBASE climbing (free solo climbing with a parachute as the only means of protection) and at the moment was trying to figure out a way to dive off a cliff, soar through the air, and land without a parachute. He said it was merely a matter of physics. Because he practiced "dark" arts, they called him the Dark Wizard.

His real name was Dean Potter. Jenny introduced us in January

2010, and he invited us to the small cabin he rented in Yosemite Valley. He called it "the shack."

I had heard — and read — about Dean, how he sought to alter his consciousness through feats of extreme athleticism and challenge. He had read *Born to Run* and saw me as a kindred spirit.

Yosemite was Jenny's favorite place on earth. I loved the outdoors. It seemed like a perfect place to go after my mother died. Dean's shack was clean and neat. His refrigerator was stocked with chia seeds, young coconuts, and spirulina powder. On his wall hung an old advertisement, yellowed with age, for Eagle Electric. In small print, it read: PERFECTION IS NOT AN ACCIDENT.

I wanted to spend time in the valley grieving, healing from my mother's passing. I also wanted to understand why I ran and to decide whether I wanted to continue. To help me understand and to help me decide, I would walk on webbing between trees. Slacklining is a discipline that requires extreme focus, yet your body has to remain fluid and relaxed. You must calm the instinctual fear that has allowed humans to survive. It teaches you to let go of your fears and forces you to trust the power of your mind — to trust a power somewhere else. Dean had started me 4 feet off the ground. Learning took time. When I stepped on the line, it would shake uncontrollably from side to side, making it impossible to balance. It was a challenge in itself to stand up on the line, let alone take a step. Progress was slow; time after time the line bucked me off until I realized that I was causing the line to shake and learned to calm it with my body and mind in sync.

I considered quitting before. I talked about it once to a nonrunner I had met a few years earlier. We were at an aid station on a ridge line 3,000 feet above Ojai, California, welcoming runners, offering them bananas, filling their water bottles, and telling them they were doing great. It was November 2008, the Rose Valley 33-Miler, and I didn't realize it, but I must have been telling the guy about my doubts.

The guy had fixed me with an odd glare.

"Dude," he said, "you had better take advantage of what you've accomplished. You're not going to be Scott Jurek forever."

There are ultrarunners who don't question why they do what they do, but I'm not one of them. Why did I run? Is ultramarathoning crazy? Is it hopelessly selfish? Can I have solitude and also love? Is there any value in winning? Competition drives me, but I know that losing myself is the real key to fulfillment. How can I win without ego?

Was I too focused on winning? Had I lost the capacity for being in the moment that had — paradoxically — brought me my greatest recognition? Or were my doubts and loss of motivation merely chemical?

Countless studies have pinpointed the source of "runner's high" as being elevated levels of endorphins and endocannabinoids, naturally occurring substances that affect the brain, produced in large amounts by exercise. This might explain the apparently large number of recovering addicts in the ultrarunning community.

I met a runner named Bill Kee when I was in Southern California in 2001, training for the Angeles Crest 100. He had long gray hair and a gray handlebar mustache. He wore cutoff shorts with flames painted on both sides. Running from one pocket to a belt loop was a heavy metal chain, holding his wallet. This was the uniform he ran in. He carried two 48-ounce Gatorade bottles and when he finished a race, he put them aside and put on his leather jacket, with its Team Death insignia, got into his big black Chevy van, and drove toward the horizon.

Kee told me that he started drinking and doing drugs when he was eighteen, and he didn't stop till fourteen years later, when he decided that life as a drunk and an addict   with its jail time, three packs of unfiltered cigarettes a day, and other wonders — wasn't working. He was living in Ojai, California, right next to the foothills of the Topatopa Mountains, and every night, jonesing for a cigarette, he'd hike into those hills. One cold night, he parked his car at the bottom of his driveway and decided to run the quarter mile to his house. Then, on a dare, he ran up a 3-mile hill, 1,700 feet of ascent. Marathons followed. He didn't know what he was doing, bonked often, learned fast.

He didn't even know what an ultramarathon was until he read about it in a magazine.

He ran his first one in 1999. He's fifty-four now. He lost a kidney in a motorcycle accident in 1980. He's been suffering from Lyme disease since 2005. But he's been sober and smoke-free since he started running. "Scott," Kee told me in 2001, "running is my new drug."

Kee has plenty of company. The mohawked, tattooed, reptile-toting Ben Hian didn't become an ultrarunning legend until he kicked his addiction to mood-altering drugs and trained his obsessive focus on running long distances. And many of the runners I have encountered in my career have talked about their struggles with marijuana, as well as eating disorders, and a general difficulty finding peace anywhere but on the trail.

Can running become its own addiction? One gruesome study showed that rats love running so much, they can actually run themselves to death. When offered food for only one 90-minute period per day, the rats in the control group (without an exercise wheel) soon learned to adapt, taking in all the calories they needed during that meal. Rats with running wheels, however, ran more and more every day while eating less and less. They eventually starved to death.

Some of ultrarunning's greatest champions seem to have burned out or just given up at a certain point. Cautionary tales abound in the ultra community, passed from runner to runner at prerace breakfasts and postrace award ceremonies like the story of Icarus and his doomed wax wings was whispered among ambitious, worried Greeks.

My hero Chuck Jones ran his last ultra in 1988, when, after watching a UFO hover over Death Valley during the Badwater Ultramarathon (he suspects it was a hallucination brought on by dehydration), he passed out.

"Now I'm a sunset runner," he says. "I work all day in the sun [laying asphalt] and then I just want to run, relax, and recover, to see what the body can do."

The great Ann Trason, who won fourteen Western States and almost beat the Tarahumara in a widely publicized Leadville 100 in 1994 (the Indians called her *Bruja,* or "the witch"), has suffered numerous injuries, and though she hasn't stopped running, she hasn't entered an ultra for several years. She lamented to a reporter, "I just wish I could go out and run every day. I think I took it for granted. I knew I'd slow down and get older, but I didn't know there'd be a cliff."

The summer after he showed me around the San Juan Mountains, in 2007, Kyle Skaggs returned to Silverton to run the Hardrock 100. He set a new clockwise and overall course record by almost 3 hours. He also set speed records for the Wasatch Front 100, circumnavigating Mount Rainier on the Wonderland Trail, and running the Grand Canyon rim-to-rim.

Then, at the age of twenty-four, he quit. He now grows organic vegetables on his farm in New Mexico. He hasn't run a competitive step since 2008.

Had I reached my cliff?

I had always been careful to rest when I needed to, especially when hurt, conscientious about treating my body right. But was burnout — or apparently happy abstinence — the inevitable price of intensely focused training like mine? Could I succeed *without* my focus? Had I been lying to myself by thinking I was living a life of balance?

Jenny thought we should take a break to process the recent events in a peaceful place. A week after my mother died, we drove the 6 hours to Yosemite.

We spent three days with Dean.

I saw that he was a balance of yin and yang: There's exquisite sensitivity and softness in his movements when he's walking a line or free soloing a granite wall. He seems to work with rock and sky, as though he's able to sense — and surrender to — currents of air that are invisible to the rest of us. At the same time, he climbs with ferocity and maintains a crushing training routine. You need that kind of ego strength to overcome fear.

Dean was married for eight years before divorcing in 2010. It was one of the things we bonded over. Another thing we had in common was our age. Like me, Dean was nearing the peak of his physical ability. At thirty-eight, he was starting to talk wistfully about the rising generation of whippersnappers with intact joints and the fearlessness of innocence—he called these climbers "monkey children"—who made everything seem so easy. I liked the way he was handling his transition. He lived in a simple cabin in Yosemite with his little dog, Whisper. His life was minimal, lit up by solitude and nature.

We talked about nutrition, and about the deaths of my mother and his father years earlier. He said he was so focused when he was on 20-hour link-up climbs of big walls that he went into a trance and was convinced he heard radio frequencies. We talked about God, the limits of technology, how in order to win, one had to realize that winning didn't matter.

I didn't think I could make it to the tree in front of me. I anticipated a fall.

"One step at a time," Dean said, as I faltered and swayed. "Stay present."

CONNECTING WITH OTHERS

If you're an ultrarunner and you spend hours and hours alone on a daily basis, training in remote, unpopulated areas, running can be a solitary undertaking. It's ironic, then, that some of the greatest and deepest joys in my running career have come from the people I have met and the things we have shared. You don't have to be an ultrarunner to take advantage of the social rewards of running. Try running—at least on some of your routes—with a friend. Join a running club or weekly group run. Enter a 5K or 10K race. Do something for running that doesn't involve running. Working at the finish line or at an aid station or joining trail work parties—all of which I've done—provided great ways for me to participate, to give back to the sport that's given me so much. Running can be a lonely activity. It can also introduce you to people worlds beyond your imagining. ▅▃

Smoky Chipotle Refried Beans

The Tarahumara eat these beans smeared on corn tortillas. They ate them on our burly 30-mile hike over and down into the Copper Canyon, and they ate them before, during, and after our race, too. At home I eat them with fresh tortillas as a snack or with a plate of chile rice, guacamole, and some salsa on the side for a hearty meal. If you have leftover beans, freeze them for future lunches and dinners.

> 3 cups dried pinto beans
> 1 medium white or yellow onion, chopped
> 2-3 garlic cloves, chopped
> 1 ½-inch piece dried Kombu seaweed (optional)
> 1-2 dried whole chipotle peppers or canned chipotles in adobo to taste
> 1 tablespoon chili powder
> 2 teaspoons dried epazote (see Note)
> 1 tablespoon olive oil
> 1½ teaspoons sea salt

Soak the beans in water to cover by 2 inches, 8 hours or overnight. Drain and rinse the beans in a colander a few times, then transfer to a large pot. Add the onion, garlic, seaweed, chipotles, and spices. Add water to cover the beans by 2 inches. Bring to a boil and simmer over medium-low heat for about 1 hour, or until the beans are soft and cooked through.

Drain the beans, reserving 4 cups of the liquid. Remove the seaweed. Remove the chiles, or leave one in if spicier beans are desired. Cool the beans for 15 minutes, then place in a food processor along with ½ cup of the liquid and process until smooth. If desired, you may thin the beans with additional cooking liquid.

Return the pureed beans to the pot with the olive oil and salt. Simmer over low to medium-low heat for 20 minutes to allow the flavors to blend. Serve warm.

Refried beans keep refrigerated for 5 to 6 days or freeze well for several months. For a quick meal or snack, spread cold beans on a corn tortilla and toast in a toaster oven for 1 to 2 minutes and top with "cheese" spread (see recipe, page 102), guacamole (see recipe, page 152), salsa, and/or hot sauce.   MAKES 7 CUPS, 8-10 SERVINGS

Note: Epazote is an herb that can make beans more digestible, as well as adding a distictive flavor. Look for it in Mexican grocery stores or near the Mexican foods at the supermarket. If you can't find it, you can substitute 3 tablespoons chopped fresh cilantro, stirred in just before serving.

21

Back to My Roots

TONTO TRAIL, GRAND CANYON, 2010

> Let the beauty we love be what we do.
>
> — RUMI

HERE WAS ANOTHER good place to stop, cold, dark, silent as a deserted cathedral. A velvety snowfall. In my running career, there had been so many of these places. This time, I would submit. Almost twenty years of serious running, more than a decade since my first Western States, a lifetime of *sometimes you just do things* and I had done them, and what had it accomplished? It hadn't prevented my marriage from failing. It hadn't warded off injuries. I had done things when I didn't think I could do them anymore. Dusty was angry. Dave Terry had killed himself, and my mother was gone. I could do things every day the rest of my life, every minute. What would it matter?

On this day, my food was almost gone. My headlamp had dimmed and was losing battery life fast. I was at least 50 miles from a phone or a road. It was 2 A.M., cold, and part of me knew that it might be dangerous to stop. Part of me didn't care.

I had been running for 20 hours. Below, a yawning chasm. Above, a black dome, smeared with stars. And there, on my right, a flat rock outcropping with a shallow cave. A perfect place to lie down, to hide from the darkness and the cold. I would lie there and wait, and rest, and in a few hours the dome would pale, and tumbleweeds would stir, and the cacti would emerge from the gloom like gentle, friendly sentries, and I would be rested and warm, and then I could run, *then* I could do things.

"Not a good idea, man. It's too cold. Once you lie down, it's going to be really hard to get up. If we stop now, we might be stopped forever."

How many times had someone urged me on? How many times did someone tell me to get up, to get moving, that even if I didn't think I could go on, he or she knew better.

"Let's go. Just a few more hours of running before the sun comes up."

Another friend, with more sensible, optimistic advice. But I was so tired. My backup light, a single, dim, LED bulb (basically a keychain light), was putting me to sleep. I would feel better after lying down. The hard sandstone would feel soft to my fatigued and sore muscles. It was such a perfect spot. I wanted to stop.

The plan had been to run free to honor my mother's passing, to recapture the feeling I had on the game trails with Dusty before I started running for belt buckles and corporate sponsors. Dusty and I were barely talking, though. So I asked my twenty-eight-year-old buddy Joe if he might want to accompany me on a 90-mile traverse of the Grand Canyon on the Tonto Trail, unsupported. No other human being in modern times had run the trail in one push, carrying his own food and water. For over a decade, I've been inspired by John Annerino's *Running Wild* and Colin Fletcher's *The Man Who Walked Through Time*. I had met Joe the year before, and he was fast and hungry for adventure. Best of all, I had a feeling he would know what I was trying to capture. He had traveled to Copper Canyon to race the Tarahumara two years earlier (he had won).

We each carried seven energy bars and thirty Clif Shot gels, as well as headlights with emergency backups. A lightweight, water-resistant shell would be our only shelter. I packed two bean burritos, some cookies, an almond butter sandwich, and a map. For water, we would drink from streams that were flowing due to the South Rim's melting snow. We had to make sure we avoided the creeks that were contaminated with uranium from turn-of-the-century mines, now dormant.

It was first light, 20 degrees. Although the Grand Canyon is known for its scorching temperatures, it was bitter cold. Our first step was straight down, and in the first 4 miles we plunged 3,000 feet, crossing cliff bands, running alongside a narrow trail lined first with ponderosa pine, then oak and sagebrush, and finally cacti. We followed drainage chutes between the rocks that marked geologic time in millions of years. By the time we made it to the Tonto Trail, which follows the broad plateau that parallels the canyon and stands watch 3,000 feet above the mighty Colorado River, our shins were shredded and raw.

It had been a while since I was so cut off from civilization, so far away from telephones and e-mail and race forms and travel arrangements. There was just us — and the empty sky and the rocky ground and the cactus. The temperature rose swiftly to a warm 85 degrees, reminding us that this place was home to desert creatures. Sometimes I took the lead, other times Joe did. We were never more than a quarter mile apart. Progress was slower than we had expected, as we learned from the hikers (the only people we saw that day) who informed us we were four drainages behind our estimated location. We weren't discouraged. We had plenty of water and food, and the abundant beauty made every mile drift by without anticipation.

By late afternoon, our shadows had disappeared, and bulging, dark clouds had filled the empty sky, bullying one another for position. We heard a low moan, which turned into a shriek. Dust and sand flew from the plateau on 50-mph winds, and then the rain started. Drops splattered sideways against the rock. At 45 miles, after running for 16 hours, lightning crashed ahead of us and behind us. There was nowhere to hide on the barren plateau, so the only option was to run. Finally, we climbed down a pebbly drainage to a campground called Indian Gardens, at the intersection of the almost highway-like

Bright Angel Trail and the Tonto Trail. We filled our water bottles in a downpour, the winds still shrieking. Thunder boomed and echoed in the canyon. A skinny bank of dirt snaked down to the valley floor, and in the distance faint lights twinkled from Phantom Ranch, along the banks of the Colorado. Above us, the Bright Angel Trail wound its way 3,500 feet up to the South Rim and the Grand Canyon Lodge at almost 7,000 feet above sea level.

There was a little unmanned ranger station next to us. It was the one spot on the trail where we could abandon the journey. Joe thought we should. He had some races coming up in the spring. I wasn't done with competition. Joe was also running low on food, and we were only halfway. Just then he dropped half of an energy bar to the ground. From his comfortable seat on a bench, he slowly bent over to pick up the sand-covered chunk. He didn't even bother to brush off the precious calories. Completely out of it, he tossed the bar to the bushes while letting out a helpless sigh. Wouldn't it be better to bail now than to risk it? Even if this storm passed, what if another came along? We both knew that too much water from above could wash us off the plateau into the canyon below or leave us hypothermic in the dark chill of the night.

I make a point to plan, to reduce risk. I measure danger against desire. I told Joe that I thought we had run through the worst. I told him we had both gutted our way through worse difficulties. I said the weather report had said the storm cell was expected to move through. Then I pointed to a circle of stars (the only one I could find) directly above us.

We ran for 3 more hours. The rain stopped, the clouds vanished. We didn't talk. My headlight went out around mile 70, and my reserve light failed an hour later. We had spent the last hour and a half in a dry creekbed searching for the now scarcely defined Tonto Trail. I had eaten both of the burritos, countless gels, and several Clif Bars, but I was hungry. And cold. Mostly, I was tired.

When I saw the rocky overhang, I measured desire and danger again and came to a conclusion. This would be a good place to stop. Just for half an hour. Just to get a short nap.

Joe didn't think so. (Obviously, Joe was right.)

"C'mon, we just have a few hours before sunup and 5 hours until we finish," he said.

It turned out to be 12 hours. There were no aid stations. No crowds. No challengers. No race directors. Just the earth and a friend and the sky and movement. The landscape diminished us. Nature's arena has a way of humbling and energizing us. I had never felt so tiny. I had never felt so big.

The sky grew colder and darker, and then I could see my breath. My shadow returned, along with the neighborly cacti, the warming, welcoming sky. Explosions of red, orange, and yellow blasted the canyon walls above us and lit up the great formations across from us. The great chasm opened below. Yesterday melted, and with it all yesterdays. To consider the future seemed as silly as trying to divine meaning from the melting morning dew.

Joe and I would literally claw our way, at times on all fours, almost 5,000 feet out of the canyon on the New Hance Trail. Some 30 hours after we entered, we stumbled into a tourist trap, gorged on guacamole and chips, and washed them down with Negra Modelo beers. Joe excused himself to go to the bathroom, where he promptly fell asleep on the toilet. After I pounded on the door and awakened him, we both pushed the seats back in the rental car and slept for an hour and a half. Afterward, we drove to Ian's place in Flagstaff and told him what he had missed.

But we didn't know that when we ran along the wide plateau, chasing our shadows, alone on a giant ledge 3 miles from the ancient river, 3,500 feet below the humanity-packed rim.

For those hours on the Tonto Trail, we didn't know anything except the land and the sky and our bodies. I was free from everything except what I was doing at that very moment, floating between what was and what would be as surely as I was suspended between river and rim. Finally I remembered what I had found in ultrarunning. I remembered what I had lost.

Salsa Verde

This brilliant green salsa adds a delicious tang to a wide variety of dishes, such as grilled tempeh or tofu and rice. Though I appreciate raw foods and greatly prefer some items (cabbage, carob) uncooked, the vegetables in this dish — delicious on their own — reveal hidden tastes and treasures when roasted. And for the practical-minded, this salsa freezes well. Omit the jalapeño if you prefer a mild salsa.

Coconut oil or canola oil
12 medium tomatillos
3 garlic cloves, unpeeled
1 small white onion, peeled and quartered
1–2 jalapeño peppers (optional)
1 poblano pepper
2 sprigs fresh cilantro
1 teaspoon sea salt

Preheat the oven to 425°F. Oil a baking sheet. Place the tomatillos, garlic, onion, and peppers flat on the baking sheet and cover with foil. Roast for 20 to 30 minutes, until the veggies are lightly browned on the edges. Remove the foil and cool.

Peel the garlic and slice the peppers, removing the stems and seeds, unless more heat is desired. Add the roasted veggies to a blender or food processor along with the cilantro and salt. Process until smooth, about 1 minute. Serve over refried beans (page 213) and brown rice, with beans and corn tortillas, or with tortilla chips. Salsa keeps refrigerated for 5 to 6 days or freezes well for several months.

MAKES 6 CUPS, 10–12 SERVINGS

Epilogue

WORLD 24-HOUR CHAMPIONSHIPS, 2010

> Sometimes the best journeys aren't necessarily from
> east to west, or from ground to summit, but from
> heart to head. Between them we find our voice.
>
> — JEREMY COLLINS

W E ALL LOSE sometimes. We fail to get what we want. Friends and loved ones leave. We make a decision we regret. We try our hardest and come up short. It's not the losing that defines us. It's how we lose. It's what we do afterward.

I decided I would make another attempt at a 24-hour race, and chase a new American record. So I flew to France for the 2010 IAU World 24-Hour Championships.

There were hundreds of other runners, never farther than a few feet away, all circling (in this particular event) a 1.40-km (0.9-mile) course of pavement and hard-packed dirt through the village of Brive-la-Gaillarde. The course was shaped like a snake twisting its way through the park (even doubling back on itself with hairpin corners), and on its longest stretch, it passed a street filled with bars and restaurants. There were two tiny rises that added up to 10 feet of elevation change per lap. Barely noticeable to a spectator, the hills would feel, after a few hours running, like constant, painful pinpricks.

. . .

People — even many ultrarunners — wonder why anyone would run a 24-hour event. The overarching question people ask usually takes the form of one word: Why? The more particular questions in my case, as articulated on Internet message boards and blogs, in magazine articles, and sometimes put to me by friends and acquaintances, were more pointed: Why now? Do you have something to prove? Are you running away from something?

The answers were more complicated. I did want to win again. (But I wasn't all that worried about a single year without a major victory, especially in the context of my career.) I did want to find that place of egolessness and mindlessness that only the monotony of a 24-hour race can produce. But mostly I wanted to run because of my mother. If she, after decades of losing nearly all her muscle control, in the last hours of a grueling last week could proclaim her toughness, then I could do my best to live up to her example. Much of her life, she couldn't walk. I would run for her.

Jenny and I arrived nine days before the race, and spent six of them in a tiny village outside Paris called Boutigny-sur-Essonne, 5 hours and two train rides from the race site. I wanted to re-create at least the spirit of my Western States preparations. I wanted the quiet and the solitude.

We stayed in a garden apartment owned by some friends of ours. It had been a mill hundreds of years ago, built above a small river next to multicolored vegetable gardens and a field of rapeseed yellow as egg yolks. The streets were narrow and cobblestoned, and the night sky was brilliant with stars. Jenny spent many of those days climbing in nearby Fontainebleau, and I loped through the outlying fields — of more rapeseed, of wildflowers, of young wheat and rye. Together, we slacklined in an area of Fontainebleau called "the sea of sand."

Except for the tiny travel blender I had packed — and our computers — it was a quiet, simple existence. We would wake and have smoothies every morning with fresh whole-grain bread from the small bakery in town, then run and climb and take walks together, and catch up on e-mail in the evening before we went to bed and talk about food and music and life and death and meaning and love. We fell asleep to the rushing of the stream and the cool spring breeze wafting through the window.

Most mornings I would run 6 miles through the woods to the nearest village with a natural food store. I prepared simple meals from the local produce and traditional French herbs. I love how the French value good food and the basic necessities of life. The rustic cobblestone village felt like stepping back in time before we overcomplicated our lives.

By the time of the race, on May 13, I had done my best to empty my mind of everything but my goal — to run as hard as I could for 24 hours. I wanted to push my body as far as it could go without going too far. Once again, I was seeking that elusive edge.

The city buses carried signs blaring details of the event. Teams brought acupuncturists, physicians, and athletic trainers. The patrons at the bars and cafés on the long stretch of the course cheered whenever we passed. I was part of the U.S. men's team, made up of seasoned veterans and solid newcomers. We would be competing against the Japanese, South Koreans, Italians, and runners from twenty other countries in Europe, Asia, North and South America, and Australia. The Japanese were the perennial favorites, although this year many of their top runners would be competing in a 48-hour race the following weekend, so a lot of unknown runners were ready to shake things up.

A Spaniard I didn't know jumped out in front and I — along with 228 others — followed. After just a few miles, the Spaniard had dropped back, and the lead was changing hands every lap around the twisted course. With that many runners on that short of a course, misunderstandings are almost inevitable. But this international crowd kept the peace. Since I didn't know anything but English, whenever I passed someone, I would just shout the international Nordic skiing words for passing: "Hup, hup."

I started out too fast (I could tell because the timing chip triggered the clock, and my splits were just over a 6-minute-mile pace), but after a few miles I fell into an easy rhythm of 7-minute miles.

Lee Dong Mun of South Korea lapped me around the marathon mark, along with Shingo Inoue of Japan a few laps later. I let them go. I wasn't racing against them. I was racing with myself and against the ticking clock.

The next 6 hours my life was stripped to its essentials — eating, drinking, and running. I avoided music for the first 8 hours because I wanted to be open to everything around me and because when the monotony became too much, I would need music. The thought of tunes became something to look forward to, the snowcapped mountain that marked the forward progress in my mind.

Researchers speculate that music suppresses pain by, basically, focusing the brain on something else — tunes. In one study, researchers found that listening to music created the same pain-easing results of taking a tablet of extra-strength Tylenol.

An ultrarunner needs a finish line to stay sane, but if it obsesses him, he's doomed. I avoided thinking of the hours ahead. I avoided thinking of Shingo. When memories of my mother coursed through me, I used them to press me on. I wanted to lose myself and by doing so to discover new limits and to go beyond them. I wanted to pry myself open, going beyond the body and beyond the mind.

Shingo stayed two laps in the lead, and even when shadows lengthened and beers and wines replaced the small cups of espresso at the streetside tables, I stayed with my pace. Revelers shouted and cheered all through the night.

The rhythm continued until it wasn't even a rhythm. It was just being. It was everything and nothing. The great Yiannis Kouros — who holds the world record of 180 miles at 24 hours on the road — has spoken and written of looking down on himself as he ran. I didn't leave my body. But I saw my father in the woods and watched him mime God letting dirt slide through his fingers. There was my

mother, laughing, ladling my plate of mashed potatoes with butter. There were blindingly orange carrots, tomatoes redder than fire
trucks. There were mouthfuls of guacamole so rich that I started sali-
vating. I heard Dave Terry opening a bottle of beer, watched him lean
back in his kitchen and tell me that not all pain is significant. There
was Dusty, beckoning me to keep going, keep going. I saw the electric
blue of Silvino and the majestic stride of Arnulfo, and I didn't wonder
how they did it anymore, I *understood* their secret. We can all understand it. We can live as we were meant to live — simply, joyously, of
and on the earth. We can live with all our effort and with pure happiness.

I ran for 8 hours before I listened to music. The piercing clarity had left me by then. Would it return? I put on my iPod then, but
I didn't know what songs were playing. I ate noodle soup as I ran,
and as much as I loved food — as much as eating brought me unmiti-
gated joy — there were times when I couldn't taste it. I had never been
so lonely. On the edge of the course away from the revelers, there
was only the sound of the river massaging the rocks, the wind comb-
ing the leaves of the trees, and the birds about to welcome a new
day.

Nine hours. Ten hours.

Our past makes us, and we can't help but plan for the future. Some
days I feel my mother's warm, strong hands on mine. Some days I envision the time I'll slow down, even stop and rest.

Fourteen hours. Fifteen. Sixteen. Seventeen hours.

The next month, I would deliver speeches, attend conferences,
and accept accolades. In June of 2010, Jenny and I would drive to
New Mexico and pull weeds on Kyle Skaggs's organic farm, then on to
Boulder, Colorado. Shortly thereafter Dusty would show up, and we
would eat together and train together and repair our friendship. In
September I would visit U.S. military troops in Kuwait and run there,
and tell soldiers about running and listen to their stories about war.
But on the snaking French course, the future didn't matter. The past
was gone. There was only the trail, only movement. There was only

now. And now was enough. It was more than enough. It was everything. I ran. I ran and I ran.

Dawn would come. It had to. The race would end. I would finish.
I knew all that. But what should have been self-evident truths felt like
prayers.

Seventeen hours. Would clarity ever return?

Wise Buddhist teachers advise pilgrims to chop wood and carry
water until they encounter blinding, transformational epiphany. After
that moment of electric bliss, the teachers say, chop more wood and
carry more water. Running had brought me peace and clarity, and I
kept running. Then the serenity was gone, and there was only the sad,
sighing wind. I kept running.

I knew my feet were moving, but I couldn't feel them. I thought
of the Taoism I had studied, one of the many teachings that had
nothing—and everything—to do with running. Specifically, I wondered if I was at that moment practicing wu wei, or "doing without
doing."

I kept running. I thought of Jenny, and Dusty, and my family, and
Hippie Dan and Ian and Dean Potter and all the people I had met
through running. I climbed the mountains of Colorado and slogged
through the valleys of California and jogged through the markets of
Japan and the vineyards of Greece, and I saw all the people and places
running had given me. I thought of pain, too. I thought of my recent
yoga sessions, when my teacher, Big Bill, saw me struggling and said,
"This is what you came for!"

Eighteen hours.

"This is what you came for." I repeated it like a mantra. Nineteen
hours. More soup. Another Clif Shot. More bananas and big gulps
of water. "This is what you came for." As I said it, I realized that it
sounded a lot like "Sometimes you just do things."

At the end of 19 hours, I saw Team USA Coach Mike Spindler
yelling times and lap counts for the American record. If I kept up my
pace, I had a shot. Twenty hours. Twenty-one hours.

Twenty-two hours, 23 hours. The announcer called out my mileage. Other runners glanced over their shoulder as I approached and moved aside. A few French runners shouted, "*Allez*, Scott. *Allez*, USA!"

I hit 162 miles with a half hour left, and a Team USA coach handed me an American flag. I held it proudly overhead for the last five laps, the last 30 minutes.

At 10 A.M. on Friday I finished, a mile and a half ahead of Ivan Cudin, who set a new Italian record, and 4 miles behind Shingo Inoue, who set a new Japanese record (by only 300 meters).

I had run 165.7 miles—an American record. No other North American had run farther in 24 hours. I had done what I had set out to do. It was time to rest. Then I would eat. And then, run again.

They are simple activities, common as grass. And they're sacred. Pilgrims seeking bliss carry water and chop wood, and they're simple things, too, but if they're approached with mindfulness and care, with attention to the present and humility, they can provide a portal to transcendence. They can illuminate the path leading to something larger than ourselves.

It's easy to get wrapped up in deadlines and debt, victory and loss. Friends squabble. Loved ones leave. People suffer. A 100-mile race—or a 5K, or a run around the block—won't cure pain. A plate filled with guacamole and dinosaur kale will not deliver anyone from sorrow.

But you can be transformed. Not overnight, but over time. Life is not a race. Neither is an ultramarathon, not really, even though it looks like one. There is no finish line. We strive toward a goal, and whether we achieve it or not is important, but it's not what's most important. What matters is *how* we move toward that goal. What's crucial is the step we're taking now, the step *you're* taking now.

Everyone follows a different path. Eating well and running free helped me find mine. It can help you find yours. You never know where that path might take you.

Xocolatl (SHOCK-o-laht) Energy Balls

A good meal—like a good story—deserves a satisfying ending. After working on this one for years, I think I finally perfected it. The natural caffeine in the raw cacao nibs delivers a jolt, and the subtle blend of chili flakes and cinnamon will gratify the most demanding dessert lover. It's a tasty treat and an energy boost, perfect for after-dinner relaxation or on a long run.

Mesquite powder was first used by native people, including the Shoshone of Death Valley. You can find it in natural food stores in the raw section or online. It can be omitted, but it adds a subtle sweetness and robust finish.

    ½ cup raw cacao nibs
    ½ cup raw cashews
    8 medium dates
    1 teaspoon mesquite powder
    ¼ teaspoon ground cinnamon
    ½ teaspoon raw vanilla powder or extract
    ¼ teaspoon crushed red pepper flakes
    ⅛ teaspoon sea salt
    1½ teaspoons raw coconut oil (warmed to liquid
        consistency)

Combine all the ingredients except the coconut oil in a food processor and process for 3 to 5 minutes until chopped to a fine consistency. Transfer the mixture to a mixing bowl. Add the melted coconut oil and stir until well combined. Form into 1-inch round balls and place on waxed paper. Refrigerate for 15 to 20 minutes, then transfer to an airtight container. The balls will keep for 2 weeks, refrigerated.

MAKES ONE DOZEN 1-INCH BALLS

Acknowledgments

Writing a book is like running an ultramarathon. There are challenging climbs, moments where simply taking a step forward feels like the most difficult task in the world. Other times, progress is effortless, and the ease seems like it will last forever. An ultramarathoner needs a crew to get through the difficult stretches, to help locate the sweet spots, merely to keep moving. I needed one for this book, too. Without a diligent and talented support crew, *Eat and Run* would not have crossed the finish line.

This book would not exist if my good buddy and classmate in the school of hard knocks, Dusty Olson, hadn't convinced me to run my first 50-miler back in 1994. He was the first, and closest, of the small and eclectic group of athletes, free thinkers, and health seekers to inspire me. Although there are too many to mention, I am indebted to them all. They teach me that anything is possible.

Shannon Weil first prodded me to write a book ten years ago. As co-founding race director of the Western States 100, she has a knack for igniting the spark of potential. Then came along Audrey Young, close friend and passionate writer, who didn't let me get away with saying I was too busy to put together a book proposal. I doubt this book would have come to fruition if it wasn't for her generous time and effort.

My agent, Larry Weissman, and his wife, Sascha, saw something more in my story and helped me bring that first proposal to new heights. Susan Canavan and her amazing team at Houghton Mifflin Harcourt have acted as chief support crew, knowing when to lend encouraging advice and when to crack the whip.

Steve Friedman has been my pacer and humble cowriter. A longtime fan of his work, I knew that if I ever did write a book, I would want Steve and his creative keyboard at my side. Besides putting up with my ultra persistence and scattered ideas, Steve helped narrate my life in a way I never would have been able to do, this despite his never running a single step in an ultramarathon. I suspect he now harbors secret ambitions of turning vegan and running a 100-miler. If he does, I'll be there to pace him.

Sarah Deming, his lovely and diligent assistant, tirelessly researched details of ultrarunning and nutrition that I didn't even know existed. Her interviewing skills pulled gems I had long forgotten from friends and mentors. A boxer turned runner (she ran her first half marathon after working on the book), I would never want to pick a fight with her. She is indomitable and relentless. And I hear she packs a punch.

Steve, Sarah, and I owe much to friends, family, and experts who graciously gave their precious time in countless interviews. Because of you this book has one more story or one more hint as to what makes me tick. Specifically, I would like to thank Kevin Pates at the *Duluth News Tribune* for being principal historian of my early running career, Neal Barnard, M.D., and Susan Levin, M.S., R.D., at Physician's Committee for Responsible Medicine for their scientific knowledge of a plant-based diet, Timothy Noakes, M.D., D.Sc., Zachary Landman, M.D., and David C. Nieman, Ph.D., who I revere for their ceaseless quest to explain the science behind ultra-endurance. Writing sage Christopher McDougall gave invaluable input and advice on the manuscript and reassured me that there was always an end in sight.

The visuals provided by my generous and artistic friends behind the lens make my story come to life. I am thankful for all who have captured my life in photos that speak for themselves.

There are so many people who influenced my life. While I may not mention you by name, you know who you are. You led me to the rugged, less-traveled trails.

Words do not describe the appreciation I have for Jenny, my trusty partner in life and best friend. She agreed with me about getting Steve to collaborate on the book, and when it looked like the partnership might not occur, she made sure it did. When Jenny wants something to happen, it usually does. I cannot thank her enough for being by my side on many of my all-nighters. She gave this book countless hours of editing and her creative eye. She also brought to it—and me—an understanding of why I chase the dreams I chase, even though they may not seem to make sense. The journey is always more fun and fulfilling with her stride by stride.

Often we need to retrace our steps back to the beginning. I would not be able to run if not for my parents. Dad, while we may not have always seen eye to eye, you provided a simple yet profound wisdom that has made me who I am. "Do things," you told me. Not some times. *Always.* Mom, while you lost the ability to perform basic tasks that many of us take for granted, you never stopped smiling and finding the morsels of joy in life. If I can maintain that same attitude I will have succeeded. My running idols may have logged more miles and climbed bigger mountains, but you are my main inspiration. I will never stop running for you.

Lastly, I owe a huge debt to the best fans in the world—from the many race volunteers, to the young runners who write letters, to the dedicated followers who send pre-race messages and post-race high fives. I continually receive motivation and support from your stories. You all remind me why I run, why we all run.

Ultramarathon Race History

Note: This is a partial list.
* Indicates new course record at that time

1994
Minnesota Voyageur, 2nd place (7:44)

1995
Minnesota Voyageur, 2nd place (7:24)

1996
Minnesota Voyageur, 1st place (7:10)

Point Reyes 50K, 7th place (4:24)

Edmund Fitzgerald 100K (USATF 100K Road National Championships),
    4th place (7:33)

1997
Minnesota Voyageur, 1st place (7:18)

1998
Crown King Scramble 50K, 2nd place (4:34)

Zane Grey 50-Mile, 1st place (8:49)*

Ice Age Trail 50-Mile, 3rd place (6:23)

Minnesota Voyageur, 1st place (6:41)*

McKenzie River Trail Run 50K, 1st place (3:49)*

Angeles Crest 100-Mile Endurance Run, 2nd place (19:15)

Mountain Masochist 50-Mile Trail Run, 5th place (7:40)

1999

San Juan Trail 50K, 2nd place (4:25)

Way Too Cool 50K, 4th place (3:48)

Bull Run Run 50-Mile, 1st place (6:30)

McDonald Forest 50K, 1st place (4:11)

Ice Age Trail 50-Mile, 3rd place (6:21)

Western States 100-Mile Endurance Run, 1st place (17:34)

White River 50-Mile, 3rd place (6:55)

Bend Distillery 50K, 2nd place (3:05)

Angeles Crest 100-Mile Endurance Run, 2nd place (19:51)

2000

Chuckanut 50K, 2nd place (4:22)

Diez Vista 50K, 1st place (4:26)*

Leona Divide 50-Mile, 1st place (7:01)*

Miwok 100K, 11th place (9:54)

Western States 100-Mile Endurance Run, 1st place (17:15)

McDonald Forest 50K, 4th place (4:36)

2001

Jed Smith 50K, 4th place (3:26)

Way Too Cool 50K, 16th place (4:00)

GNC 50K, 4th place (3:24)

GNC 100K (USATF 100K Road National Championships), 4th place (7:28)

Leona Divide 50-Mile, 1st place (6:59)*

McDonald Forest 50K, 2nd place (4:17)

Miwok 100K, 2nd place (8:42)

Western States 100-Mile Endurance Run, 1st place (16:38)

Baldy Peaks 50K, 3rd place (6:14)

OXFAM Hong Kong Trailwalker, 1st place team (12:52)*

2002

Leona Divide 50-Mile, 1st place (6:46)*

Promise Land 50K, 2nd place (4:37)

Miwok 100K, 1st place (8:44)

Western States 100-Mile Endurance Run, 1st place (16:19)

White River 50-Mile, 5th place (7:16)

Tamalpa Headlands 50K, 12th place (4:15)

Silvertip 50K, 1st place (4:18)*

OXFAM Hong Kong Trailwalker 100K, 1st place team (12:47)*

White River 50-Mile (USATF Trail National Championships), 5th place (7:16)

2003

Way Too Cool 50K, 5th place (3:41)

Diez Vista 50K, 1st place (4:25)*

Zane Grey 50-Mile, 5th place (8:50)

Miwok 100K, 1st place (8:44)

Western States 100-Mile Endurance Run, 1st place (16:01)

White River 50-Mile (USATF Trail National Championships), 5th place (7:13)

Hasegawa Cup — Japan Mountain Endurance Run 77K, 1st place team

2004

Way Too Cool 50K, 3rd place (3:46)

Leona Divide 50-Mile, 1st place (6:45)*

Zane Grey 50-Mile, 6th place (8:57)

Miwok 100K, 1st place (8:47)

Western States 100-Mile Endurance Run, 1st place (15:36)*

Vermont 100-Mile, 5th place (16:41)

Leadville Trail 100, 2nd place (18:02)

Wasatch Front 100-Mile, 17th place (27:21)

2005

Way Too Cool 50K, 10th place (4:09)

Chuckanut 50K, 11th place (4:24)

Diablo 50-Mile Endurance Run, 1st place (9:10)

Promise Land 50K, 2nd place (4:59)

Miwok 100K, 2nd place (8:43)

McDonald Forest 50K, 3rd place (4:51)

Western States 100-Mile Endurance Run,
    1st place (16:40)

Badwater Ultramarathon, 1st place (24:36)*

2006

Copper Canyon Ultramarathon, 2nd place (6:47)

Leona Divide 50-Mile, 3rd place (6:48)

Miwok 100K, 2nd place (8:42)

Badwater Ultramarathon, 1st place (25:41)

McKenzie River Trail Run 50K, 8th place (4:32)

Spartathlon, 1st place (22:52)

2007

Copper Canyon Ultramarathon, 1st place (6:32)

Mad City 100K (USATF 100K Road National Championships),
    2nd place (7:32)

Miwok 100K, 5th place (9:04)

McDonald Forest 50K, 14th place (4:40)

Hardrock 100, 1st place (26:08)*

Spartathlon, 1st place (23:12)

2008

Bridle Trails Winter Trail Running Festival 50K,
    5th place (4:15)

Way Too Cool 50K, 4th place (3:35)

Chuckanut 50K, 3rd place (4:12)

Miwok 100K, 4th place (8:38)

McDonald Forest 50K, 3rd place (4:13)

Spartathlon, 1st place (22:20)

World of Hurt 50K, 3rd place (4:53)

UltraCentric 24 Hours, 46th place (48.7 miles)

2009

Chuckanut 50K, 11th place (4:25)

White River 50-Mile (USATF Trail National Championships),
4th place (7:13)

Ultra-Trail du Mont-Blanc, 19th place (26:07)

NorthCoast 24 Hours, 75th place (65.8 miles)

JFK 50-Mile, 11th place (6:31)

2010

IAU-IAAF 24-Hour World Championships, Silver Medal (165.7 miles),
U.S. Record

White River 50-Mile (USATF Trail National Championships),
4th place (7:02)

Notes

1. Somebody

Badwater history and course details are from the official race website and the documentary *The Distance of Truth,* Pageturner Productions, 2008.

Information on ibuprofen's harmful effects on runners is from an interview with David C. Nieman, Ph.D., director, Human Performance Laboratory, Appalachian State University.

4. "Pain Only Hurts"

The list of the benefits of a plant-based diet is drawn from "Vegetarian Foods: Powerful for Health," a publication of Physician's Committee for Responsible Medicine, 2011, and the American Dietetic Association's "Position Paper on Vegetarian Diets," July 2009.

7 "Let the Pain Go Out Your Ears"

The figure for average protein consumption is from the study "Current protein intake in America: Analysis of the National Health and Nutrition Examination Survey, 2003–2004," by Victor Fugoni, *American Journal of Clinical Nutrition,* vol. 87, no. 5, 1554S–1557S, May 2008.

The current U.S. recommended daily allowance of protein is from "Dietary Guidelines," U.S. Dept. of Health and Human Services, 2010.

The adverse effects of excess protein consumption is from *The New Becoming Vegetarian: The Essential Guide to a Healthy Vegetarian Diet* by Vesanto Melina and Brenda Davis, Book Publishing Company, 2003.

Information on the diabetes epidemic comes from "National Diabetes Statistics, 2011," available online at the National Diabetes Information Clearing-house, U.S. Department of Health and Human Services.

Evidence linking the three most common causes of death in America to the standard Western diet can be found in *The Food Revolution: How Your Diet Can Help Save Your Life and Our World,* by John Robbins, Conari Press, 2010, and *The China Study: The Most Comprehensive Study of Nutrition Ever Conducted and the Startling Implications for Diet, Weight Loss, and Long-term Health,* by T. Colin Campbell, BenBella Books, 2006.

The quote about the appropriateness of vegetarian diets for all stages of the life cycle is taken from the American Dietetic Association's "Position Paper on Vegetarian Diets," July 2009.

9. Silent Snow, Secret Snow

Information on the way cows are treated at industrial dairy farms comes from *Mad Cowboy: Plain Truth from the Cattle Rancher Who Won't Eat Meat,* by Howard Lyman, Scribner, 2001.

Course details and the history of the Western States Endurance Run were drawn from the official race website, the website of the Tevis Cup, and interviews and correspondence with race cofounder Shannon Weil.

Historical references to the Paiute, Shoshone, and Washoe peoples were sourced from "WA SHE SHU: The Washoe People Past and Present," a publication of the Washoe Tribe of Nevada and California and the Paiutes of Utah website.

Gordon Ainsleigh's story comes from "Inventing 100-Mile Trail Racing," 42K(+) Press, 1998, available online at www.marathonandbeyond.com, and from "Western States 100's Gordon Ainsleigh," by Mark Vanderhoff, *Reno Gazette-Journal,* June 2003.

10. Dangerous Tune

The biographical information on Arthur F. H. Newton was taken from *Bunion Derby: The 1928 Footrace Across America,* by Charles B. Kastner, University of New Mexico Press, 2007, and *C. C. Pyle's Amazing Foot Race: The True Story of the 1928 Coast-to-Coast Run Across America,* by Geoff Williams, Rodale, 2007.

The biographical information on Percy Cerutty was taken from "Cerutty, Percy Wells (1895–1975)," *Contemporary Authors,* Thomson Gale, 2007, and from the Herb Elliot interview on Radio National on January 5, 2001, a transcript of which is available on www.coolrunning.com.

The biographical information on Chuck Jones comes from an interview with the runner.

The value of emptiness of mind for the warrior is explored in many bushido texts, among them *The Book of Five Rings*, by Miyamoto Musashi (tr. Thomas Cleary), Shambhala, 2010.

Henry David Thoreau's famous quote about simplicity comes from *Walden*.

11. "Are You Peeing?"

The body's ability to acclimate to heat is discussed in detail in *Surviving the Extremes: A Doctor's Journey to the Limits of Human Endurance*, by Kenneth Kamler, St. Martin's, 2004.

The rate at which a body loses fluid and salt during exercise comes from "Exercise and Fluid Replacement," Position Paper of the American College of Sports Medicine, 2007.

The discussion of hyponatremia and the challenges of maintaining proper hydration during an ultra is drawn from interviews with Timothy Noakes, M.D., D.Sc., Ph.D. (hon causa), Discovery Health Professor of exercise and sports science, University of Capetown; Robert Lind, M.D., medical adviser to Western States 100, 1974–2006; David C. Nieman, Ph.D, FACSM, director, Human Performance Laboratory, Appalachian State University; and Zachary Landman, M.D., researcher and ultramarathoner.

12. Battling Bug Boy

Biographical details and the quote about running 10,000 miles were taken from an interview with James Shapiro.

The story of the remarkable pilgrimage of the marathon monks comes from *The Marathon Monks of Mount Hiei*, by John Stevens, Shambhala, 1988.

13. Of Bears and Gazelles

The study showing that vegetarians watch less television, smoke less, and sleep more per night than meat-eaters is the Loma Linda University Adventist Health Study.

Blood type O is described as a "canny, aggressive predator" on Eat Right for Your Type: Official Website, "The Type O Profile."

Dr. Fredrick Stare's takedown of the blood type diet comes from *The Food Revolution: How Your Diet Can Help Save Your Life and Our World*, by John Robbins, Conari Press, 2010.

14. A Hot Mess

The account of Al Arnold's run comes from "The Road Goes On Forever," by Bob Wischnia, *Marathoner,* Spring 1978.

Biographical details of Sri Chinmoy come from his official website and the article "Sri Chinmoy Seeks to Claim a Title: Stunt Man Supreme," by James T. Areddy, *Wall Street Journal,* January 13, 1989 (reprinted on www.rickross.com).

Details of the self-transcendence race come from the Sri Chinmoy Marathon Team website, "The 2011 Self-Transcendence 3100 Mile Race."

Accounts of the Divine Madness group are drawn from the articles "A Running Club Is 100 Miles Outside of the Mainstream," by Jere Longman, *New York Times,* July 28, 1997; "Running Like Hell," by Michael Finkel, *Women's Sports and Fitness,* November 1999; and "Ultrarunning: Runner's Death Places Sport Under Scrutiny," by Jere Longman, *New York Times,* March 7, 2004.

The body's adaptations to altitude are described in *Surviving the Extremes: A Doctor's Journey to the Limits of Human Endurance,* by Kenneth Kamler, St. Martin's, 2004.

The detailed description of the stresses of the ultra, from the loading on bones and muscles to the cascade of stress-related hormones, is culled from interviews with Timothy Noakes, M.D., D.Sc., Ph.D. (hon causa), Discovery Health Professor of exercise and sports science, University of Capetown; Robert Lind, M.D., medical adviser to Western States 100, 1974–2006; David C. Nieman, Ph.D., FACSM, director, Human Performance Laboratory, Appalachian State University; and Zachary Landman, M.D., researcher and ultramarathoner.

15. These Guys Again?

Some of the information regarding Caballo Blanco and Copper Canyon comes from *Born to Run: A Hidden Tribe, Superathletes, and the Greatest Race the World Has Never Seen,* by Christopher McDougall, Vintage, 2011.

The study demonstrating the dangers of sitting is "Leisure Time Spent Sitting in Relation to Total Mortality in a Prospective Cohort of U.S. Adults," by Alpa V. Patel, Leslie Bernstein, et al., *American Journal of Epidemiology,* 2010 doi: 10.1093/aje/kwq155.

16. The Central Governor

A fascinating discussion of VO_2 max, lactate threshold, and efficiency in both humans and animals can be found in *Why We Run: A Natural History,* by Bernd Heinrich, Harper Perennial, 2002.

The central governor theory of neural recruitment is explained in *Lore of Running*, by Timothy Noakes, M.D., D.Sc., Human Kinetics, 2002. Noakes is Discovery Health Professor of exercise and sports science, University of Capetown.

17. Hunted by the Wasatch Speedgoat

Biographical details of the Skaggs brothers were taken from "Rogue Runners," by Adam W. Chase, *Running Times*, June 2009.

Hardrock horror stories come from interviews with past participants, the official Runner's Manual, and the article "It's Gonna Suck to Be You," by Steve Friedman, *Outside*, July 2001.

The biographical information on Rick Trujillo comes from an interview with the runner.

The biographical information on Laura Vaughan comes from an interview with the runner.

18. In the Footsteps of Pheidippides

Course details and the history of the Spartathlon come from the official race website.

Plutarch refers to the Marathon run in his essay "De gloria Atheniensium," tr. Frank Cole Babbitt, via Perseus Digital Library, Tufts University. The full quote is as follows: "The news of the battle of Marathon Thersippus of Eroeadae brought back, as Heracleides Ponticus [an earlier historian whose works have been lost] relates; but most historians declare that it was Eucles who ran in full armour, hot from the battle, and, bursting in at the doors of the first men of the State, could only say, 'Hail! we are victorious!' and straightway expired."

The references to Pheidippides in Herodotus's *Histories* occur in Book 6, chapters 105–6. We cite the A. D. Godley translation available online via the Perseus Digital Library, Tufts University.

The biographical details of John Foden were taken from the online articles "Irishman Is Co-founder of Spartathlon" on www.ultrarunningireland .com and "John Foden — A Life Devoted to Ultrarunning" on www.ultralegends .com.

Yiannis Kouros's biography and records were taken from his official website.

Kouros's definition of ultrarunning is taken from "What Is Ultra-running?," by Yiannis Kouros, March 2008, downloadable from www.yianniskouros.com.

The myth of the founding of Athens is recounted in *Mythology*, by Edith Hamilton, Bay Back Books, 1998.

Hippocrates's quote about food and drink comes from *On Ancient Medicine*, tr. Francis Adams, via the Internet Classics Archive.

The research on soldiers by Dr. Andy Morgan at Yale Medical School was reported in "Lessons in Survival," by Ben Sherwood, *Newsweek*, February 13, 2009.

Dr. Kenneth Kamler's book about the factors that separate winners from losers in the world's toughest environments is *Surviving the Extremes: A Doctor's Journey to the Limits of Human Endurance*, St. Martin's, 2004.

19. Lost

The historical background of the 24-hour race was taken from "History of the 24hr Race," by Andy Milroy, www.ultralegends.com, November 4, 2008.

The importance of the sun in Native American ceremonial running is discussed in *Indian Running: Native American History and Tradition*, by Peter Nabokov, Ancient City Press, 1987.

20. Secrets of the Dark Wizard

Dean Potter's biography was taken from "The Aerialist: Dean Potter," by Matt Samet, *Outside*, July 2011.

For a discussion of the research linking runner's high to endorphins and endocannabinoids, see "Phys Ed: What Really Causes Runner's High," by Gretchen Reynolds, *New York Times*, February 16, 2011.

The biographical information on Bill Kee comes from an interview with the runner.

The study about rats running themselves to death is cited in *Activity Anorexia: Theory, Research and Treatment*, by W. Frank Epling and W. David Pierce, Psychology Press, 1996.

The biographical information on Chuck Jones and his Badwater hallucinations comes from an interview with the runner.

Ann Trason's quote about the cliff comes from "Catching Up with Ann Trason," *TrailRunner Magazine*, January 2009.

Recipe Index

Index

Note: S.J. in the index refers to the author, Scott Jurek.